LIFE, LETTERS, AND SERMONS OF
JESSE DELVES

Mr DELVES
In the early years of his pastorate

LIFE, LETTERS, AND SERMONS OF

JESSE DELVES

MINISTER OF THE GOSPEL

PUBLISHED BY
THE CHURCH AND CONGREGATION AT
EBENEZER STRICT BAPTIST CHAPEL
CLAPHAM, LONDON
WHERE HE WAS PASTOR FROM
1935 TO 1977

Obtainable from

Mr S. A. J. Collins, 3 Parkthorne Rd.,
Clapham Park, London SW12 0JN

ISBN 0 9508506 0 8

Printed in Great Britain
at the University Press, Oxford
by Eric Buckley
Printer to the University

CONTENTS

LIST OF ILLUSTRATIONS

FOREWORD

WITH some reluctance, due to lack of grace and ability, I venture to comply with the request for a brief foreword to this memoir of the Lord's servant whom I knew and esteemed for so long as Pastor. I do so, as humbly trusting that it was Divinely ordained that, in the late summer of 1934, two things (one in grace, the other in providence) 'worked together' to lead to the beginning of my acquaintance with, and love for, him. I hope it was then that the Lord laid eternal realities in my heart (so different from my former contentment with correct religious notions) and also about that time I was moved in providence to S.W. London and guided, in answer to prayer, to Clapham chapel. I was then unknown to any there, and they to me, but it became the 'house of bread' to me and the ministry was, I believe, blessed to the deepening of those exercises already begun.

Truly 'the memory of the just is blessed' and the manifestation of the grace of God in His servant (which alone we would desire to magnify) will be remembered by the many who similarly knew him and for whom a word of introduction is unnecessary. But this foreword is intended to express the sincere desire that this account of Mr Delves' life and labours which his successor in the Pastorate has, with the help of others, lovingly and prayerfully compiled, may redound to the glory of a Triune Jehovah and have His approbation resting upon it; that it may be the means also of emphasising the need for that personal and inward revelation of the truth upon which our late friend so often insisted, delivering from false religion, vain hopes and resting upon notions of naturally acquired truth.

Mr Delves' tender and exercised spirit shines in the account of his life and in the letters which follow. The sermons are 'ordinary' examples (i.e. not specially selected) of the ministry with which, week by week, Clapham was favoured for so many years. They set forth the 'main things'—sin and salvation; the glory of Christ's Person and His finished work on behalf of the church, and the vital work of the Spirit of God in them. The ministry was indeed the 'savour of Christ', but it is solemnly to be remembered—either 'the savour of death unto death' or 'the savour of life unto life' (2 Cor. 2.16). Some of the earlier sermons we can personally remember.

May these truths be savingly revealed in their power and unction in the hearts of many who read this memoir.

J. C. NEVILLE

HIS LIFE

CHAPTER ONE

Early Days; Call by Grace and Call to the Ministry

His birth and early life

'I was born into this world on 18 November 1891, of godly parents, in the village of Rushlake Green, in the parish of Warbleton, Sussex. My father was a member and deacon at "Mount Hermon" Chapel, Warbleton, which place of worship I was brought up to attend. I well remember the Pastor, and a number of godly people that were connected with that cause, in my young days.

'Through mercy I was blessed with consistent and God-fearing parents, setting before us as a family (there were four sons, Edgar, Nelson, Jesse, and Stanley) a good example, training us in the fear of the Lord, in truth and uprightness. I often reflect upon the days of my childhood with thankfulness to the Lord for this blessing, daily reading and prayer with the family present whenever convenient, his children always having a warm place in my father's petitions at the throne of grace.

'In my infancy, owing to my mother's illness I was mistakenly given an adult dose of sleeping medicine which sent me unconscious for many hours. I was not expected to revive, but in time I regained consciousness and recovered. Through the watchful providence of God I was preserved on another occasion from what could have resulted in an early grave but have been brought safely thus far.'

He leaves home

'I left home at the early age of twelve to work in the boot and shoe trade at Burwash Weald in Sussex, where I stayed for about four years. During this period I was the subject of some solemn religious impressions, once particularly when an old man died suddenly. This old friend used often to come in the shop, and naturally I became quite attached to him; his sudden end quite affected me, producing solemn reflections as to my own case and state before God if I should suddenly die, but these early impressions faded away, and I have no reason to feel there was anything spiritual or saving in them.

'In time I left this situation and went to work for Mr William Tingley, at Scaynes Hill, Sussex. I was very happy there, and have pleasant memories of those days, and the godly friends that would come in the shop and have spiritual conversation. Mr Main was the Pastor, and his sober gracious ministry has left its memories, but as this was but a temporary arrangement these happy days came to an end and I went to work at East Grinstead. Here my life was quite different to Scaynes Hill, though I attended the chapel there, and heard different supply ministers. I did not stay in my situation very long, circumstances arising which necessitated making a change, my desire at that time being to obtain a post nearer my home and parents, but this was not the Lord's purpose, for this marks one of the most memorable providences of my life.'

A remarkable leading in providence

'One evening in the summer of 1908, a man passed the shop calling with evening papers, but I decided not to purchase one; after the man had gone, a sudden impulse seized me to hurry after him and obtain one. In that paper was an advertisement for a young man wanted to work in the boot and shoe trade at Hove. As the advert. rather attracted me I wrote in reply, not expecting any response, but a letter came, the man stating that he liked the way I had written, and though he had a number of applicants, he decided to give me a trial. This leading of the Lord's providence brought me to Hove and Brighton which affected the whole of my future life. As I look back, how clearly I can see the truth of that Scripture: "I will bring the blind by a way that they knew not; I will lead them in paths that they have not known; I will make darkness light before them, and crooked things straight. These things will I do unto them, and not forsake them" (Isa. 42: 16).

'I came from East Grinstead to Brighton in 1908 at the age of 16. I had never been to Brighton before, but I found my way to Hove, and soon commenced in my new situation. I soon found I was in a worldly atmosphere, sabbath breaking, horse racing, and other things, which brought me into many dangers and temptations.

'Certain things were suggested to me in which, said they, I might enjoy myself. On one occasion I went to a theatre, and another time took a cycle ride to Worthing on a Sabbath morning, to attend the service there. When I arrived an old man was in prayer; he appeared to be under a blessed anointing, for a sense of the goodness and mercy of the Lord filled him so that he was quite broken down. These things impressed me, and my effort to do what I knew was not right brought conviction and guilt on my conscience and consequent unhappiness. My father's prayers for his sons often confronted me, for it was his daily practice to kneel down at his armchair and pray for his "boys". As I look back to those early days what cause I have to be thankful for godly parents, a watchful eye over our movements, and good family training.

'I was in this situation four years, snares and temptations continually attended me, but through the forbearance and tender mercy of a Covenant God, I was preserved from falling into some things that could have brought much ultimate grief and sorrow both to myself and to my dear parents.'

His call by grace

'I began to attend Galeed Chapel, and continued to do so for some time without feeling any real attraction to the ministry, being very lonely, often having resentful feelings while sitting in the gallery, both towards minister and people.

'Once I was sharply spoken to by one for using a hymn book which did not belong to me, and I came out of chapel in such hatred and rebellion against the people that I determined not to go to the place again. However I could not stay away.

'About this period a great gloom came over my spirit which it is difficult to describe. I became very depressed and lost the interest I previously had in things about and around me; in fact I became so low in mind and depressed in spirit that my life became a burden to me, and yet I could hardly have given a reason if asked, as there was no outward cause. Added to this I found a terrible temptation besetting me, which was to put an end to my miserable life, as there seemed nothing to live for. But while in this wretched condition, one day while walking the street, I found myself begging and pleading before the Lord to deliver me, when I felt instant relief, and the temptation seemed to be just lifted from me. Thus I believe the Lord appeared for my help and delivered me, for it did not return again.

'This was followed with much self examination, a deep concern relative to my state before God, secret prayer, confession of sin, reading the Scriptures for myself, a felt need of mercy, and a sense of what my sins deserved. I began to entreat the Lord to teach and instruct me, to open my eyes and not leave me to be deceived. At this time I had some discovery of the nature and character of a just and holy God, of the law in its spirituality, of what it requires in a perfect obedience, and this word followed me continually in condemning power in my guilty conscience: "Whatsoever is not of faith is sin" (Rom. 14: 23).

'I was now brought in guilty before God, condemned by the law. I saw and felt sin as against God alone, and I had to confess with David, "Against Thee, Thee only, have I sinned, and done this evil in Thy sight; that Thou mightest be justified when Thou speakest, and be clear when Thou judgest" (Ps. 51.4). I felt that one impure thought in my whole life would bring me in guilty in God's sight without anything else, but I proved and felt my whole nature was defiled.

'At this time it seemed as though the Lord overturned the privileges which I had had, such as being brought up under the truth, attending the means of grace, being outwardly moral and upright; death seemed to be in all this. Nothing could help me now but the free mercy of God. I felt myself lost.

'One night in reading Psalm 31, the 7th verse was made good to me: "I will be glad and rejoice in Thy mercy, for Thou hast considered my trouble; Thou hast known my soul in adversities." I began to feel my hard heart soften, with some sweet feeling sense of the Lord's mercy, that He knew my case, and hope sprang up that the Lord would one day appear to me and deliver me.

'I now began to attend Galeed with an earnest longing in my soul that I might get something through the preaching. Sometimes I felt helped, sometimes condemned. I have sat in the gallery at Galeed hearing the awful consequences of living and dying ignorant of God and salvation and have felt that Mr Popham spoke as he did because he could see me in the chapel. I remember some seasons in those days though, when I got helps, renewings, and the ministry began to be life and teaching in me.

'While in that situation I had everything around me to draw me away. I have often roamed the streets till late at night and then been afraid to enter the house, as the atmosphere was so worldly (and I was very sensitive to scorn) and yet here God in mercy began His work in my soul: "Bless His holy Name."

'One Sunday morning very early, feeling in much darkness and trying to seek the Lord, I felt the publican's prayer so fitting my case. The words seemed just to embrace all the religion I possessed, and I felt I could say them from my heart. I went to chapel, and after Mr Popham had been a short time preaching, he said, "Perhaps someone here feels he can only say the publican's prayer, 'God be merciful to me a sinner'. If so, go on, you are in the right way, and it will be made manifest in the Lord's time." I felt such power enter my heart by this that I could hardly keep my seat, but felt I must get up and say, "That is where I am".

'One night I had an attack of haemorrhage, not violent but serious, and being in bondage and darkness about my state, I felt a cold sweat of horror come over me in the prospect of death, as I feared. This I believe was on a Sunday morning. I got up and went out, earnestly entreating the Lord to appear for me. I got some encouragement in the morning. I went again in the evening. The text was: "He that loveth not knoweth not God, for God is love." Mr Popham was very special *to me* that night. I felt much power in hearing, and seemed to come to the border of liberty, but the time had not come.

'I shall never forget my Pastor's first visit to me. I was in such bondage I could hardly utter a word, but he quoted two verses of that hymn "Prepare me, gracious God" (Gadsby's selection, 471). Each line seemed to pierce me through. After I had stammered a word or two in respect of needing a right preparation, he spoke very kindly to me, saying he hoped the day would come when we should rejoice together, which came to pass later.'

Commences his own business

'In the year 1912 I commenced in business for myself at 140 Preston Drove, Brighton. Of this important step I have reason to feel that the good hand of the Lord went before me in a particular way; this property being empty, was advertised in the "Gospel Standard" and at the first opportunity I went over to see it; as I was in the shop, I had a persuasion that this was to be the place for me to start in business. The owner of the property, an attendant at Galeed Chapel, kindly agreed to let me the premises on a three year lease. Here I worked and prayed; work soon came in, and when the first rent became due, I was able to pay my landlord, and continued with the business from 1912 to 1935.'

His marriage

'In reflecting upon these providential leadings I must retrace my steps a little, and recall another important event in my life. Before I left Hove I had made the acquaintance of a dear young friend who later became my wife, and in December 1914 we were married at "Hanover" Chapel, Tunbridge Wells, by Mr J. K. Popham.

'This was one of the happiest days of my life, though it was a pouring wet wintry day. As I was going in the train to Tunbridge Wells, I felt such a nearness to the Lord, and I believe He gave me that blessed promise, "I will never leave thee nor forsake thee". What a happy day it was. The Lord had granted my request in three things: to have a wife, a home, and a business.

'In earlier days at Hove, after the evening service at Galeed I used to roam the streets of Brighton till about 10 p.m. before I would go into my lodgings. This made me long for a wife and home of my own. My dear wife and I have been spared together now for 55 years, for I am writing this in January 1970.'

Deliverance from soul trouble

From the period when Mr Delves first became spiritually concerned he states, 'It was about five years before the Lord Jesus was revealed to my soul as my blessed and adorable Redeemer, during which time I had many "hopes and fears" alternate rising, but the deliverance came in January 1916. On the Sunday, Mr Dickens had been preaching at Galeed. I had a good time in hearing, and in the evening felt a particular desire to write a few lines to my pastor. I did so late that Sunday night, and sent it.

'I was much troubled in mind the next day as to whether it was a right step; consequently it was a day of examination and prayer. In the evening about seven o'clock, meditating on these things while working at the bench, I felt suddenly such light shining into my heart, and all my past experiences brought vividly before me from the time I was first convinced of sin, together with a clear witness in my own soul that what I had passed through was the work of the Holy Ghost. The convictions, the helps, prayers, the hearings, all seemed to shine before me, the Lord putting His seal to the work. These words were applied with power: "I have loved thee with an everlasting love; therefore with lovingkindness have I drawn thee" (Jer. 31: 3). All my soul exercises I felt and saw to be the drawing power of His lovingkindness.

'While absorbed in this sweet realization of the love of God in bearing His witness with my spirit thus, the veil seemed to be taken away, and I saw by precious faith the Lord Jesus Christ upon the cross as my blessed and glorious Redeemer, bearing my sins. I looked upon Him whom I had pierced. Blessed sight indeed it was! So real was He to me that I felt my sins were pardoned, and coming to myself I said, "Where are my sins that have been my burden?" They were gone. I felt my conscience clean. In my experience that memorable night it was like a sky without a cloud; there was no bar between my soul and my God. I said, "My Father". I felt these words too: 'He that hath seen me hath seen the Father' (John 14: 9). Thus I believed in the Trinity in Unity; one God in three Persons, co-equal and co-eternal; God my covenant Father in Jesus Christ; the Lord Jesus the eternal Son of God in His Divine nature from all eternity; and the Holy Ghost a Person in the Godhead, the revealer of Christ in the hearts of God's living family.

'That night I tried to read a part of John 6, but it was a new book to me. Everything in it seemed for me. I was quite overcome with such love and manifested mercy. Truly it was sweet liberty that night!'

Joining the Church at Galeed Brighton, and baptism

Mr Delves often recounted the circumstances of his joining the Church and of his baptism. Following the letter which he had ventured to send, Mr Popham came to see him. He entered the shop, and finding Mr Delves alone, he said to him, 'You have had a blessing', to which Mr Delves responded, 'I have, and I can tell you about it.' When Mr Delves had related the Lord's mercy to him Mr Popham said, 'We have a Church Meeting tonight and you must come.' On that occasion two elderly gentlemen who had previously been named to the Church were coming to give their testimonies. In view of their age their experiences were rather lengthy so that Mr Delves was waiting in the vestry for more than an hour and a half. Mr Delves was evidently graciously helped in declaring what the Lord had done for his soul, and doubtless the freshness of the blessing upon his spirit added to the savour of his relation. At least one member of Galeed (still living at the time of writing—1982), who was present at that Church Meeting, has never forgotten the savour of Mr Delves' testimony that evening.

He was baptized in the same month, January 1916, but of his baptism Mr Delves told us that he did not enjoy any particular sense of the Lord's presence.

The commencement of exercises about the ministry

It was from this period of especial blessing that Mr Delves dated his exercises relating to the ministry. His own record continues: 'At this time my exercises relating to the ministry commenced with the impression that the Lord had a work for me to do and that I was to be a witness that He does visit and bless poor sinners.'

The First World War

The marked deliverance with which Mr Delves was favoured and his initial exercise relating to the ministry were soon sharply tried by his call-up for service in the First World War: 'The War was then raging and shortly after I was called upon to leave home and go into the army.

'It is impossible to relate the trials of such a life to those who have the fear of the Lord in their hearts and the anguish of mind after joining instead of trying to get exemption. However, I had cause later to feel that it was the right time as I was kept in England and enabled to meet with the people at Canterbury and Aldershot for a season of about two years.

'During this time my faith was sharply tried with temptations to give up all religion, but I trust the Lord sustained me and kept me alive, and I was favoured at times with seasons of refreshing at the Prayer Meetings mostly, and sometimes under the preaching of dear old Mr Hewitt. During this time the Lord made that sweet revelation of His love to me a great help in time of trouble, though I could not rest in it. When at Swanage one night in great distress of mind the Lord appeared to me [whilst Mr Delves was walking alone on the Downs overlooking Swanage pending his embarkation for France] and spoke this word: "I am with you alway, even unto the end" which so calmed my mind that though I was in trouble it was as though I had no trouble. How sweetly it confirmed the precious words [which Mr Delves had on his wedding day as before related], "I will never leave thee, nor forsake thee". Shortly after this I was sent to France, and though constantly in danger, my life was preserved and I was brought home again safely.'

Mr Delves related on more than one occasion the particular time of his posting to France. His company was under instructions to report on the Sunday night as their ship was to sail the following day. Prior to leaving, the company was granted 48 hours leave, so naturally Mr Delves went home, and to chapel on Sunday morning. Mr Popham asked him when he had to return, to which Mr Delves responded 'We are supposed to report tonight, but as we do not sail until tomorrow midday, most have said that they will have an extra night at home'. Mr Delves, in relating this incident implied that he was inclined to adopt a similar course, but Mr Popham said, 'Well, *you* must go tonight'. Accordingly Mr Delves went, and he proved the benefit of having heeded his Pastor's counsel, for he was permitted a measure of choice as to his duties, which those who reported late were not.

Four letters follow, one from Mr George Wariner, one from Mr Popham and two from Mr J. H. Gosden. The first is of particular interest as Mr Delves said that Mr Wariner was the first person to take any kindly interest in him when he went to Galeed. Mr Wariner was a sidesman who eventually handed a letter to Mr Delves inviting him to spend the Lord's day at his home.

The letters provide some indication of the spiritual affection subsisting among the pastor and friends at Galeed, as well as giving an impression of the mutual anxiety at that time of national stress.

(Sent while Mr Delves was still stationed in England)

120 Havelock Rd,
Brighton
July 1917

My dear Jesse,

I was surprised, and also equally pleased to see the post-lady bring me a letter from you this morning. Now as I am at home this afternoon on account of the rain I will try and drop you a few lines in answer to it . . . Yes, we had Mr Hazelton at Galeed yesterday, a very good substitute but not like our own pastor. His text in the morning was from Proverbs 13. 12 'Hope deferred maketh the heart sick; but when the desire cometh, it is a tree of life'. In the evening he spoke on the Lord's will that His people shall be with Him, to behold His glory, when time with them shall be no more. Speaking for myself how we need continually to be weaned from seeking for satisfaction in the things of this life, yet I trust I can come in with the last verse of our second hymn at the prayer meeting yesterday morning, 973:

'Lord, there are no streams but thine,
Can assuage a thirst like mine,
'Tis a thirst Thyself didst give
Let me therefore drink and live'

Our dear Pastor spoke well on Wednesday evening on Christ being the light of life. He was at Godmanchester on Thursday and Gower Street yesterday. I hope he has been and will be preserved from harm whilst in London, and return to us in safety on Wednesday. He is preaching at Gower Street on Tuesday evening . . .

We are glad you are keeping well and also hope that you may continue to see the good hand of God in removing you from the cooking so that you may spiritually profit in having a little more spare time. Our sympathies are with you in the various trials and separation from those you love in respect of army life. We desire the time to hasten, if the Lord will, when you may again be with us, to enjoy the spiritual communion and conversation. I unite with you in gratitude to the Lord that He has still kept you here, for the sake of yourself and dear wife. We cannot yet see the end of this terrible war; I much wonder what is yet before us, and have many fears of yet darker times unless we as a nation turn to Him, and acknowledge His dealings with us as just for our sins against and neglect of Him, feeling there is much truth contained in Ps. 81.13 and 14, which it would be our wisdom and mercy as a nation to follow. I am glad to say we are all well. We have seen your mother during her stay in Brighton, and feel much for her loneliness. Mr Banfield's youngest son joined the army last week. Curwen Tucker is in France, and has been having rather a rough time. I heard from Tom Tingley the other day—he is still at High Wycombe. I am sorry to hear that Mr Jenkins is suffering from shell shock . . . Peter Read has received instructions to present himself at the Town Hall on Tuesday week for the army unless his governor can get him off by appeal. Now I think I will conclude. You will probably think this to be a very mixed letter, so with our united love and desires that amid all your uncongenial and distasteful surroundings your soul may be kept alive to the Lord, that you may often find His presence in your heart, and thus grow in grace and a knowledge of Him as your Lord and Saviour.

Hoping to see you shortly, and to hear from you when opportunity and inclination meet,

I remain
Your affectionate friend,
George Wariner

13, Surrenden Road
Brighton
17th July, 1917

My dear friend,

I have often wished to write a line to you, but having little time and several brothers away in the Army to write to, have put it off till now. When I heard that you had been subjected in a more than ordinary degree to persecution and injustice, I felt a wish to sympathise with you by letter. I do not know that I can say that I have much of one requisite for sympathy; it is necessary I think for real sympathy, to have been in the same place. Well I have had some few things to put up with whilst in this Corps. Yet to be honest I very frequently feel fearful lest because I am not properly separate from the world, therefore I am not subject to persecution which is the lot of all those who will live godly.

This fear often, as I reflect, makes me deem those who are enabled to walk in proper separation and are consequently persecuted, to be favoured people, and the persecution an honour. In this view you will not think me callous if I say I am glad you have undergone this trial, for whilst you no doubt have no great self-complacency, yet you will I trust have been strengthened in the grace of God and have proved the sufficiency of it. 'My grace is sufficient for thee; My strength is made perfect in weakness.' If so, painful though the trial has been, yet it has had a good effect, and I trust you will feel it to be so. Unworthy as I am yet sometimes my very soul is stirred with desire to be for the Lord's glory: 'Let your light so shine before men that they may see your good works and glorify your Father which is in Heaven.'

But in this consideration, as in all others, one has to come to the painful conclusion that one fails sadly. Who can express the desire, when hope in the Lord's mercy is felt and some of His goodness and love made known, to live to His praise? But personally it has to come to this constantly: 'No flesh shall glory in His presence.' Christ and His merit alone are sufficient. Guilt and demerit attach to *all* I do, although I would live exactly according to His will in all things.

Well my dear friend, may you be strengthened and brought well through the refining fire. How we do need patience and grace to wait upon the Lord during these dark days. He is good, can we not say, and deserves our praises. Alas that I so fail in gratitude for all His mercies.

I do hope we shall soon see you home again on leave. But whatever is before you, I wish you may feel His presence to support and comfort. We have lost nearly all our 'A' men from hospital now, they having been replaced by 'C', to which category I belong. Our united Christian love,

Your affectionate friend,
John H. Gosden

5th. February, 1918

My dear Jesse,

I am very glad to have your letter. It is a letter of remembrance, a looking-back letter, and very profitable it is to remember all the way the Lord has led us, when we are enabled to do so by the Spirit. In the review there is much to humble and abase us, and cause unspeakable shame. Corruptions dark and foul have blackened and marred us. O it is most painful to remember one's own part of the way! How extremely unlike a child of God have I been in my spirit! How wayward, unthankful, untender, unbelieving, prayerless and unsavoury! It is a dark side, one's own is! But the Lord's side: His mercies new every morning; the leadings, teachings, touches and helps of His Spirit; the views of Christ; the hope in His blood and righteousness; the humbling sense of an interest in the covenant which is ordered in all things and sure; the new warm love which enlarged our hearts; the sacred confidence in God both for time and eternity—O how sweet, how encouraging is such a backlook!

And your outward references I like. It was a time to be much remembered when divine pardon and heavenly love filled you and made a willing captive of you, and I rejoice in you as one God has given to me. This rejoicing has a jealousy in it. I pray you may be kept in the fear of God. I see you are so now. Follow on. May you ever be low in your own eyes. And your love for us at Galeed is pleasant to me. We are in affliction in the removal of you and all the other dear young men, and in the infirmities of our aged members, but withal we have such mercy. Specially is this so just now. Mr. J. H. Gosden's case is a wonderful one. He is undoubtedly an anointed minister, but I miss him much.

Archie Hayler's case is a very good one. He knows both sides—sin and salvation. May many more be brought among us of the same stamp.

It is wonderful to see God's goodness to your dear wife. I am very pleased to see His goodness to you in that particular. She said to me the other day she had had some good helps lately in hearing. O that the one thing she needs and seeks may soon be given to her!

God be with you, preserve you, and restore you to us.

All at the chapel would send love to you if they knew of my writing.

I am,
Your affectionate pastor,
J. K. Popham

7th. February, 1919

My dear friend and brother,

It seems selfish of me not to have written for so long, seeing you are still in a foreign land and isolated from all your friends, whilst I have been released from the army and am now, in that sense, a free man at home. They demobilized me under the scheme releasing all who had been in hospital twenty-eight days and over. I feel it to be a great mercy and a very wonderful providence to have been brought through so safely. My leg is practically well, except for a very slight weakness which I shall always have but which does not affect me much, and is not worth mentioning.

I often think of you and sympathize with you. How thankful I am you have been kept safe! It is indeed a great mercy. You have, as you said in your last letter, been favoured in days past with sweet gospel liberty. If I may claim to have been so favoured in a small degree (and I trust it is not wrong for me to do so), I with you do truly want another such blessing. At times I am almost indifferent, but at other times feel I cannot go on without some renewed token of God's favour. It is an infinite mercy for us that He does not change as we do, but that He is faithful and true. And if He has reconciled us to Himself in the body of the flesh of Jesus through death, He will never leave us to sink. He paid too high a price to lose one of His own. 'Ye are bought with a price.' But what we want, dear friend (is it not?), is a constant renewal with power of a sense of our interest in His love, the love which brought Him to die for sinners. For sin so often defiles us and separates between us and our (as we hope, our) Redeemer, God. This at least is my sad experience, and no power on earth can bring nearness and cleansing again; only I do believe the blood of Christ can, as applied to the conscience. I wish I knew by experience more of what Hart sets out in those lines (concerning the blood of Christ):

> 'If guilt removed return and remain,
> Its power may be proved again and again.'

I hope it is well with you, and that my barren state will not be conveyed to you by this note. Remember me, if you can, in your prayers. I am a poor fearful creature, and need in many ways the help of God. The Lord bless you and prosper you in your soul, and bring you home again soon if His holy will.

With Christian love, my wife joining,
Yours sincerely in gospel bonds,
John H. Gosden

Trials at home and soul exercise as to his own case and the ministry

Relating to the period following his release from the Army, Mr Delves writes: 'My dear wife was in a very run down state of health and after some time she underwent an operation in hospital in London. During this affliction I was much exercised both for her and myself; one evening while alone reading, this word was fastened upon my mind with much sweetness: "Unto you therefore which believe He is precious." The word was so opened up to me—what a believer really was, and how Christ in His Person and work was made so precious to him and I had a powerful impression that I should one day be called to speak in His Great Name. On the Sunday following the 54th chapter of Isaiah was made most precious to me, my soul entering in a blessed way and manner into the promises contained in it. That day I went up to London in the afternoon [presumably to visit Mrs Delves in hospital], happy in my soul.

'At another season I was favoured with a love visit on a sick bed by our pastor's article in the Standard on Philippians Chapter 3 [probably *Gospel Standard* (1921), p. 235]. Whilst reading I felt my heart melting with His love to such a polluted wretch as I felt myself to be.

'During these years my mind was often tossed about relative to the work of the ministry, the exercises at times weighing very heavily. It would work chiefly in some word being especially opened up, and some sweet liberty of spirit in meditating upon it.

'At other times I had such apprehension of my own ignorance and foolishness that I tried to cast off the exercise, feeling that it could not be of the Lord; and comforted myself in the thought that I would let my mind settle, but this I could not do for long, for the trial would begin again and some word would come that would convince me that the matter was of the Lord. At one time this word constantly followed me: "Go preach the preaching that I bid thee", which I felt to be "Jesus Christ and Him crucified!"

'3/3/21. During this time I was favoured at times with some touches of the Lord's love to me and at other times sorely tried in my mind.

'The prayer meetings have been a very heavy exercise of

mind, often having to beg my way to chapel, and fearing I should be put to confusion before the people and that my mouth would be shut, but in this I have proved the enemy a liar and God faithful to His Word; He has most graciously helped me many times and lifted me above my fears.

'I travelled in this path with this burden of the ministry laid upon me for seven years without speaking a word to any fellow creature; my feelings were that if this matter was of the Lord He would lay it on the minds of His dear people without my touching it; and my prayer was that I might not mention the matter to any person, not even my own wife. In this I believe the Lord kept me though it seemed as though it would never come to pass: it appeared impossible.

'In this month of January 1923, one evening after the service one of the brethren spoke to me saying, "I would like to see you privately"; this remark went through me as I felt at that moment what was on his mind; shortly after, coming home from a funeral, he asked me if I had any exercise concerning my future; if the Lord had spoken to me in any word of direction. I then felt compelled to tell him what was on my mind, that although I had been for a long time tried about this matter, I could not feel clear about it as I had not had any distinct word. At that time he told me he had felt it on his mind for some time.

'I was now brought into great exercise of mind. I did try to beg of the Lord that I might know His will, and not be left to my own will in this thing, and not be deceived. That night this word kept coming to me "Unto me, who am less than the least of all saints, is this grace given, that I should preach among the Gentiles the unsearchable riches of Christ" (Eph. 3: 8).

'The word abode with me some time, then I would call it all into question again. After this we were brought into the path of affliction, my dear wife having to undergo an operation in July and another one the July following. During this season of affliction the Lord brought me into fellowship with many portions of His Word that might [otherwise] have been passed over. I passed through much furnace work, under this chastening at the time. The following January [1924] one Tuesday morning, feeling to have come to the end of everything in my feelings, I begged of the Lord to settle my mind about the matter so that I could rest, when this word was powerfully spoken to me, I believe from the Lord, "For the work of the ministry, for the edifying of the body of Christ" (Eph. 4: 12); I came downstairs and found the passage and it seemed plain to me then what the Lord intended me for; the next Thursday was the quarterly Church Meeting. I went with these words on my mind. When Mr Popham read that chapter and commented on the very verse that had been spoken to me (as I felt), I felt such a solemn power pervade my very being that night, that that was the mind of the Lord concerning me.

'After that memorable time I went on for some time; occasionally brother Pocock would speak his feelings and I would tell him mine.' [Of such visits Mr Delves said that Mr Pocock would enter the shop and often greet him thus: 'Is it still Joshua 1.8?'] Mr Delves continues: 'At times I felt such a sinful wretch before the Lord, that the thought seemed only like presumption to think of such a work as the ministry for such a poor ignorant wretch as I felt. But in my abjection the Lord would answer with some word that would close my mouth and cause me to feel I must leave the matter with Him.'

Sad family bereavements

'At this time my dear wife not being able to attend chapel I felt constrained one day to speak of some of the things we had heard in the morning; in that, I felt a peculiar liberty in following it up which surprised me, when perhaps my mind just before was quite dark.

'Another trial was my mother's illness which was a great strain to us; I hope it was that in reading by her bedside I felt compelled to speak my thoughts on a portion of the Word when it opened up which I have reason to believe was a comfort and help to her. I have sometimes continued it in our family circles.

'I now often travelled in darkness and such confusion prevailed in my mind, though frequently some word would be brought to my mind and I would find myself, in meditating in it, led into some of the truths in the Scripture, and also see how the Lord's tried and afflicted people are called to walk it out in experience. In the year 1926, my mother died and we feel we can say with respect to her that she is "with Christ which is far better".

'My mind was constantly tried concerning the solemn work of the ministry, at times asking the Lord to remove it if it were not His will. Nothing particular occurred after this till, I think, in February 1927, when a sudden and heavy trial fell on us in the untimely end of my brother Nelson. He took his life one Tuesday morning with his gun in the stone shed on the farm. This trial brought me into the most solemn consideration of the sovereignty of God and of the unspeakable greatness of one's own soul-state. The sovereignty of God was very solemn to me, and is still; "One shall be taken, and another left".'

A sacred view of Christ; further trials and confirmations concerning the work of the ministry

'After this I was again brought into great trial in my mind and it seemed more than I could bear but one day the same friend called to see me who had been travelling with me in this exercise, and we had a little conversation together.

'In the afternoon the Lord in His mercy came and blessed my soul. A solemn sacred view of Christ suffering in the garden rose up before me. I saw Him there by precious faith, sweating blood, in great agony, and was favoured with a sweet view of the eternal Sovereign Love of God the Father in the gift of His Son; and of the Son in His willingness to die for lost and ruined sinners, and of God the Holy Ghost, to whom be eternal praises for making known to me in some measure that it was all for love,

"For love of whom?, of sinners base,
A hardened herd, a rebel race
That mocked and trampled on Thy blood,
And wantoned with the wounds of God."
(Gadsby's 153, pt. 2)

'I was obliged to leave my bench and be alone, and Oh what a hatred against sin did I feel, and my soul was melted with the love of Christ shed abroad, and I blessed God for such infinite love, and Christ's words then came with power, "Father, if it be possible, let this cup pass from me: nevertheless not as I will, but as Thou wilt" (Matt. 26: 39). I felt my spirit brought into a sweet conformity to the will of God, just willing to be something or nothing as He would have me be, and so sweetly enabled to cast my care and the heavy exercise of my mind upon Him and to say "Thy will be done".

'This sweet appearing of the Lord to me so settled my mind for a time that I felt some rest and quiet, and was enabled to leave it with the Lord, believing that if it was His will, He would help me and if not that it might be otherwise.

'A little time after this Mr Popham called to see me and said he had heard I had an exercise about the ministry, but that it came as a surprise to know. He wished me to tell him a little which I did and he received it kindly, and gave me some most affectionate advice, saying he would be afraid to hurt my feelings in any way, but that many had those feelings when blessed, but that it was not of the Lord; whether it was in my case time would prove, advising me to wait and watch the hand of the Lord in the matter; so we parted in love and union.

'After this I came into much bondage again in my spirit, feeling as though the Scriptures were closed against me and my mind so dark and ignorant that nothing but confusion seemed to belong to me, I wished the matter could be stopped and nothing more said of it. I had hardly any light into the Scriptures and there was not a text in the Bible that I felt I could speak from for ten minutes.

'Here I could see nothing but that I had mistaken the way, and it was but the workings of my mind. I felt I should be confounded before the people if I was brought before them; my mind was in great bondage and this caused many cries to the Lord not to let me be deceived.

'One evening while out walking and labouring under this darkness, the word dropped so sweetly into my heart, "If the Son therefore shall make you free, ye shall be free indeed" (John 8: 36).

'The Lord showed me that I had no liberty in myself, I was trying to walk in my own strength, looking within for something more than looking to and trusting the Lord. I was shown what true liberty was, that Christ procured it by His sufferings and death and resurrection, that He fulfilled the law and made it honourable and that if we are one of those for whom Christ was made a curse, and for whom He died, we have true liberty; an experience of pardon by His blood applied by the Holy Ghost brings liberty when received by faith and every intimation of love and mercy manifestly brings with it, if felt in sweetness and power, a measure of liberty. What sweet meditation I was favoured with for some time by this word of the Lord Jesus.

'After this, opening the Bible one morning I opened on to this word: "I will go before thee, and make the crooked places straight: I will break in pieces the gates of brass, and cut in sunder the bars of iron:" Isaiah, 45.2. This word confirmed me in this, that the Lord would bring me into the ministry, and that I should have much opposition; but that the Lord would be sufficient for me in spite of all that might oppose me. I saw much in this, the Lord going before, and being with a sinner and also being His rereward.'

'June, 1927. During the last few days I have felt some sweet nearness to the Lord and a little light into His word; it is just as the Lord is pleased to reveal it to me, for I have nothing in myself, poor dark ignorant creature, sin mixed with all I do, in my thoughts, in my actions, what a weak foolish thing I feel to be in every way.

'Last Saturday I went out for an early morning walk. I felt a sweet nearness, and had a sight of the human nature of Jesus. The line of the hymn (950) "Wrapt in humanity, to die", was so sweet to me. Oh to have right teaching, and to be well set down in every Gospel truth and in our own sinfulness that we may by the Spirit's teaching be taught to worship Him in spirit and in truth.

'June 12, 1927. On Sunday was Mr Popham's 46th Anniversary of his first preaching at Galeed. May he yet be spared to us if the Lord's will for a long time, and his labours abundantly blessed.'

Further domestic trials and sore spiritual temptation

'June 13th, 1927. My dear wife left home for 10 days or so to help nurse her mother, who has kept her bed now for nearly a year; may she have journeying mercies and be brought back to us safely, and be strengthened in body, and if the Lord's will "filled with joy and peace in believing" and feel the pardon of all her sins, for His Name's Sake, Amen.' That this prayerful desire was abundantly answered, the sequel will shortly show.

'August 1st. I feel the Lord has not spoken anything special relating to the ministry, but I have sunk again into deep waters, this time in a way almost terrible to think of, being beset by the most blatant temptations, that is I now feel them to have been temptations, of a most awful nature which shook me to the very foundations; it seemed as if my little religion I had was ebbing away. I was tried on this point, that there was no such thing as real religion; even that there was no hereafter (awful thought), that when I died I should die like a dog after all. Now my mind was at times racked by these temptations; at times I could hardly bear to go down on my knees; it would be thrust into my mind, "there is no God to go to", that I had not an immortal soul; the most wicked and insidious seeds of infidelity I had in my nature. Though at this time I hope there was a violent struggle going on in my heart, yet I sometimes feared I should be overcome after all, and prove to be nothing more than a hypocrite.'

Mrs Delves sweetly blessed with spiritual deliverance

'I was plunged into deep waters, I fell into deep mire where there was no standing. But Oh blessed be God, He was pleased to deliver me and raise me up again by giving me a blessed answer to prayer (the cries of years' standing) by opening the windows of heaven and pouring out a blessing on the soul of my dear wife who had long been in captivity. Oh how sweetly did He bless her soul, so that she was raised up to bless and praise Him and her tongue loosed and her mouth opened that she was enabled to declare what God had done for her soul. And truly I can say that in blessing her He blessed me also. It was like another deliverance to me, for faith was again given and the precious Gospel again made life and power in my soul. I felt again led into the Truth in much sweetness and made willing to speak in His Name if it was His will.'

Mrs Delves wrote some account of her experiences and these were published in the *Gospel Standard* (1976), pp. 283–8. She passed peacefully away on 11 May that year. A short extract from the account will convey something of the sacredness of the season to which Mr Delves refers.

Mrs Delves writes: 'Then came a wonderful season when my heart was softened and prepared for His coming, to make Himself precious to my soul. How I had longed for full forgiveness, sweet gospel liberty, but feared that if it should ever be, it would be near the end of my days knowing my sins richly deserved His wrath, and to be banished for ever. Well do I remember feeling, especially on one occasion, there was nothing but hell for me, and really I feared I should soon be there. Never can one express these terrible feelings. Every word of God seemed written against me—when in the early hours of one morning that sweetly came—that, "still, small voice". This sweetened the bitter cup and gave a hope in Him, even for me.

'Under this feeling I could truly say, "I looked for hell, He brought me heaven". Blessed be His Name, He came in love and broke my heart all to pieces, speaking peace and pardon, full and free. Wonder of wonders! I found my heart completely softened with His wonderful Love. Blessed Jesus! It came like this: "Is not this a brand plucked out of the fire?", again, "And ye are complete in Him". Again, "O Naphtali, satisfied with favour, and full of the blessing of the Lord: possess thou the west and the south" (Zech. 3: 2; Col. 2: 10; Deut. 33: 23).

'O the sweetness of the wonderful love of God! "He brought me to the banqueting house, and His banner over me was love" (S. of S. 2: 4). Better felt than expressed! Food for the body was not my attraction or need, but Jesus was precious to my soul. He loved me, He would love, and I could not refuse to be loved—that is the best expression for that wonderful season.

"Sweet the moments, rich in blessing,
Which before the cross I spend"
(Gadsby's 158)

'To think of the cost, what it cost Him, our Dear Redeemer, to save my soul! O to live nearer and nearer to Him! Dear Jesus, sweet name! Holy Spirit, open up more and more Thy sacred truths. Blessed Trinity, Father, Son and Holy Ghost!'

After relating some further experiences and her visit to Mr Popham Mrs Delves speaks of her baptism: 'When I went before the Church, I felt to lose the sweet comfort, and could not tell out my feelings or speak well of a good God as I would, who had been so precious and done so much for a vile sinner. I just felt to go into darkness. My bodily strength also was small and I collapsed. This was a bitter trial. I remained in this dark, troubled state for three days. During the third evening, I was lying on a bed in the garden when the darkness of mind began to leave me—sweet feeling! The Lord drew near; His precious Word came into my heart once again. My dear husband came to be with me for a few minutes and I told him of the change. His answer was, "Well, you know, the Lord Jesus was in the grave three days". O what that was to me words cannot express! I could with heartfelt gratitude praise Him for allowing me in a very small measure only just a touch of fellowship and communion with Him in His sufferings, and to be a follower in a path of trial and to bear the cross. I began to be stronger in body and was helped to be baptized the following week, August 10th, 1927.

'On the morning of August 10th, I awakened early as in a dream. It was so sweet. I dreamed I heard a multitude of voices, singing, "Hallelujah, praise ye the Lord". It was distinct and beautiful. I wakened my husband to tell him. I felt I must speak of it. I said, "I do hope they will sing warmly at Galeed this evening, but they cannot sing like that". To my great relief that wonderful hymn was sung (Gadsby's 730): "All hail the power of Jesus' name".'

Fruits of patience from long exercise concerning the ministry

Mr Delves's writings continue: 'April 12th, 1928. About eight months have passed since then and I hope it has many times been sweet and profitable to look back upon the way the Lord has led us in Providence and Grace. I was at the time of writing this alone under two providential trials which pressed heavily. The Lord has now been pleased to grant relief from both in a great measure. How much I have to mourn the workings of my own wicked heart, and rebellion and unbelief; how slow we are to trust in Him. To trust in Him at all times is more than is in my power. I have to prove that God alone can give me that faith to trust Him; we may often think we can trust Him till the trial comes to test the matter, and then we find how little faith we have.

'During the past few months I have been through a great deal of exercise of soul relating to the matter of the ministry, but it has been a sifting time indeed, and those things that I had believed

I felt and received of the Lord touching this solemn matter have been very much called into question; much opposition has been brought against it in my own heart, and I have sometimes come to this point, Was it of God or of man? knowing that many of the Lord's people have had exercises about preaching, but that it has come to naught; therefore it is doubtful if it was more than a leaning that way in themselves only.

'In looking back over this period, I do not feel to have had anything from the Lord further with respect to it, so that I feel now to want another confirmation and token from Himself if it is to be His Will. There was a time with me when I frequently felt like a bottle wanting vent, and I have felt liberty in my spirit, and the Scriptures were opened up in some measure to my understanding; but a cloud has come over it and it has had to be tried in the fire; the enemy has often suggested that if ever the Lord intended me to speak in His Name, He would have opened a door before this time. "See", says he, "here is the best part of your life ebbing away, and it seems less likely now than before", to all which I quite agree, and I do certainly see and feel myself more than ever now to be such a poor, ignorant, weak, stupid creature, that for me to ever preach seems impossible, and sure I am that is, in and of myself, for I believe I should be utterly in confusion if brought before a company of people unless the Lord was with me and that to bless. He would indeed have to be mouth, matter and wisdom, yea All in All to me; but though I feel such a poor thing myself yet I have been encouraged by these words "I can do all things through Christ which strengtheneth me", and again, "With God all things are possible". What I feel to need now is for the Lord to come again and shine into my soul as I hope He has done in days past, and then how soon is darkness made light; crooked things straight and rough places plain.'

A visit to Biddenden

'In July 1928 I went to Biddenden and on the Monday evening went to see Mr Kemp, the Pastor, and what to me was very remarkable almost at once he fell to speaking of the way the Lord had led him in his call by grace and to the ministry, and some of the afflictions and trials that followed. This was very striking to me as so far as I knew he had not the slightest knowledge of my having any such feelings. I was encouraged to find, however, that there were things that very much resembled my own case, especially his feeling that he would never be able to stand up before a company of people. After speaking some time he turned and said "Now I think it is your turn". I felt constrained to tell him a little from the beginning till the time of my deliverance, but avoiding anything relating to the ministry— This was very marked to me.

Invited to speak at Shoreham: trial and deliverance

'After this a friend [Mr Pocock] said to me one day, "If you were asked to go and help the friends at Shoreham by reading and expounding on the chapter, would you do so?". Said he, "You think the matter over". My answer to him was that if the Lord opened a door for me and gave me a direction in the matter I feel that I should not dare to refuse. Some weeks after this one morning, I received a letter from Mr Funnell, the deacon at Shoreham, to this effect: "Some months ago he had been told that one of the members at Galeed was exercised about the ministry, though no name was mentioned; Mr Pocock had since also spoken to him about the same thing mentioning my name, and having an evening vacant on Tuesday 25th September, he would be glad if I would come and speak to them, and might the Lord's presence be felt among us." This letter brought me into great trouble; I had never before been asked to speak, but here was a letter asking me to speak to them in the Name of God. Oh how I sunk. It had never come home so clearly to me before. After breakfast I felt I would try to read of the call of Jeremiah, and how it touched my case: "Then said I, Ah Lord God, behold, I cannot speak: for I am but a child. But the Lord said unto me, Say not, I am a child: for thou shalt go to all that I shall send thee, and whatsoever I command thee thou shalt speak."

'I felt it my duty as promised before to take this letter to my pastor which I did the same morning. Mr Popham pointed out that this thing was not in order, and did not approve of the action; I had, said he, no right or authority to go to any place to preach as I had not received the sanction of the Church of which I was a member, and that it was my plain duty to write and decline the invitation. I told him I should be very grieved to walk in any way inconsistent with Church order and discipline, and that I should decline it in accordance with his request. Mr Popham said the deacons were coming that evening and that he would lay the matter before them.

'This seemed to cut me down at a stroke, and I believe the enemy set in upon me sorely. Thinks I, "Now here has been all these years of trial and exercise about preaching, and now as soon as you receive a call the thing is crushed", and moreover I felt I had swerved from my conviction that if the Lord opened the door, I should sin if I refused. Oh what a death it seemed to bring upon it all. It brought me into great trial which continued till the Thursday afternoon when I went out after dinner, and walking down Stanford Avenue I felt in a dreadful state; it seemed the Lord was dealing hardly with me. I felt like Jonah when he said, "Out of the belly of hell cried I". When I reached Beaconsfield Road, suddenly this verse dropped right into my heart so wonderfully:

"No harsh commands He gave,
No hard conditions brought;
He came to seek and save,
And pardon every fault."
(Gadsby's 448)

I began to feel different; the hard rebellion I had melted like wax before the sun, it brought me down at His feet, confessing, and confessing, and still the words kept coming, "He came to seek and save, and pardon every fault"; what a blessed exchange it was. My faith saw His great love in coming to suffer and die for such wretches as I felt myself to be; how I loved Him; sweet meditation I had in the busy traffic, of God's wonderful love, a full complete pardon for all and every sin past, present, and to come. This continued till the next evening, when sitting in my chair such darkness came over me that I cannot describe. It was just like being shut up in a dark room, I felt it; I could never preach, and I secretly hoped that the thing would be stopped. The next day was a heavy day and when Sunday came I felt I could not bear to meet any of the people, especially the Pastor; and I seemed to go that day for life or death, but during the prayer Mr Popham was so earnest and I felt near the Lord, that

I began to hope that I should not be cut off, and when he stood up to give out the text it seemed as though everything hung upon it, and it was this, "I am the Lord thy God, which brought thee out of the land of Egypt: open thy mouth wide, and I will fill it" (Ps. 81: 10). How well I heard that day and I believe I can say I have done each time since.

Visits Biddenden again: the fleece wet and dry

'We went for a holiday to Biddenden for a week, and here I again became very tried as to whether I had received it from the Lord, and the case of Gideon was much upon my mind. He had had the sign of the fleece wet, but Gideon said, "Let not thine anger be hot against me, and I will speak but this once: let me prove, I pray thee, but this once with the fleece; let it now be dry only upon the fleece, and upon all the ground let there be dew. And God did so that night: for it was dry upon the fleece only, and there was dew on all the ground" (Judg. 6: 39, 40). I did in my heart desire that if it was from the Lord, there might be a further sign as I was there where my exercises were not known.

'The first thing I had was a sermon put into my hand preached by the late Mr McKenzie, from Acts 20.28: "Feed the church of God, which He hath purchased with His own blood." This was very applicable at this particular time, but on the Sabbath morning at the prayer meeting the deacon read Isaiah 6, relating to the call of the prophet, and the confirmation of his message. Following this the first hymn at the service was 374, originally occasioned by the death of Whitfield. Mr Kemp then read Acts 5 where there stood up in the council a Pharisee named Gamaliel, and concerning the Apostles he said, "If this . . . be of men it will come to naught: but if it be of God, ye cannot overthrow it; lest haply ye be found even to fight against God".

'In his prayer he especially prayed for any that might be exercised about the ministry, and prayed that they might be rightly directed. In the evening he preached at Grafty Green, and his text was Isaiah 41.14, 15 "Fear not, thou worm Jacob, and ye men of Israel; I will help thee, saith the Lord, and thy Redeemer, the Holy One of Israel. Behold, I will make thee a new sharp threshing instrument having teeth: thou shalt thresh the mountains, and beat them small, and shalt make the hills as chaff."

'This was a very remarkable day to me and I felt I could say no more.'

Sent out into the ministry with the approbation of the Church at Galeed

'Feb. 21, 1929. Since the above, as week after week has worn away I have been up and down, sometimes feeling an inward encouragement and at other times very cast down. Nothing further occurred till Mr Popham called to see me and said the deacons wished to hear what I had to say. He was very anxious it should be kept secret; accordingly in about a fortnight I was invited to attend the Pastor's house and relate my exercises. I felt much sinking of heart before the time came to go, but as I was walking to the house these words came very sweetly: "Wait on the Lord, trust also in Him, He shall bring forth thy righteousness as the light and thy judgement as the noonday."

'I felt helped to speak to them and I have reason to believe the Spirit brought those things to my remembrance which I believed I had tasted, handled and felt.

'March, 1929. After this I had a dream, and I dreamt I was to preach in Galeed Chapel, but that I had great difficulty in getting to the pulpit; I was in chapel and Hymn 320 was given out, "God moves in a mysterious way etc.", and I had to pass out the back of the chapel and go up the passage; I met Mr Popham on the stairs and waited for him to pass me, when he turned and seemed as if he would have spoken but said nothing. By the time I entered the pulpit the people were singing the last verse,

"God is His own interpreter,
And He will make it plain."

'I had no text but as I took the Bible down these words came powerfully to my mind, Psalm 23, 'The Lord is my shepherd, I shall not want.' I could not find the psalm in the Bible, so as the people were waiting I stood up and gave it out, when I felt such power and liberty that my voice quite startled the people. I began to speak with boldness, when I noticed the Bible was covered over. I awoke, feeling it would only be possible for me to preach by the power and unction of the Spirit of God, and not by books or natural arguments, though I feel it right to use what means are at my disposal as ignorance is nothing to be proud of; but I feel that if I have to stand up in the Lord's Name, He and He alone will be all sufficient.

'April, 1929. In the Providence of God I went before the Church at Galeed on March 7th, Thursday evening, and my testimony was accepted by the Church. I spoke before the Church from the words in Isaiah 28.16 speaking in great conflict of mind, of the Lord Jesus Christ as the Foundation etc., for about thirty minutes. To my surprise the Church received me.'

After the meeting Mr Popham was taken ill. He wrote to Mr Delves as follows:

Normandien,
10, Harrington Road,
Brighton.

March 8th, 1929.

My dear Jesse,

On arriving home last night almost immediately I became unwell, and this morning the doctor said I had influenza, and that I must make arrangements for the Lord's Day as I should not be fit to go out.

Now, as the Church sanctioned your going out to preach you must take my place.

Two words of advice I have to give you:

1. Lay a good foundation of doctrine in your sermons.
2. Try to open your mouth and let every word be distinctly uttered.

The Lord help you! If you are invited to preach at Shoreham I wish to see you before you go, if you feel led to accept the invitation.

I hope your wife is better and that you have recovered from the exhausting exercises of last evening.

Your affectionate Pastor.

Of this sudden development Mr Delves has given his own account: 'The Lord alone knows what I went through from Friday to Sunday evening. I seemed as one plunged into deep waters; everything swept away; no religion left. I could not go forward, and could not turn backward. That Friday night was a night of terror, trial, and testing of the whole thing. The pains of hell gat hold upon me; I found trouble and sorrow.

Everything seemed to be called into question; sometimes I felt I had been presumptuous. But in the morning, I believe the Lord gave me some relief in that terrible fire. It was as though He gently whispered in my ear: "I will strengthen thee".' Mr Delves often referred to that memorable Lord's Day evening at Galeed. (He had been too weak and overwrought to venture in the morning.) All fear was taken away when he began to speak and to him, if not to others, the contrast between the occasion and the preceding Thursday evening when he felt to be in such bondage, was most marked. His text on the Lord's Day evening was Phil. 3: 10. In referring to that time, Mr S. F. Paul, until his death in 1971 a deacon for many years at Galeed, wrote: 'Some of us who had travelled with him in his exercises can testify to the wonderful way in which he was helped on that memorable occasion. It seemed as though the whole Church was praying that he might be helped, and that they might not be put to shame in their decision to send him forth in the Lord's Name; and truly the Lord heard their cries, and endued His servant with a gracious power, the influence of which was very evident.'

Mr and Mrs Delves
(at about the time he began to preach)

CHAPTER TWO

The Ministry, Early Years and Call to Pastorate at Clapham

WE have a little insight to the domestic burdens which arose as a result of the ministry: Mrs Delves wrote, 'My dear husband was thrust into the ministry. It was a heavy path indeed, each day for a time "strength enough and none to spare". But, blessed be His Name, He alone was our strength and stay. Satan is a cruel foe, but God is greater than the enemy of souls. Things looked so cross-handed often, but all was wisely ordered and managed. I had inwardly to ask God to manage my heart. I felt all would be well if He would but do this.

'On one occasion my husband had to leave home at 5 p.m. on Saturday for a long journey. This was a great trial for we were usually very busy on Saturday evenings, and if severe weather, there was more trade than usual. As the time drew near for him to leave, customers came in freely, and it looked impossible to manage with one pair of hands less; indeed extra help was needed. I felt teeming with rebellion. O my wicked heart! Only God could see—when this came distinctly: "Wist ye not that I must be about my Father's business?" (Luke 2: 49) Immediately I felt to let all go. My husband was in his right place. I could say nothing, and I felt willing to see him go to the work to which he was called. And though it was a long busy evening until late, I felt helped all through.'

One of the first places to which Mr Delves went to minister was Ebenezer, Clapham. The Thursday following Mr Delves' first sermon in public on the Lord's day evening referred to, Mr. S. F. Stevens a deacon at Ebenezer Clapham, wrote as follows:

To Mr. Delves
Dear Friend,

I am a stranger to you personally, yet not a disinterested one, and having heard of your speaking at Galeed on Lord's Day evening last and having a good report of the same from a godly friend, as we at Ebenezer, Stonhouse Street, Clapham, have still three vacant dates this year, we three deacons are unanimous that we might ask you if the Lord will to come and speak the word of life to us, as you may be helped of the Lord so to do . . . Your dear aged and honoured and beloved pastor has been to us annually for I suppose about 30 years, and we hope if the Lord will he may be able to visit us on Whit Monday next. We are very sorry to know he is so unwell, but 'The government is upon His shoulder', and we know not what purpose He had in opening that door for you last Lord's Day, but it may be unfolded later on.

This letter coming so soon, I feel may make you tremble, and cause you many misgivings, and Satan may try to prevent, but I hope the Lord may direct you. No doubt venturing forth in this solemn work, will mean many new trials, new temptations, and much painful (but I hope prayerful) exercise. Doubtless not every one will receive you, but may the Lord open your eyes that you may see, greater is He that sent you forth, than all the host that may oppose you. I think no greater honour can be placed upon a poor sinner than to be a servant of the Most High God, and He never makes a mistake, nor does He ever create anything in vain; therefore if He sends you forth He has a purpose in it and will accomplish that purpose, and you have His promise which still stands 'Lo, I am with you alway even unto the end'. May He give you to prove He has chosen the weak things of the world to confound the mighty and dear Paul says 'When I am weak, then am I strong', 'Not by might, nor by power, but by my Spirit saith the Lord'. May the Lord make and keep you faithful, and encourage you to go forward, by giving you seals to your ministry, and make it manifest in the hearts of His poor people that you are His servant.

Well, I feel I am but a poor ignorant sinner and know not what to say or how to write so please forgive me. I would write to your encouragement if I could; well, our open dates are, May 19th, June 9th, August 4th 1929. The Lord's Days are all filled for 1930, but if convenient to you we may fit in a few week evenings next year, G.W. These three Lord's days have been a great exercise to me and many letters have I written, but God moves in a mysterious way, and who knows what it may mean. I hope we may meet together at a Throne of Grace on this matter, I mean in our homes, and may the Lord direct you in the matter, and should it be His will for you to come to us, I trust He may be in our midst and touch with compunction, and sprinkle with blood.

With Christian love, and shall be glad to hear from you as soon as you can, I remain yours sincerely, S. F. Stevens.

Mr Delves responded to this letter by agreeing to engage for the first of the vacancies. Subsequently he took all three dates, and in the following years increased his engagements with Clapham. In the early part of 1933 he was laid aside with a serious illness, as a result of which a number of engagements had to be cancelled. Mr S. F. Stevens wrote frequently during this illness, and his letters reflect a tender and loving concern for Mr and Mrs Delves, as well as manifesting anxiety lest this affliction, and consequently Mr Delves's absence from their midst, was a chastisement from the Lord of the Cause at Ebenezer. A few extracts from Mr Stevens' letters follow:

To Mrs Delves,

. . . may the Lord comfort your dear husband that he may feel 'The government is upon His shoulder' and no mistake is possible with Him. 'Jacob alighted at a *certain* place', not one which he had marked out and chosen, but a lonely spot, a hard pillow, but it was a certain place where the dear Lord had chosen, that He would bless him there. May our dear friend feel that though he would not have chosen this affliction yet that it is the place where the Lord will meet him and bless him . . . I trust he may soon be recovered and if the Lord's will be able to be with us the following Lord's day, even if only for one service, but that we must leave at present . . .

To Mr Delves,

. . . I hope it may be the will of the Lord soon to raise you up and strengthen you in your poor body and in your inner mind by His Spirit that you may again go forth even like a giant refreshed with new wine, the wine of the Kingdom. Your affliction is a matter of exercise to us here; is the Lord chastening us, by withholding His servant from us? Let us search and try our ways and may we be humbled in godly confession of our sins . . . I am sure it is a trial to you to have to disappoint your friends, but you must try and not worry about it. It is hard sometimes to believe to our own comfort and rest, that all things work together for good, but if the Lord whispers a word and says 'I am with thee thy troubles to bless' that will put things right . . .

Another to Mr Delves,

. . . Well I believe the Lord has been with you in this affliction, and I trust sanctified it to you and so it may prove a blessing both to yourself and also to those amongst whom you minister: 'Afflictions make us see, what else would 'scape our sight'; they bring us to reflection, make eternity a solemn reality . . .

Such gracious letters, whilst doubtless strengthening to Mr Delves, evidence the personal exercise of the writer, and it was only three months after writing the last letter from which an extract is given above that Mr S. F. Stevens was taken to his eternal rest. In Volume 1 of the *Further History of the Gospel Standard Baptists*, Mr S. F. Paul writes:

Before he passed away, however, he was the means of setting on foot those proceedings in the church at Ebenezer which issued in Mr Delves becoming the pastor. In June of 1933, the latter received the following communication from the church: 'At a church meeting held at Ebenezer Chapel on April 19th., our late and much esteemed friend, Mr. Stevens, gave notice of a church meeting to be held at one month from that date, when he proposed to bring before the church the following proposition: "That Mr. Jesse Delves be asked to supply the pulpit for three months in 1935, with a view to taking over the pastorate." His exercises concerning this matter were not merely just for the time, but rather they had occupied his mind for some years, and for yourself in particular for some long time, and we hope he was not alone in this matter. Owing to his death, the deacons in conjunction with Mr Midmer who was asked by them to take the chair at their meetings, considered it advisable to postpone the meeting to such a date as should be announced. The meeting, duly convened, was held last Wednesday evening, after the service. The proposition was then put to the church with the following result: For the proposition 18, against 9, thus giving the necessary majority to enable the deacons to write to you. We therefore, on behalf of the church, have pleasure in asking you to give this matter that weighty and solemn consideration that it demands, and much hope you may receive the necessary leading from the Spirit, so that you may feel clear in moving in the matter. We can but believe that you have found at times unusual liberty in the pulpit, and a union to us as a church. We hope there has been a mutual growing of attachment yet to be increased. May the Lord make it increasingly clear that this is the work of His hands and that the union, if right in His sight, may be blessed to many souls.

On 22 July, Mr Delves replied as follows:

Your very important letter . . . has been the matter of much heavy exercise, inward conflict, and prayerful consideration. I trust my desire has been to know and do the will of the Lord in this matter.

Many anxious days have been spent, and many cries put up to the Lord, beseeching Him to show me the way wherein I should walk, being fearful of my own choice in coming to a decision. During this anxious period of waiting and watching three things have weighed upon my spirit.

First, the Lord has at times favoured me in preaching amongst you, with freedom and liberty; there has been a measure of unction and feeling, which has resulted in a growing interest in you as a people, an increasing union to you as a church, which has produced in me an exercise towards you in relation to the matter now proposed.

Secondly, my labours among you appear not to have been in vain, and though it is a day of small things, there have been some signs following, several added to the church, and some confirming evidence that the hand of the Lord has been in the ministry to some cases.

Thirdly, as a church you have Holy Scripture on your side in a mutual desire for a pastor, which has been observable when some appear more content to continue with the Supply system, though you have been consistent in not disclosing your feelings as being toward me in particular . . . Further, the portions of Scripture that have had considerable influence on my spirit have been as a direction, and on occasions I have felt a willingness to labour statedly among you if the will of the Lord be so.

At other times, this influence has been opposed by the following considerations:

First, the lack of unanimity has weighed heavily, causing much turmoil and disquietude of mind, so as almost to 'turn the scale'; but of late my feeling has been more concerned that it would not be right, in view of what has been felt toward you, to decline on that account.

Secondly, my painful sense of the lack of grace and gift so necessary for the pastoral office, many recurring apprehensions that the preaching will not stand the test, that in a short time the ministry would dry up and become burdensome to the people; and yet when so concluding I have felt condemned, in that it is yielding to unbelief in doubting the power of God, who alone is sufficient for all my need.

Thirdly, the fear that my coming amongst you may be a cause of strife and disunion in the church, has almost moved me to decline; but I desire grace to pray for the spiritual welfare of those unfavourable as well as those in whose heart it is to invite me.

These considerations have now brought me to the following decision—to accept your invitation to supply probationally for the first three months in 1935, provided a mutual understanding be agreed upon that, if as time proceeds it does not appear according to the mind of the Lord, the matter need go no further.

May the Lord be with us each, giving grace to be much in prayer and watching thereunto, well exercised, much and often in confession of sin, tender in His fear, and walking worthy of the vocation wherewith we are called.

During the year 1934, there were signs of the Lord's approbation in several additions to the church, as well as the feeling of an increasing union between the people and their prospective pastor.

Of this time Mr Delves wrote:

On one occasion I had a telegram to say that Mr Midmer was ill (he passed away later, on 3rd July) and would not be able to preach or preside at a particular Church meeting and could I come . . . I came, and preached and presided at the Church Meeting that followed, and that evening always stands out in my mind. (Two friends gave in their testimonies.) I felt for the first time in a particular way that I could give myself to this church, and I went home under a sweet sense of the goodness of God. Then a trial followed, that I feared I had not grace to preach constantly to the same people. It appeared to me that it must inevitably result in the congregation becoming weary of me long before the three months expired. But in this even the Lord was good to us; as one Sabbath followed another, things seemed to follow on in the ministry and I began to carry the people in my heart, prayers and affections, so that it tended to liberty, and I felt wonderfully helped through those three months.

At the commencement of the probationary period on the first Lord's Day in 1935 Mr Delves gave a brief introductory address to the congregation (as Mr Paul recounts in his 'History'):

He defined the position and exhorted them to prayer and watchfulness that the mind of the Lord might be made abundantly clear. At a church meeting following this period on April 17th. Mr Delves was given a cordial invitation to the pastorate, which had now become unanimous, showing that his continuous ministry for the period of probation had been the means, in the Lord's gracious hands, of removing the opposition which had previously existed. Mr Sawyer of Mayfield presided at this meeting, and the same evening preached a very appropriate sermon from the blessing of Asher in Deut. 33: 24, 25.

During this period of solemn exercise Mr Delves received a clear confirmation of the Lord's will concerning his acceptance of the pastorate. He related it with feeling, as being 'a word from the Lord'. He had been preaching at Southampton on the Lord's Day and returning home to Brighton on Monday morning was waiting for the train at Portsmouth station, sitting pondering and seeking another word of direction in this solemn matter, when these words were given to him, 'Feed the flock of God which is among you, taking the oversight thereof, not by constraint, but willingly; not for filthy lucre, but of a ready mind' (1 Pet. 5: 2). They were to him as the fleece being dry, after many indications of the Lord's purposes for him.

The 'History' continues:

> The commencement of the new pastorate was signalized by special services held on Whit Monday, June 10th. The evening service was taken by Mr J. K. Popham, but in the afternoon he sat in the rostrum with Mr Delves, to hear the latter preach and relate his call by grace and to the ministry; and a wonderful sight it was to see the aged pastor of 'Galeed', Brighton, sitting beside one of his sons in the faith, looking intently at him, and listening with impaired hearing to catch every word. Mr Delves took for his text: 'Uphold me according to Thy word, that I may live; and let me not be ashamed of my hope' (Ps. 119: 116). After referring to his need and desire to be upheld in Christ, the eternal Word, as well as in the written Word, and to be made to live in true exercise and in the ministry, he proceeded to refer to his hope that the Lord had called him by grace and into the ministry, and placed him in this pastorate, desiring not to be ashamed of that hope.

CHAPTER THREE

Clapham Pastorate

THE first Lord's day following the Church's unanimous invitation to Mr Delves to become their pastor, he addressed the assembled Church and congregation in a manner characteristic of the tender oversight which he displayed in his office throughout the ensuing forty-two years. A few extracts follow:

> Now, I wish to say to you, that you have conferred an honour upon me, of which I feel unworthy. I accept the invitation, feeling persuaded in my own heart that it is according to the Lord's gracious purpose. There is no need, really, for me to keep you waiting to know my mind. In view of the unanimous vote of this church, it would be hypocrisy for me to say I must wait and see what the will of God is. God has made His will known in this; therefore by His grace I will come to you, and even now, I believe we may say (without presumption), I stand here as your pastor. You are my people now, my charge; I am your pastor. May God give me grace to exercise the office. I am sensible of my need, and may He give me wisdom to exercise the authority that the office confers upon me, in the spirit of Christ, and in love.
>
> May the Lord help us to walk together. You will need patience with me. I am new to this office, but my eyes are up unto Him for wisdom and grace, and if He is pleased to supply my need in the ministry, we may see His great goodness towards us in building us up and establishing us. May it be His good will to increase us with a godly increase, but the greatest of all things is the presence of Christ. If we have that, we have the substance.

The years immediately following witnessed a gracious fulfilment of those desires, a number of godly additions to the Church taking place.

It was not long, however, before the ominous clouds of the impending War brought a train of trial and anxiety to the beloved Pastor and his wife. A number of young men were called to serve their country, one or two of whom had just been enabled

'Ebenezer' Chapel, Clapham

to follow their Lord in the path of obedience. With what loving concern must the pastor have watched and prayed for the safe keeping of his flock, especially those involved in active service. But fear for the safety of his people was not confined to those actively engaged, but for his congregation generally, some of whom suffered bomb damage to their homes; others were actually bombed out, whilst a number more lived alone in flats without any suitable shelters. For such the pastor's home, Firs Cottage, a short distance from the chapel in Fitzwilliam Road, became a second home, the cellar often affording a place of retreat during the severe raids in the area. Mr Delves customarily cycled round to the members of his flock to ensure they were still preserved. He stayed at Clapham continuously throughout the war years, only occasionally visiting friends in the country for one or two days to provide much needed respite from the stress and strain. One such refuge in the country was the home of Mr and Mrs Clark at Barton-le-Clay. Mr Clark was the pastor there for many years, having known Mr Delves since first making his acquaintance at Brighton a long time previously. Mr Delves took the Anniversary services in August at Barton for many years until failing health prevented. In his prime, during the post-war years, three of those annual occasions were marked by a visit to Barton of a coach-load of Clapham friends accompanying their beloved pastor to the services. For an equally long period Mr Clark made an annual visit to Clapham for a weekend, until increasing age and weakness forced him to remain at home. Some remember with thankfulness those annual visits.

In due time the war gave way to peace, and in the Providence of God, to outward prosperity to the Cause at Clapham. The return and settlement of some young men and women who had just prior to the War been directed to the chapel provided a nucleus for a larger congregation than the chapel had had for a number of years. Several couples with their young families lived within a short distance of the chapel, which—certainly in the cases of some—became the pivot of their lives. A number were added to the Church so that by the end of 1946 there were more than forty regular members, at that time two additional deacons being elected. One of these was Mr Tingley—referred to in the letter from Mr Wariner quoted previously. Mr Tingley was brought up at Scaynes Hill chapel, but through a love to Mr Popham's ministry settled for a time at Brighton, until returning home to carry on his father's business after his death. Later he settled in London and attended Clapham just prior to Mr Delves' settlement. One or two members still remember the savour of his humble testimony before the Church, when having been blessed under a sermon from Matt. 11: 28–30 he was constrained to come forward. More particularly the relation of his sad backslidings and merciful restoration appear to have impressed the Church at the time of his testimony, as referred to in the minutes of the Church Meeting. Doubtless it was such a deep experience that made his place so valued by his beloved pastor, and consequently his sudden death as a result of an accident was the more painful. He was taken home 31 May 1948, aged 52 years. (For further details see *Gospel Standard* (1948), pp. 179, 180.)

* * *

An account of this nature should above all things be faithful to the truth, and the period we have reached seems to mark—at least, from the outward aspect—the height of Mr Delves' pastorate. In following years there was a continued building up in the Church and congregation, but compared with the initial years at Clapham, the subsequent period saw a gradual decline. For example, excluding members who had to be withdrawn from, there were as many additions to the Church in the first ten years as there were in the following thirty years of the pastorate; more pointedly there were as many additions in the first 18 months, as in the last twenty years. These facts are mentioned not to deprecate the ministry or loving pastoral affection of the gracious subject of this record, but to reflect faithfully the course which the Lord had designed for him to walk out. As John the Baptist had to prove the truth of his own prophetic words 'He must increase, but I must decrease', so in a measure did our late dear friend and pastor. The wisdom of the Lord is unsearchable; to be given grace to bow to His sovereign purposes is the humble lot and privilege of the Lord's afflicted and poor people: for even 'Christ glorified not Himself to be made an High Priest'; in all things He did those things that pleased His Father (John 8: 29). We think it may be rightly felt that this sacred Pattern was in a gracious measure exemplified in Mr Delves.

Although the late 1940s and early 1950s witnessed encouraging additions for the pastor, from then on there were matters to balance days of prosperity with days of adversity; some things painful to bear and walk out in the tender fear of God. Mr Delves' life-long friend, Mr J. H. Gosden, was not unacquainted with the trials attending the pastoral office. It may be appropriate at this point to give an extract from a letter he wrote affectionately counselling Mr Delves at the commencement of his pastorate. Apart from its gracious tone the letter reveals that Mr Gosden recognized that his friend's tender disposition would need to be balanced by a due attention to firmness:

> . . . Doubtless you will find many trials, but the all-sufficiency of God can only be known in and through trial and emptying processes . . . My natural disposition feels some things very keenly. But all such things when they drive one closer to God's Throne of Grace, are not without profit.
>
> In the pastoral office there seems so much wisdom and tact needed together with *firmness* and faithfulness; that very wisdom which is from above described in James is absolutely indispensable. May the Lord endow you with this and every other grace as your needs require . . . It is an exceedingly solemn and yet honourable position to be a professed servant of Christ and an undershepherd in His Church, but if we can truly realise that *we are* His servants, that will be a strength when faint and weary . . . Pray for us as we would desire to for you.
>
> Yours affectionately,
> J. H. Gosden

In a letter years later Mr Delves wrote: '. . . There are many sad and strange things in these days; my heart is often grieved, much conflict in the night, wondering where the scene will end . . . I have had to walk in some things enough to make a Pastor's "heart bleed", but have been helped till now. . . .' Such heavy matters, as well as personal sins and sins of Church and Nation will cause the Lord's true people to 'sigh and cry'.

Moreover, the almost unrelieved—as it seems in this day—withholding of the Spirit's power (lamented by Mr Delves, and briefly mentioned in Letter VIII), will be a particular burden to every graciously exercised reader. We know that Mr Delves felt these things as he walked out this period of his pastorate—years of gradual decline, but nevertheless years which reflected a ripening of the ministry. Although his had largely been graciously experimental, it cannot be doubted that, under the Spirit's blessing, Mr Delves' trials and afflictions brought forth in his later ministry the tried fruits of a real manifestation of mercy, and a personal knowledge of Christ—blessings which, in his early years, he had been singularly favoured to experience, as before related.

In 1954 years of exercise were brought to a head when the Church gave its unanimous vote that Mr J. C. Neville's exercises concerning his call to the ministry were of the Lord. He and Mr Delves had walked in mutual exercise about this matter for about eight years, Mr Delves watching with loving anxiety but not 'pushing' the matter, whilst Mr Neville waited, not for the approbation of man—for he had evidence of that in his pastor and others—but a clear token from the Lord and a spirit of willingness in consequence. This was largely brought about finally through the ministry of Mr Delves one Lord's Day in February, when on both morning and evening occasions he spoke of Jeremiah's call to the work (Ch. 1), and laid particular stress upon the blossoming of the almond tree (v. 12). (It would seem that the Lord used the literal fact of the almond blossom suddenly appearing—between the services—on the tree in Mr Delves' garden at the Cottage, to confirm the subject in his mind, which proved of such blessing to our friend.) In the weeks before the Church Meeting references by Mr Delves to different texts which Mr Neville had had applied years previously, but of which Mr Delves did not know, were used of the Lord in sealing the matter and enabling him to make his exercises known publicly to the Church in April.

Whilst a manifest evidence of the approbation of the Lord upon Mr Delves' ministry, the solemn step necessarily deprived the pastor of the presence, and to a degree the assistance, of one of his deacons, Mr Neville having been elected to that office a few years previously. Three years later, following Mr Neville's acceptance of the call to the pastorate at Richmond, he and his family were removed from Clapham. Subsequently other deacons were elected in 1955, 1958, and 1966, in later years two removing in Providence to other parts of the country.

In 1960 the church and congregation recognized their pastor's 25th Anniversary by a presentation to him and Mrs Delves and on the Lord's Day following Mr Delves preached from 2 Sam. 7: 18. In January 1962 Mr Delves entered hospital from where he wrote to his flock on a number of occasions. Whilst there he felt some sweetness in the recollection of the truth he had been enabled to preach at the Northern Meetings of the Gospel Standard Societies the previous September from Luke 24: 45–47 (see *Gospel Standard* (1961), p. 321). In one of his letters he wrote:

> O think of what sin cost Him, and if we have an interest in His vicarious sufferings, then they were our sins—but O what a gospel is this:
>
> 'We bruised His body, spilt His blood,
> And both become our heavenly food.'

In another letter, whilst recovering in hospital, he wrote:

> Earlier this afternoon hymn 871 quite broke me down, especially verse 4:
>
> 'For this correction render praise;
> 'Tis given thee for thy good.
> The lash is steeped He on thee lays,
> And softened in His blood.'

They were indeed a few sweet moments . . .

> The Lord has been with me in the furnace of trial, but how has it been with some of my hearers? Has the Lord sanctified the trial to you as a congregation? I am indebted to you for your prayers and practical kindness, but has the Lord spoken by my silence? Have you as a people, under my pastoral care, had heart-searching before the Lord? any real sanctified profit and purging of the living branches of the Lord's vineyard to bring forth more fruit? For myself, I have much to confess before the Lord for my own sins, but bless His holy name, He has come over it all and poured in the oil and wine.
>
> Please accept a pastor's love to his flock . . .

Mr Delves resumed his ministry at Ebenezer on 1 April when he preached from Ps. 116: 7: 'Return unto thy rest, O my soul; for the Lord hath dealt bountifully with thee.'

In 1969 Mr Delves was again laid aside for about a month and upon his return preached from Ps. 17: 15. He was then in his 78th year and, naturally viewed, it did not seem that he could be spared much longer, but instead he was to be spared for another ten years, during which time the church and congregation were privileged with his tender oversight and gracious counsel, and for most of the time he was enabled to fulfil his pastoral office.

On 29 December 1969 at the Monday evening prayer meeting Mr Delves recounted a particular blessing he had just received. Having read Ps. 119: 81–96 he said:

'The reason I have read these verses, and commenced with hymn 582, is because I felt some confirmation in my heart this morning when reading before I came downstairs.

'I had sought the Lord for another confirming token of His favour toward me in these my latter days. While I was pondering matters over, this came: "All is ordered well." "All is ordered well." Then I began to think upon this when the line came: "And my soul approves it well," but I knew there was something before this, yet for the moment, I could not think what it was; then it came upon my spirit so sweetly, "All is settled".

> All is settled,
> And my soul approves it well.

That was followed by this particular word of Scripture: "For ever, O Lord, Thy Word is settled in heaven" (Ps. 119: 89). It was as though the Lord said to me, "I have given you tokens and I shall not take them away. They are all settled, they are settled in My divine purposes toward you." "All is settled." It was these three words that were so particularly good, and I was able, in some measure, to feel that all had been settled well for me in the Lord's divine purpose, yea, in His covenant of grace before time ever was.'

This sweet appearance of the Lord to him was an evident support to Mr Delves during his declining years; years made heavy in a personal way by the increasing weakness of his beloved wife. Mrs Delves' memory began—at first occasionally but progressively more markedly—to fail, and it was painful to see the weakening and distressing effect which this had on the dear pastor. He himself, probably as a result of this strain, suffered occasional bouts of weakness and giddiness so that his 40th anniversary in May 1975, was to a point overshadowed by the anxiety which was felt for him and his wife. However, Mr Delves was able to preach on the Whit Monday occasion, when he took for his text the same one from which he had spoken forty years previously; Ps. 119: 116. A special meeting for prayer was held on the previous Saturday at which Mr Delves was presented with an illuminated address and a cheque.

In February 1976 it was felt essential that Mr and Mrs Delves should have a thorough rest and accordingly with the kind co-operation of the Gospel Standard Bethesda Committee (of which, with other Denominational bodies including the Gospel Standard Committee, Mr Delves had been a gracious and loyal member for many years), they were admitted to the Home at Hove. Initially they went for a month, but Mrs Delves' health deteriorating, it was needful to extend their stay. Dear Mrs Delves passed away in the Home there, on 11 May, aged 84 years, leaving a particular fragrance in respect of her gracious walk as a pastor's wife.

As already recorded Mrs Delves had been singularly favoured, but she had to walk a heavy pathway of bodily affliction in earlier days, and she also knew the plague of her own heart. These things enabled her to act so tenderly and faithfully to others in similar circumstances. One instance may illustrate to a point her wisdom in honouring the Lord while helping the tempted. A friend, having been particularly favoured, called some time later at the Cottage. Mrs Delves opened the door and said, 'I hear you have got some good things to tell us'; the reply, somewhat sharply was, 'O but I have not lived there', to which Mrs Delves quietly responded, 'What you mean is that you *did* live there'. Perhaps she was looking back to her own conflicts, some of which she experienced when she had to leave her spiritual home at Brighton, and move to Clapham. Of the time, some $2\frac{1}{2}$ years after Mr Delves came to Clapham, when she felt constrained to transfer her membership she wrote: 'I was looking with envy in my mind at Galeed, when this came: "Is Christ divided?" and I felt reproved and glad to go into Ebenezer to the evening service, feeling that I deserved to be banished—"My wicked heart no small part"—and had to confess and confess. After this my mind and heart turned to Ebenezer and the friends here, and no longer to those left behind, and I had no wish to go back to them.' She was undoubtedly a great support to Mr Delves in his office, not only in prayerful exercise but in very practical ways. On one occasion Mr Delves had been sorely provoked by an adversary, and said, 'I am going round to see him now'; Mrs Delves going to fetch his coat, quietly quoted 'Vengeance is Mine; I will repay, saith the Lord' which broke the dear man's spirit.

The passing of Mrs Delves instead of further weakening Mr Delves in fact relieved him of the distressing anxiety which had been his lot for some time; indeed, there were times when his own mind tended to wander, but he seemed especially supported at her funeral and afterwards expressed a wish to return home to Clapham. Friends kindly fetched him back and he was enabled to address his people again on Lord's Day evening, 18 July 1976 from 2 Cor. 13: 14. Thereafter he was able to preach a few times and to take some of the prayer meetings. The unctuous savour of his brief sermons and addresses in those, his last days, will not quickly be forgotten. He was able to administer the ordinance of the Lord's table on most occasions until December 1977 from the end of which year he resigned his honoured pastorate, as explained in the concluding chapter.

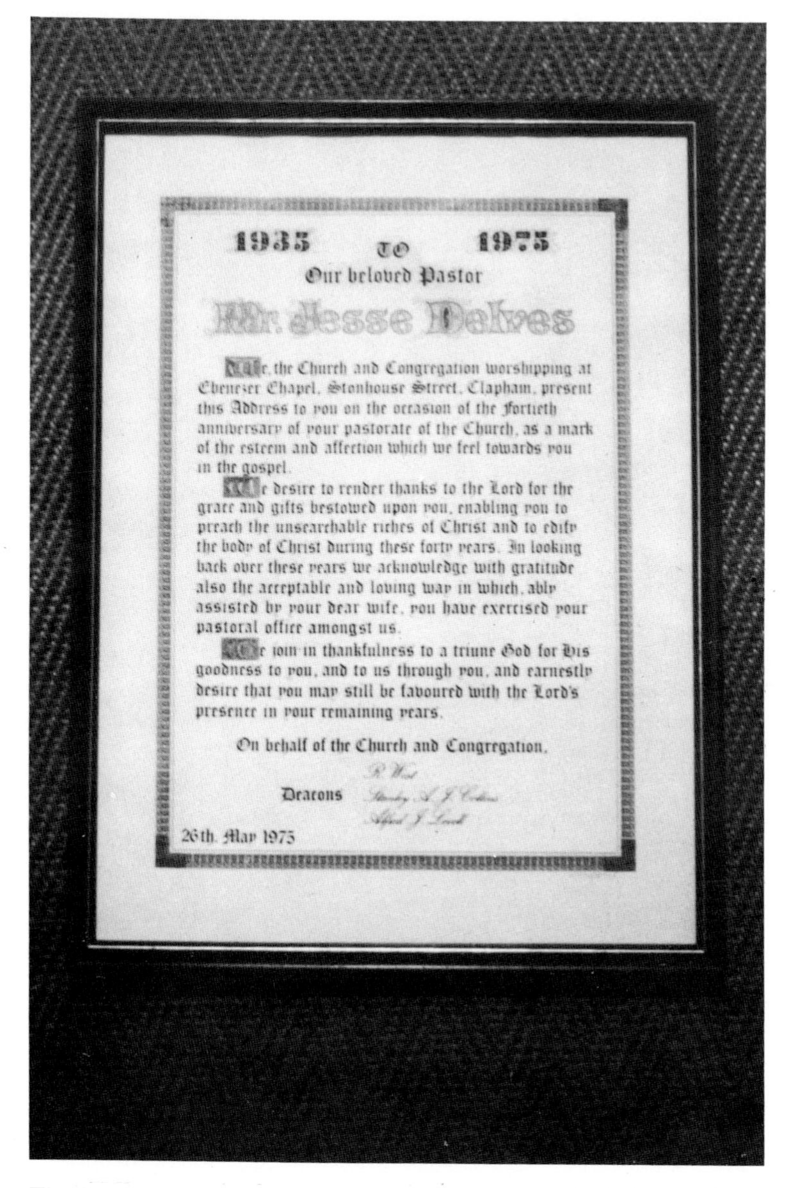
1935 TO 1975

Our beloved Pastor

Mr. Jesse Delves

We, the Church and Congregation worshipping at Ebenezer Chapel, Stonhouse Street, Clapham, present this Address to you on the occasion of the Fortieth anniversary of your pastorate of the Church, as a mark of the esteem and affection which we feel towards you in the gospel.

We desire to render thanks to the Lord for the grace and gifts bestowed upon you, enabling you to preach the unsearchable riches of Christ and to edify the body of Christ during these forty years. In looking back over these years we acknowledge with gratitude also the acceptable and loving way in which, ably assisted by your dear wife, you have exercised your pastoral office amongst us.

We join in thankfulness to a triune God for His goodness to you, and to us through you, and earnestly desire that you may still be favoured with the Lord's presence in your remaining years.

On behalf of the Church and Congregation.

Deacons

26th. May 1975

The illuminated address presented to Mr Delves on the fortieth anniversary of his pastorate May 1975

CHAPTER FOUR

Last Days

Mr and Mrs Delves were never favoured to have any children, but they did not pass their days in isolation, their home always being open to any friends in need. In a particular way their home became the home of a few friends who lived with them for many years. Miss V. A. Gurney originally moved from her native Eastbourne to Brighton in 1925, to assist Mr and Mrs Delves on a temporary basis, but what was expected to be short lived in fact became a permanency, Miss Gurney moving with them to London in 1935. She transferred her membership to Clapham with Mrs Delves in June 1937 and remained a most meek, loyal, and discerning member until failing health necessitated her removal to the Bethesda Home in 1966. She passed away on 6 October 1969, an obituary notice being published the following year in the *Gospel Standard* (p. 159). Her earlier help to Mr and Mrs Delves was lovingly repaid by their devoted attention to her for a number of years until, as mentioned, she needed the care provided by the Bethesda Home.

During this later period in Mr and Mrs Delves' life, it became evident that they would need someone, at least to provide regular, if not continual, help. A younger friend whom Mr and Mrs Delves lovingly received, had lodged with them many years, but at this period it was necessary for her to attend to her own parents, and consequently she removed from London. However, in the Lord's merciful providence Miss Freda Rolph, who had been a loyal member for many years, was willing to devote increasing time to her beloved pastor and his wife, and for several years she lived permanently with them. It was to Miss Rolph that the Church owed, through the Lord's mercy, the unwearied care and attention which was such a comfort to their beloved pastor, especially in his last days following the loss of his dear partner.

The care he received was the repeated subject of Mr Delves' gratitude until his end. It is a responsibility rightly to convey Mr Delves' state of mind in the last two or three years of his life, but it is true to state that almost invariably he was graciously placid. Whilst yet able to attend chapel, and still carry out most of his pastoral duties, he had been actively concerned in the settlement of the Church's new pastor. To allow this to proceed in accordance with the wishes of the Church he had graciously relinquished his responsibilities and resigned his office with effect from the end of 1977. That this step was not premature was evident as from that time he began to fail. Although able to listen to all the services which were relayed to his home, he but rarely attended chapel, and his weakness increased so that he was often confined to his bed.

This long period of weakness was borne with gracious patience; this, through the Lord's enabling, was, to Miss Rolph and others who were often with him, the outstanding characteristic of his closing days. Over his last two years he uttered a number of gracious sayings, and some of these were published in the *Gospel Standard* (1981), p. 89, but it would be unfaithful to the facts to suggest that those reflected a state of mind which was largely joyful. Many were the days, if not of darkness, yet of silent exercise. For the most part he spent his time in quiet meditation and reflection; when otherwise—either through some little reviving touch, or a measure of darkness—it was evident on his countenance, and to those close to him such occasions provided openings for conversation. On other occasions he would be quiet, sometimes spending a whole day in complete silence: it was this sacred, though silent, witness to the vital work of the Holy Ghost which was so attractive. Mr Delves reflected, without any dissembling, the state of his soul, and yet in his most reserved periods the promise was manifestly fulfilled: 'The Lord shall never suffer the righteous to be moved.' Against this background we subjoin a selection of those expressions which fell from Mr Delves' lips, in this latter period of increasing weakness.

'I have no doubts or fears. The prospect is a good one. Now we see through a glass darkly, but then face to face without a veil between.'

'Ah it is evening time but I *know* it will be well.'

One afternoon when feeling very poorly, twice he quoted:

Yes, I shall soon be landed
On yonder shores of bliss,
There, with my powers expanded,
Shall dwell where Jesus is.
(Gadsby's 483)

At another time he quoted the same verse to a friend who came in to see him, and said, 'I have seen Him by faith, and He was the chiefest among ten thousand and the altogether lovely, *but soon* I shall see Him face to face'.

Very poorly, he said, 'Not much strength! The prospect is a good one. All is settled! Nothing to do but await the Lord's time.' At another time: 'I am ready to go when it is the Lord's time. Nothing to do but leave earth for heaven'!

May 1979. One quoted:

If once the love of Christ we feel
Upon our hearts impressed,
The mark of that celestial seal
Can never be erased.
(Gadsby's 344)

to which he responded: 'I have been marked with a celestial seal.'

'It shakes me sometimes when I think of eternity—not just a short space of time.'

'My days are closing in and I shall soon be in that place [looking up] where sin no more defiles' (Gadsby's 850).

A few weeks before he died he asked one to read the whole of that hymn. The deacon was led to announce the same hymn on the evening he died, the service as usual being relayed to the Cottage, and the singing had just concluded when Mr Delves passed away on 16 January 1980, aged 88, to be for ever with the Lord. Two of his latest remarks stand out: when feeling a measure of darkness, faith was manifested in a humble testimony as to the faithfulness of God and the immutability of the Covenant: two themes, with the precious Atonement, on which he delighted to dwell in his ministry. He said, 'Our standing is not dependent upon great ecstacies of joy but upon the finished work of Christ'. A week before he died 1 Pet. 2: 7, 'Unto you therefore which believe He is precious', was quoted to him. When he heard the word 'precious', he turned over on the pillow with effort and looking one full in the face said, 'He has been many, many times'.

Thus ended the life of one who towards his end declared, 'I am looking forward to a house not made with hands, eternal in the heavens'. He had sober views concerning heaven: the prospect of eternity to him was to see and be with Christ. He used to relate two experiences which greatly influenced his mind about heaven. Once he had a dream which occurred some time after his father died. He dreamt that he was back home in the old forge at Rushlake Green, and his father appeared at the window and began to converse upon spiritual things; after a time Mr Delves remarked: 'Father, don't you know me? you remember you had four sons, Edgar, Jesse, Nelson and Stanley', to which his Father replied, 'We know no man after the flesh', after which he was no longer to be seen. This made a lasting impression upon Mr Delves, as did a remark by an old minister he remembered from his youthful days. The minister was asked whether he thought we should know one another in heaven, to which he replied, 'When I get there and see Him as He is, I will not want to look at anyone else'.

The funeral service was taken in Ebenezer Chapel, Clapham on 24 January 1980—Mr J. C. Neville officiated. In doing so he was able knowledgeably to reminisce on the long pastorate of over forty-two years, having attended Clapham from its commencement. It was fittingly remarked: 'We hope, as I believe our late dear friend would have desired to be said, that what we have said concerning him is what he was by the grace of God.' In sending forth this account it is likewise our fervent desire that what has been written will, through the Spirit's power, tend to the glory of God's grace, in His sovereign disposing of His grace and gifts. Whilst desiring to retain with affection the memory of former days, we would wish to do so in the spirit of a view once given to an aged friend of our late

Mr and Mrs Delves' grave at the 'Dicker' Chapel
burying-ground, East Sussex

pastor: 'I had', he said, 'a sight of Mr Delves as a star in the hand of the Lord' (Rev. 1: 16, 20).

The subject of this memoir had a right foundation to his religion. Recalling past years, when preaching on the occasion of his 40th anniversary, Mr Delves said: 'It is a mercy to have a real foundation . . . When I was in the army in the First World War . . . I found myself being shaken about my religion; but one day that word came so sweetly, "Because I live, ye shall live also".' It was felt fitting that those words (John 14: 19, to which Mr Delves often referred) should be put on his gravestone in the Dicker graveyard, Sussex, where in accordance with his wishes, Mr Delves was interred by the side of his late dear wife.

LETTERS

THE following is a selection from Mr Delves' later years. Although he frequently met the correspondent of Nos. II, III, IV, V, and VI, almost total deafness precluded any conversation. We would humbly desire that the Lord's wisdom in this afflictive dispensation (undoubtedly sanctified personally to the friend concerned, who, though of another Cause, was accustomed to call Mr Delves, 'My Pastor') might more widely be manifested in making the reading of these letters profitable. The remainder, to friends at Clapham and elsewhere, will not, it is hoped be unacceptable—not only regarding their content, but as giving a little view of Mr Delves' gracious character, and also his personal exercises.

I

11.8.61

My dear ———,

Our minds often run to you, and we hope it is well with daily strength and grace for your needs . . . The service I hope was profitable last evening; speaking from Acts 5.31–32 I had, I hope, a little opening up of the sacred truth involved, and just a little softening from a verse in hymn 1149, latter part of verse 2—'unless I were sure He is God'. The eternal Godhead of Christ as well as the characters 'Prince and Saviour' were so attractive, and what great need have I of what follows: 'Repentance and forgiveness', even continually in myself: what depths of sin, and yet what heights of mercy to reach a case like mine. I feel less able to preach than ever, and sometimes wonder how much longer it can continue, but our sufficiency is of God. May the Lord graciously favour you with the 'Light of His countenance', giving you to hear the Shepherd's voice in some confirming token of your interest in His precious love and blood . . .

We miss you very much from . . . the services, but are glad you can have this very needful break . . . We were very thin last Sabbath; but the greatest blessing and honour is to feel that the 'Lord is there'. I hope you may get some good help at the chapel . . .

My love in the Gospel,
Your affectionate Pastor,
J. Delves.

II

Tues. April 10, 1962

Dear ———,

My mind has been much upon the profitable time we spent together last Monday evening at your home. You were so graciously led and helped to tell us of those good things which we believe the Spirit of the Lord has revealed and made known in your heart of those things that accompany salvation.

Those are things you have 'tasted, handled and felt of the good word of life', that has extended over a period of many years, undoubtedly from quite early days, though, as you told us, attended with much uncertainty as to their reality, but now confirmed by a clearer light and hearing the Lord's voice in your heart saying, 'I know the thoughts I think toward you, saith the Lord, thoughts of peace, and not of evil, to give you an expected end' Jer. 29.11. The Lord has graciously removed the cloud that has for so long hung over you, and under which you have been assailed by many temptations by that enemy of souls, and sweetly favoured you with those tokens of His great love to a great sinner, as you will feel to be, and so utterly unworthy of His goodness which softens the hard heart, and produces those tears the Lord 'puts into His bottle' Ps. 56.8, and then, under His gracious unction you offer the best sacrifice which the Lord accepts, Psalm 51.17. How great, immutable, and free then is His love—'swallowing up' ten thousand sins, as His glory appears before the eye of your faith in coming over the mountains of your (our) black sins and pouring in the 'oil and wine' of His gospel. This is to 'sit under the Apple tree'—Song of

Solomon 2.3, 4. How sweet it is then to 'repent and sing, rejoice and be ashamed', Hymn 241. This is the 'south wind' that causes the spices to flow out—Song 4.16.

May you 'still enjoy this feeling', Hymn 158, and in a right and gracious way, under the sweet constraint of Christ's love, follow in His ways. I hope the Lord will be with you in this also, in a view of the solemnity and beauty of Gospel obedience, having in your heart a single desire to 'honour Him' and 'not be ashamed'—Hymn 427.

It may be the enemy will attempt to hinder you in this, but I trust you may be helped to 'look straight on' and that it may be 'Jesus only', for He has said, 'If ye love Me keep my commandments' . . . I have just written this because I was not able verbally to respond to the good things you told us last evening.

We reached home safely about 5 pm today after a very pleasant stay with our mutual friends—who have been so kind.

Please accept our very kind wishes.

Very sincerely yours,

J. Delves

III

Oct. 6. 1962

Dear ———,

How very kind of you to think of us in the acceptable gift of eggs which I know we shall enjoy . . .

I trust you may often be favoured with some sweet renewings, which will enable you to 'hold fast' and endure to the end.

With the Lord's people there is a 'Covenant Union' wherein are living communications of grace, which revive the soul, make Christ precious, and help us to 'press on' in the face of much opposition. In Rev. 2.17 the promise is to the 'Overcomer'. What a mercy it is that the victory is 'gained *for* us and given *to* us' 1 Cor. 15.57. You will have many battles with Reason, Self, Satan, Sin, Unbelief and other enemies. How we need grace to 'fight that good fight of faith' 1 Timothy 6.12; 'strength to do all things'—Philippians 4.13. One felt able to say:

'Yes, I to the end shall endure,
As sure as the earnest is given;
More happy, but not more secure,
The glorified spirits in heaven.'
340, Gadsby's

Mr Popham used to say, 'If you fear you may lose the blessing you hope you have received from the Lord, *ask Him to keep it for you*'.

I was speaking last night about 'working out our own salvation with fear and trembling', and how this is done by God working in us by His Spirit. By grace we work out what the Lord works in.

The Lord grant you much of His favour, and being unable to hear, very graciously sanctify the reading in your quiet home.*

Our united Christian love,
Sincerely yours,
J. Delves

IV

26.12.1962.

Dear Friend,

. . . It is good that you have been favoured with some sacred and profitable meditation on the 'things which accompany salvation'. In these favoured moments one can for the time lose sight of earth and its passing things, and contemplate hopefully the ultimate enjoyment to the full of those eternal and abiding realities that will never cease. How true it is that 'We in this tabernacle do groan being burdened' 2 Cor. 5, but a mercy indeed if we can hopefully feel that 'When this earthly house shall be dissolved we have a building of God, a house not made with hands eternal in the heavens'.

It is our mercy that the sovereign eternal purposes of God in the Covenant of grace cannot be affected by our personal feelings. His Word is for ever settled in Heaven—Ps. 119.89. In ourselves we only see sin, ruin, death, and everything that

* This should not be understood that the friend neglected attendance at chapel; on the contrary, though quite unable to hear, she has always persevered whenever health and strength has allowed.

is vile: 'Woe is me for I am undone' Is. 6. But in Him, Christ, we see (by faith) all a poor undone sinner needs, even for time and eternity. May your meditation of Him often be sweet—Ps. 104.

Wishing you every blessing for 1963.

Yours sincerely,

Jesse Delves

V

Dec 31. 1963

Dear ———,

Thank you so much for your good and profitable letter. How confirming it is when we are favoured to feel a little renewing in our souls as you have done of late. Does it not prove that the gospel is as a 'well of water springing up into everlasting life' John 4.14, and when a little of its saving power is felt in the heart we can say 'We want no other Gospel, but desire to know more of this'.

What a revelation of mercy, grace and peace is this gospel to poor sinners, lost and ruined in themselves, helpless dependants on the sovereign bounty of a Covenant-performing God. Were not His thoughts thoughts of peace from everlasting to His spiritual Israel—Jeremiah 29.11?, and what is the 'expected end', but eternal life which is the gift of God—Romans 6.23. It must be one of the two with us, either the 'wages of sin' or the 'gift of eternal life'. What a mercy if those 'thoughts' prove to be the latter with us. It was remarkable that you were able to hear those words when Mr ——— was reading, notwithstanding your deafness; it would seem there must have been a particular purpose in this. Your meditation of Him has been sweet in those particulars you mention.

I was speaking here recently from Isaiah 9.6. 'His Name shall be called, Wonderful, Counsellor, the Mighty God, the Everlasting Father, the Prince of Peace'. In all these and many besides Christ is 'Wonderful'—wonderful in the glory of His eternal Godhead; wonderful in His pure humanity; wonderful in the view of faith as Immanuel, able to save unto the uttermost, exalted a 'Prince and a Saviour to give repentance to

Israel and remission of sins'. As this view of Christ opens to faith so does He become the 'Chiefest among ten thousand and the altogether lovely' Song of Solomon, 5.10 & 16. Some time ago now Hymn 21 was made very sweet to me on a 1st Lord's Day, so that I gave it out at the Lord's Supper; at the opening the first five verses, and at the close, the last five; but, although in poetic strain, it was the 3rd verse which was particularly sweet ('White is His soul, from blemish free; Red with the blood He shed for me; The fairest of ten thousand fairs; a sun amongst ten thousand stars').

May the Lord often sanctify your solitude and affliction although so much alone, yet not alone, for no company can be so choice as the presence of Himself. John 14.18.

. . . Please accept our united Christian love and best wishes for the coming year.

Yours very sincerely,
J. Delves.

VI

July 12 1965

Dear ———,

We are all very sorry to hear of your fall, and having to be taken to hospital with a broken leg. I understand that there has been an operation, that you are comfortable, and getting on satisfactorily. What a mercy this is, is it not—is not the Lord a stronghold in the day of trouble? . . . What a gracious promise is it not, '*I* will be with thee'. I do hope my friend is proving something of this, and I seem to feel that you are. This evening at our little prayer meeting I read a few verses in Acts 7, to verse 9, and spoke a little on that last sentence, '*But* God was with him'. But it was a path of heavy trial was it not? I know how once in my little life, though I was in the midst of trouble—and indeed I *was* just then—yet the Lord appeared, and I was favoured to feel as though I had *no* trouble. How 'sweet to lie passive in His hands'.

I remember you mentioning that line at the time of your baptizing, 'You're safe in your Redeemer's hands' (Gadsby's 82). I hope you feel safe in His hands now, though with a broken leg. All our *times* are in His hands, all events at His command. How true it is that we know not what an hour may bring forth. What a mercy it was that your fall was in the garden, where you were noticed. Is not all ordered well?

My wife joins with me in Christian love and our sympathies, desiring for you healing mercies (and much inward help) though we know it must take time. If you have a hymn book you may find it good to read Hymn 329. The friends at Chapel will miss your attendance with them, and I believe many prayers will be put up for you. I remember how broken down I felt when I was in hospital reading Hymn 871. I cannot bring it back, but it was very sweet then especially verse 4. We believe there is a 'needs-be' in the Lord's purposes for these 'manifold temptations', 1 Peter 1.6. It is, I think, Rutherford who says something like this: 'He never lays a cross upon us but He bears the heaviest part Himself.'

Accept our love in the Gospel, and may the Lord be your strength and stay.

Yours very sincerely,
J. Delves.

VII

October 17. 1967

My Dear Friend,

In a prayerful desire that the best of blessings may be yours in the matters of this life, and your future prospects, and also in the great and important matters of eternal salvation, I venture a few lines in the desire to be of some encouragement in your present exercises . . . Some of us can understand your feelings, attended it may be with much conflict and at times temptation from the great enemy of souls, and many questionings, but I hope you may still be graciously helped to 'wait on the Lord for He shall strengthen thine heart' Ps. 27.14; also in Ps. 62.8: 'Trust in Him at *all* times', even in the darkest times. For our encouragement the dear Lord said, 'All things whatsoever ye shall ask in prayer, *believing*, ye shall receive' Matt. 21.22. It may be that you feel that the Lord is silent, but this is not really so; even the poor woman who came to the Lord had her faith tried for 'He answered her not a word', Matt. 15.23, yet eventually commended her faith. I well know that the (apparent) delay in an answer to prayer can be a sharp trial of faith, but the 'Vision is yet for an appointed time' etc. Habakkuk 2.3. He will not fail thee: 'Wait on Him then, take courage still.' It was in 1916 when I believe the Lord appeared to me, at work in my shop, but it was 11 years after this before my wife felt to have the blessing she desired, and then it was very real; but in 'the trial of faith' (1 Peter 1.7) which we are sure to have, God is a Sovereign: some have long waiting, while others are more favoured as we feel. Yet if we wait a life time, we shall be richly blessed if and when we 'See Him as He is' (1 John 3. 1 & 2) Dear Friend ———, the Lord be gracious unto thee, and help thee to 'press toward the mark', Philippians 3. 'Without cessation pray, your prayers will not prove vain, Our Joseph turns aside to weep, But cannot long refrain', Hymn 308. Pt. 2 . . .

Yours affectionately,
J. Delves

VIII

19/11/68

My Dear Friend ———,

I can hardly tell you what a comfort it has been to me to receive your good letter today. I have had it strongly on my mind that I must try and write you again. To me your letter is indeed a word in season, for I had been very, very low myself, and in great conflict of mind relative to my personal case as well as my ministry. The solemn fact that the power of the Holy Spirit is largely withheld is to me a heart-searching question. Is it I? is a penetrating question. The fact that I heard not a word about the Wednesday sermon* sent me into great conflict in which Satan was busy with his suggestions, and fearing I had said things I ought not to have said distressed me, so that when I began to read your letter it was as a 'word from the Lord' to poor unworthy me, and I desire to thank Him for moving you to write to me.

*Ps. 118: 25.

Perhaps I may now say that your deep soul exercises have weighed heavily with me, not because I doubt the reality of the Lord's gracious dealings with you (God forbid), but because the long desired blessing is as yet withheld, that is, the sweet and full liberty of the precious Gospel in a revealed Christ personally, so that you can feelingly say 'He loved *me* and gave Himself for *me*'. Now, dear friend, I do not doubt but that this is the case as to your blessed standing in union with Christ, though you may still feel to be 'with no sweet enjoyments blessed', but may the Lord help you to press your case, spurning doubt, the Holy Ghost your witness, for I feel persuaded that 'the time of love will come', and then you will say 'He was worth waiting for'—even if years are involved. His presence felt and enjoyed is that true soul prosperity, which is of more value than 'numbers' though we desire to see this. O dear friend it is good to me to have your letter, I feel softened as I write, and can but feel that the blessing is not far distant. The Lord help you to press on though hosts of enemies rise up; look alone to Him; Satan will try to force things on you to drive you to despair so that as Paul you can say, 'O wretched man that I am, who shall deliver me?', but the Lord can, and I feel sure He will. Look to no creature, friend or minister, but to the Friend of sinners, keep your eye on Jesus Christ, and plead the blood that does for sin atone. O when you can feel, as you say 'a precious Christ within you, and all about you', then will He be the 'Chiefest among ten thousand' in the possession of Him as He is now in the desire for Him. The *nearness* you have felt at times in pouring out your heart to Him means that He is 'shewing Himself through the lattice', and must soon bring you 'to the banqueting House'.

Yours affectionately,
J. Delves

IX

February 3/70

Dear Friend,

. . . To *see* the Lord's goodness in temporal things is a favour worthy of notice, for some who are favoured with the blessings of this life do not *see* the good hand of the Lord therein. Is it not therefore a token of the Lord's favour to you that you cannot rest here? Your soul has known something of that sacred communion with your Lord, some softening, that 'good hope through grace', so that you could say:

> 'To know my Jesus crucified,
> By far excels all things beside'

and now that the Lord has laid this 'Foundation Stone' in your heart the cruel enemy is attempting to overthrow it, and would drag you to despair, but of this I am persuaded that he never will; yet even so clouds come over, and the soul is in heaviness through manifold temptations. All—it is suggested—is sentiment, pride, vain confidence or just some emotion of nature. I know myself what these heavy days are, yet I am persuaded that the Lord has a set time to bring your soul out of prison to bless and praise His Name, and though the days of trial and conflict continue I am convinced that deliverance lies ahead . . . I remember so well how (on the same night that I hope the Lord appeared to me) I tried to read with my wife in the 6th John, but when I came to the verses from 32 on, they seemed to fill my soul. I could not read any more; but, sad to say, since those days, O what a sink of sin and iniquity has my wicked heart been. Divine forbearance alone has spared and brought me hitherto . . .

Your affectionate Pastor,
J. Delves

X

Sept 25—70

My dear Friend ———,

As I have to be leaving shortly to go to Welwyn, I can only just gratefully acknowledge your kind letter, and say what *heartfelt* joy I felt in reading it as you relate what a sweetness you felt in that verse of Hymn 708:

> 'Thy whole dependence on me fix;
> Nor entertain a thought
> Thy worthless schemes with mine to mix
> But venture to be nought'

May I not say, if not presuming, that your letter brought an answer to many prayers that the Lord would 'open the prison doors', Ps. 142.7; also as in Isaiah 61.1.

. . . I know how true it is that that great adversary (1 Peter 5. 8, 9) would destroy it all if he could, and bring you to the verge of despair, but does not this prove that 'This is the *Lord's doing* and is marvellous in our eyes'?

I pray you may continue to read in the Song of Solomon prayerfully, even though the devil may tempt you it is hypocrisy; but can you not say 'Draw me, we will run after Thee'—and has not the Lord brought you into His chambers (of communion)?—do not the assaults of Satan prove its blessed reality?—you have the 'earnest'. May the Lord shew you even greater things than these. I believe He will—one day I am persuaded He will bring you into the 2nd Chapter of the Song, verses 3–6.

I know you will fear to presume but, as my late Pastor used to say, 'Sing while you can for the days of darkness are many'. O may the Lord favour you still yet with a sweet blessed view by faith of Redeeming love and grace in the *wonders of Calvary*—and the precious blood of Christ filling you with joy and peace in believing; but '*hold fast that thou hast* that no man take thy crown', and may the glory of Christ in His blessed Person and work shine before your eyes and keep you close to the cross . . .

Affectionately yours,
J. Delves

XI

11.1.72

My very dear Friend,

We are very sad to hear that you are brought so very weak and low in body. I desire to send just a line to my friend, in humble thankfulness for that union of spirit we have enjoyed together from the 'first day until now'. We would bear you before the Lord, as helped, and may you feel very sweetly in this 'valley of the shadow' (Ps. 23) that 'underneath are the everlasting arms'; may you feel in spirit (so to speak) to be

Mr Delves at the opening of the Bethesda Home, Hove
18 March 1972 (aged 80)

'coming up from the wilderness, leaning on your Beloved', and, 'He brought me to the banqueting House, and His banner over me was love'. I have thought of the verse you have sometimes mentioned to me

> 'But let not all this terrify;
> Pursue the narrow path;
> Look to the Lord with stedfast eye,
> And fight with hell by faith'
> Gadsby's 305

May it please the Lord to spare you a little longer to your dear daughter especially, and to the Cause of God, the dear little Sanctuary, and all of us if it be His will; but whatever the Lord's purpose may be, we need grace to say even in this, 'Not my will, but thine be done'. Many times through your long life you have been helped, guided, and supported in and through trials and 'hard things', and now the Lord has brought you to this day and I believe you would say, 'He hath done all things well': you have a good hope through grace, and we know that now 'He will not fail thee nor forsake thee'.

I have cause to be thankful for the kindness and affection you have shown to unworthy me, and to my wife, for so many years. May 'the Lord cause His face to shine upon thee and give thee peace'. The best is to come: 'Eye hath not seen nor ear heard what God hath prepared' etc.—Everlasting Salvation.

. . . All at Firs Cottage unite in sending our love in the Gospel and all kind wishes,

Yours affectionately,
J. Delves

XII

9th November, 1972.

Dear ———,

Our minds have been with you in this time of trial and affliction, and I trust our prayers also that it may be the Lord's good will to restore and raise you up again, and we are indeed thankful that this has so far been granted unto us, but we realise it has been a heavy path indeed, and attended with much discomfort and suffering. In a particular sense it has been 'through much tribulation', but hitherto the Lord has been your helper in *many* times of need. What I believe you long for above all besides, in this aspect, is the Lord's gracious appearing, and some sweet feeling of His presence and blessing. We sincerely hope and pray this may be granted, but even so 'Though with no sweet enjoyments blessed, His covenant stands the same'. As the Psalmist, you have to say, 'My house is not so with God'; it has been a mingled cup, but a mingled cup is in your heavenly Father's hand—did not our Lord Himself say this? and truly His way was much rougher and darker than ours. I do desire for you (if but for a few minutes) some sweet fellowship with a suffering Saviour. Did not He bear a heavier load, carry a heavier cross, walk a darker path, drink a more bitter cup? He Himself had 'strength enough (it is said) and none to spare'—so with the Psalmist; 'The sorrows of death compassed me', Ps 116, but afterward, 'What shall I render unto the Lord', etc. We hope your convalescence will be helpful, and a measure of recovery be given—and then you will be glad to return to your 'own company'.

. . . We are all fairly and send our love,

Yours very sincerely,

J. Delves

XIII

22/12/72

. . . Although in much bodily weakness my dear friend is still spared and brought thus far, and ——— able to care for you. What a blessing this is for you as provided in the Good Providence of the Lord in your last days. My desire for my friend is that this may be a favoured season in the 'best sense', in a sweet manifestation of a Saviour's love shed abroad, and to very sweetly feel 'He loved me and gave Himself for me'. Looking back over the trials of the past years—long ago—you can see a supporting Hand, helping, guiding, and supplying your need amidst almost insurmountable difficulties. Truly 'the Lord has done great things'—and now it is evening time, may you often be favoured with some sweet foretastes of immortal joys—Hymn 472, verse 3, and all the verses.

Very affectionately yours,
J. Delves

XIV

Jan 24—73

Our Dear Friend———,

... we are greatly relieved to know you are better and will, we hope, soon be quite well again ... These afflictions that come to us have a voice in them that 'this is not your rest'. ——— has given me another sermon to look through and revise—the text is Ps 90.12. This subject can and does bring a sober and prayerful concern as to how matters stand in the prospect of an unending eternity. At about 5 a.m. this morning I had a little sweet feeling in thinking of the heavenly Jerusalem, from Isaiah 27.13 as connected with Revelation 21.2–7, and the Hymn 934. In the midst of much conflict and temptation it seemed to bring *a hope of the future*—there was something attractive. It is sweet to *feel* a little *real worship* here, but what must it be to *be there*? 'Blessed are they which are called unto the marriage supper of the Lamb', Rev 19.9. What a mercy it will be to be *right with God* and to *be ready*. I feel so far off and do need another token—a view by faith of the great and blessed Redeemer, and to feelingly say, 'He loved me and gave *Himself* for me'.

Your affectionate Pastor,
J. Delves

XV

March 19, '73.

My very dear kind friend,

Please accept my appreciation of your kind thought in writing to me in the loss of my eldest brother. It has brought a sadness, a breach in the family, leaving my brother at Crowborough 6 years younger than myself. Edgar was 86. Not long before he died he asked for his Bible, and read aloud Psalm 37 ('My psalm', as he termed it) and engaged in prayer with some feeling and access, as I am informed. Soon after he began to breathe heavily, and at 12.30 departed this life. I have a comfortable feeling that it is well, and that he was prepared. He was living alone and would not leave his bungalow for a Bethesda—and we can feel thankful that he did not have to be taken to hospital. It is a solemn voice to me for the 'time is short'. I long for another token—one of *Heaven's blessings*, then I could feel like Simeon, Luke 2, 'Lord, now lettest thou thy servant depart in peace, according to Thy word, for mine *eyes have seen* thy salvation' etc. I attempted to speak from these words yesterday and felt I believe some sweetness. The good man was 'Waiting for the consolation of Israel', and not in vain.

What a wonder it will be to be right and as dear old Mr Pocock used to say in prayer sometimes—'When we come to die, may we have nothing to do but to die.'

It is sweet to look back on our long friendship, as also I can with your dear Pastor: 'His Providence unfolds the Book'—

> 'Sweet to look back and see my name
> In life's fair Book set down;
> Sweet to look forward, and behold
> Eternal joys my own'
>
> Gadsby's 472

—*when we can*

The Lord graciously sustain you in your lonely path—and yet I hope, 'not alone'.

. . . Yours very affectionately,
J. Delves

SERMONS

Prefatory note

ALL the following sermons were preached at 'Ebenezer', Clapham. During the first 25 years of the pastorate, the Church was favoured to have a good shorthand writer, the late Miss H. Stevens. The late Mrs D. M. Tingley (widow of Mr T. Tingley, the deacon) performed a labour of love for many years in transcribing and typing the sermons taken down by Miss Stevens. All but a few of the following sermons came from that era, when also Mr Delves was in his prime. Since then another friend has continued the labour of love by taking down and typing the sermons, and many of these, as well as some earlier ones, have been duplicated and circulated widely. In view of this, it seemed desirable to give more of the earlier sermons which have not previously been published.

THE PRAYER OF THE DESTITUTE

23 September 1934

'He will regard the prayer of the destitute, and not despise their prayer.' (Ps. 102: 17)

IT has not been, and it is not, easy for me to come here this evening. The things of God, and the unutterably solemn position I occupy in standing here before you to speak of them, weigh upon my spirit very heavily. I have some little perception of the importance of truth, and of the woe pronounced upon those who do not speak right things concerning God. I feel too, upon my spirit, the difficulty of a mortal man speaking of immortal things, things that are so incomparably beyond us, that, as has been expressed, the most we can know is but as a child going to the seashore and filling a tiny bucket. Yet, it is a mercy for us if in any degree, we have our eyes opened to what is before us, and to the tremendous issues.

'He will regard the prayer of the destitute, and not despise their prayer.' This Psalm appears to have been written about the time when the Jews came out from their seventy years' captivity, and the verses preceding evidently describe the prayer and condition of those grievously afflicted, in their captivity and destitution. And one, a prophet (who he was is not clear), a gracious man, prays under a state of heavy distress; yet he takes comfort in the eternity of God. The unchangeability of God is his comfort and strength. 'Thou art the same, . . . Thou shalt endure . . . Thy years are throughout all generations.' He believes that deliverance is attained in respect of the Jews. The time to favour Zion, yea, the set time is come. God was able to deliver them and bring them out of their captivity, they were to return to their own land, which some of them did. There was a rebuilding both of the walls and of the temple of Jerusalem, according to this word, 'When the Lord shall build up Zion, He shall appear in His glory. He will regard the prayer of the destitute.'

There is a connecting link between divine decrees, delivering mercy, and answers to prayer. If we rightly view the matter of prayer, we shall view it in this light; that God has eternally decreed to bless His people, to deliver them, and to comfort and teach them in answer to their prayers. The time was appointed of God. The time was set; it was not an indefinite time, when He should deliver them. It was a time decreed in His eternal mind. But how was it to be done? It was to be by a sure instrument, the prayers of destitute people. Now our prayers will never alter divine decrees, but we are not to sit down and say, 'Because God's purposes are fixed it is no use praying', because if there is something we are needing, He has decreed to supply that need in answer to prayer. He uses means; it is according to His will, and praying is one of the principal means. Prayer brings heaven's blessings down into our hearts. 'For this will I be enquired of by the house of Israel to do these things for them.' Happy is that person, who, either in regard to matters in providence or more particularly in grace, can say, The Lord heard my prayer. Divine decrees are fulfilled too, by the use of means appointed by God, and this in particular, the crying and groaning of sinners.

'Prayer was appointed to convey
The blessings God designs to give;
Long as they live should christians pray,
For only while they pray, they live.'

Now if the Lord will help me, without any further prologue I will apply myself to this text. It divides itself into three parts. There is a destitute person or destitute people rather; they pray; the Lord regards their prayer. Now first, their destitute state. He will regard the prayer, not of a rich person, not of one who is sufficient in himself, who feels no need of anything, who is rich and increased with goods, but He will regard the prayer of the destitute person. Very fitting to some of us when we feel our poverty. Now what is it to be destitute? It is to be in want, to be in need, to lack that which is necessary for our comfort. It is so naturally; if a person is in extreme poverty, with perhaps hardly sufficient food, and living in a deplorably mean condition, we say he is destitute. He is lacking the ordinary comforts of this life. Now if we view it spiritually, we may say it can be examined in a twofold sense. Spiritual destitution may be considered absolute or comparative. First, there is such a state as absolute destitution, that is, spiritually viewed. It is a state described by the Apostle Paul in the Ephesians where he says, 'You hath He quickened who were [he describes their state before quickening] dead in trespasses and in sins'. Further, they walked according to the course of this world, according to the prince of the power of the air, strangers from the covenants of promise, without hope and without God in the world. This destitute person, absolutely destitute, is without any vestige, trace, or evidence of spiritual life or quickening grace. He may be a wealthy man, he may possess houses and even millions of money, but if he is without God, he is destitute. What will all earthly possessions, though good and desirable in their place for certain uses, avail us when we have to meet God? A destitute person is one who is separated. 'Your sins have separated between you and your God.' I do not want to be in such a condition—a destitute person. The image of God is defaced in such a person, he is corrupt, he is lost, just lost, but the painful aspect of the case is, he is in a way insensible to his condition. He is destitute, but is not sensible of it. Such a state is sad indeed, and I hope it may not be true of anyone here this evening. To live and die utterly and entirely destitute of any knowledge of God or desire for Him means eternal perdition, separation from Him, and ultimately that terrible word, 'Depart from Me, ye cursed, into everlasting fire prepared for the devil and his angels'. He is not only destitute here, but he will be eternally destitute; his destitution does not cease by his decease, but he will be without God in eternity, lying for ever under His just wrath in hell. So Holy Scripture declares.

But we may consider destitution as it is felt in a quickened person, one who is a possessor of God's electing grace. You may say, 'They are not destitute'. They are not in one sense, because if they have God and His grace, in however small a degree, they are 'rich to all the intents of bliss'. Nevertheless, there is with gracious people, a painful sense and experience of destitution.

They feel to lack and come short of that which they are convinced they must have. Their destitution arises from teaching, from the light of the Spirit of God shining into the heart, whereby the inward depravity and evils of the heart are discovered. They are destitute. Now this may be described in two or three ways. One feels this destitution when in some degree one feels condemnation, which we speak of sometimes as the terrors of God in a broken law, the wrath of God seen in His inflexible justice. When the law of God is applied to an awakened conscience, that brings a sentence of death there, and this is spiritual destitution. O, the emptying such souls experience! They are just emptied from vessel to vessel. They lose things they had been clinging to, good works, good frames, many things, until they are just brought to this; to feel they have nothing at all; to feel they are just utterly lost. Now this is spiritual destitution. You see by the Spirit's teaching, the spirituality of the law, with its claims. You feel you have broken it, and feel the condemnation of it in your conscience; you feel to be emptied from vessel to vessel, and you are destitute.

Now this destitution may be in a person who knows the things of God. A person naturally may become destitute, who has been living in affluence and had abundance; he may lose it and become destitute in regard to the things of this life. Now where God gives His grace He will never take it away. A stake in Zion will never be removed, neither shall the cords thereof be broken; but there is sometimes a sense, a painful sense, of divine desertion. In this way, sometimes, believers are brought a little into solemn fellowship with Christ when He said upon the cross, 'My God, My God, why hast Thou forsaken Me?' The Spirit of Christ will never really and finally forsake a gracious person. When He once comes He will remain, but there is sometimes a painful experience of the withholding of His divine operations, which are felt to be desertions. Believers do experience this, they sometimes feel that the Lord has left them. He has not left them really, but there is a withholding of communications, and if we do not have a supply given we die. We can only live really by the supplies of His grace communicated to us, not from anything derived from ourselves; but if this is withholden for a time, we languish and weaken and become destitute in our souls. There is a cessation of that influence, unction, sweetness, and power of the Spirit of God that we have previously felt, and we have sometimes to say,

> 'O, where is now that glowing love,
> That marked our union with the Lord?'

There is a sense of destitution and desertion. We may sometimes feel this by a lack or absence, a spiritual absence. We may be destitute, or feel to be destitute, of a living exercise in respect of the things of God. We vary a great deal in our experience; our standing does not alter, but we alter greatly in our own individual cases often. How we change! Sometimes we have a zeal in the things of God, and are earnest in seeking Him, and yet at another time we may become careless, indifferent, and almost unconcerned about things, destitute even of a gracious exercise of soul before God. We may be destitute of those communications which keep our souls alive, fresh, vigorous, and active in the things of God. This is not a comfortable state, not a desirable state, but in one sense a necessary state, because God will make us feel our destitution, make us feel our need. We may, for a time be abandoned for a purpose.

'He will regard the prayer of the destitute.' Now this is certainly not in an absolute sense, because such an one even in his destitute state is enabled to pray. A destitute person may pray. Now is not that a comfort to you and to me? Notwithstanding all that we may feel to lack, our destitute state, our spiritual poverty, our sinfulness, our distress, we may pray. But we may be destitute of prayer. Is not that the case sometimes? Have we not felt to be destitute even of a desire, even of a wish?

> 'I could not to a wish aspire,
> If one good wish could purchase heaven.'

So destitute of life and feeling we may be that we cannot raise, of ourselves, a spiritual desire, so helpless are we in regard to any movement in holy things. Yet such a person, in that condition, is, by the reviving and renewing power of the Holy Ghost in him, compelled to pray. He prays. What is prayer? It is really approaching the throne of grace, by praying in the Name of Jesus and pleading for what we need for His sake. Now, you see, before you can really pray, you must be destitute, sensibly destitute, and that destitution sanctified and rightly wrought in you will bring you to pray. A person self-sufficient will not pray. 'Few, if any, come to Jesus, Till reduced to self-despair.' Here is the destitution, and here is a destitute person praying. He comes because he is compelled to come with all his destitution. Now how else can you come to the mercy seat for a supply of grace? Is it not when you feel your destitution, your poverty, your lack, and your need? There is no limit in regard to this coming of a poor creature to Christ, no, there is no limit.

'The vilest sinner out of hell
Who lives to feel his need,
Is welcome to the Throne of Grace,
The Saviour's blood to plead.'

You may come then, and you may come with your destitution. You are not going to leave it behind, no; you are not to wait until you are in a better frame, or till you can obtain something to come with, or some ground in yourself to stand upon. No! You must come needy, helpless, loathsome, and bare; you must come just as you are. This destitute person prays. He must. He has no alternative; if he does not, he dies; his eyes are open to the source of supply; he has faith given him to believe there is a supply in Christ, and being emptied from vessel to vessel, he comes with his emptiness and his poverty to Christ for supply, a destitute praying person. Perhaps it may fitly describe some of us here; we feel destitute, but that does not shut us out. We feel our poverty, our need, but that is a qualification. It is all the fitness He requireth, to feel our need of Him. Is not that a mercy? Can you be too bad for Christ? Bunyan says, 'Many people talk about not being good enough for Christ, but find me a sinner bad enough.' Is it not a mercy that we can come with our failings, our wretchedness, to the Throne of Grace? What will He do with us? Why! He will take our rags and give us a perfect robe of righteousness. As it is expressed in the prophecy of Zechariah, the man had his filthy garments taken from him, and he was given a change of raiment. He was not destitute then, he had all he needed, a perfect righteousness, and a fair mitre set upon his head. But it is such hard work to come when we feel so destitute, it seems such a contradiction. If we were more spiritually minded, we could pray. If we had more grace, we could do something. But that is not the Lord's way here. He brings a poor thing to feel he can do nothing, but he will never allow him to shelter under his own helplessness. You will not be able to sit down and say, 'I can do nothing without Christ, so I shall be excused'. No, you will never be allowed to do that. What can you do? Come with your destitution, your weakness, your sin, and your guilt. Will He receive you? He will if He is true to His own Word. 'This Man receiveth sinners, and eateth with them.'

Now have you sometimes lost your destitution at the Throne of Grace? Could you follow me in an experience something like this? You have sometimes had, as it were, to struggle hard against your own feelings, the buffetings of Satan, inward temptations suggesting that it is no use to come, and even infidel suggestions that there is no God to come to, and no reality in religion after all. You are disposed to give it all up, and yet there is a moving in your heart beneath all that by which you are compelled to come. Now the Lord may favour you with a little nearness. Perhaps you begin feeling very cold, distant, and hard; you get a little softening. The Name of Jesus begins to be very precious in your heart; you get a little view of the atonement by faith, and He allows you to come to Him, favours you with a little sweet holy familiarity. You lay your case before Him; He receives your confession and blesses your soul, and you lose your destitution. He takes your poverty and clothes you with the riches of His grace; He refreshes your spirit and you are blest. This is a destitute person praying, and though it is not a comfortable state, yet it is really wholesome for us to feel our destitution and our poverty. But it is not desirable that we should continue in, or be satisfied with, our distress, or lack, or poverty, in spiritual things; but if we are rightly affected by that teaching it will arouse in us a firm desire to get something from God. If you are destitute, you will be after something you must have. It is so naturally. If we are destitute, we are lacking something necessary for our comfort. So it is spiritually. There may be a true seeker after God, who feels to lack something necessary, who is destitute. He has not the clear experience and teaching others have; he feels to come short, to be destitute, to be out of the secret. What about such an one? Why, He may come in such a condition, and plead for all that heaven has good. Yes, and when you get hold of God in prayer it is for Christ's sake, always for Christ's sake, you will never have anything apart from Him. 'Every grace and every favour comes to us through Jesus' blood.' There is such a strength in faith sometimes in a believer that he lays hold of Christ in prayer and will not let Him go. That is not presumption; it is a holy boldness, a boldness of faith, and he says like Jacob, 'I will not let Thee go except Thou bless me'. What will the Lord do with such an one? Why, He will clothe you with His grace; He will take your hell, and give you His heaven. You will never despair in coming, nor will you ever come in vain. You may say, 'I am still destitute'. That is nothing against you whatever; you may still come. You may say, 'I have come many times'. That is nothing against you; it may be for the exercise of patience. The Lord may see fit you should wait upon Him for a lengthy time set by Him; but the time of deliverance will come, when you shall clearly see, not only that He shed His blood, but shed it for you. You will not be destitute then.

If you get Christ in your heart you will have all you want both for time and eternity, and you will want nothing besides. If He comes, He will make Himself all in all in your heart, infinitely blessed, and you will not be destitute then. He will regard your prayer; He will regard it favourably. You might take notice of something someone said to you, but notice it unfavourably; but here it means He will regard it favourably. A person might make a request to you and you regard it very favourably, but perhaps you would have to say, I would relieve and help you if I could, but I have not the means to do it. This would never be the case with Christ; no, because grace with Him is infinite and you will never be sent empty away for lack of means in Him. He will regard your prayer. He has regarded mine, therefore I can speak experimentally. I am not speaking lightly when I say I believe God answers prayer. He will regard the prayer of the destitute person, and when it says, He will regard it, it does not mean just that He will take notice of it, and go no further. We might hear and receive a person's request, and never answer it. But this will never be the case with God. If there is a real prayer wrung out of one's heart, it will be answered in the court of heaven. For this purpose, the Son of God is there in our nature, as the great High Priest of the Church; therefore a destitute person's prayer will never be turned away. Now the ground upon which we may come is the fulness and merit of His precious blood, and that will always be sufficient because there is an infinitude of merit in a precious Christ, and He will never be the poorer for what He gives a destitute sinner. We might be able to help one, but no more; but whatever He gives, so infinite is the merit in Himself, that He will never be the poorer. He will regard your prayer favourably, and that means He will answer it. 'The prayer of faith shall save the sick.'

But I will apply this in matters of salvation. You must pray in faith. You say, I am destitute of faith. Ask Him to give it to you. It is a grace, and a grace for which we often have to come. But notice that word, 'Whatsoever ye shall ask in prayer, believing, ye shall receive'. Now you see, 'faith is the substance of things hoped for, the evidence of things not seen'. If you feel to need a spiritual blessing, say, forgiveness, the appearing of God to you, liberty from the law, the sealing of the Spirit whereby you may know your interest and standing; if you have grace to come to Him in faith, upon the ground of His own promise, believing in your heart that He will grant your desire, you will get it. You will be sure to get it in the Lord's time. He may for a purpose keep you waiting, and He may wait Himself too. He waits, but what for? He waits to be gracious unto you. Now you will get what you want, if you, in the strength of faith, can lay hold of Christ. You may have the blessing in your hand, though perhaps not as yet in the fulness of it received, you may have it in the hand of faith, and be as certain that you will receive it as though you had already possessed it. 'Faith is the substance of things hoped for.' You may have a thing in faith without having the real thing you are hoping for, as yet. Thus you may believe, and be fully assured in your own heart, that you will receive it. 'He will regard the prayer of the destitute, and not despise their prayer.' No! It does not matter how destitute you are, the Lord will not despise you for that, not if you can come in prayer with your destitution. He will not despise your prayer, He will regard it, hear it, and answer it, and then you will not be destitute.

May He grant it to us. Amen.

THE RIGHTEOUSNESS OF GOD REVEALED

13 January 1935

> 'For therein is the righteousness of God revealed from faith to faith: as it is written, The just shall live by faith.' (Rom. 1:17)

I made, last Lord's Day, some attempt to speak a little of the gospel of Christ, and to give some reasons why we should not be ashamed of it. The reasons are affirmed by the Apostle himself in the context: 'For it is the power of God unto salvation to every one that believeth, to the Jew first and also to the Greek.' My friends, does that definition embrace us? Could we, if we examine our own hearts and experience, affirm or have any reason to believe that we have received the gospel by faith and felt it to be in our experience 'the power of God unto salvation'? It is this to every case, every individual case, where the Holy Ghost so applies it effectually and savingly.

Now I read this verse, I believe, last Sunday evening, but did not speak upon it, and purpose if the Lord help me, to endeavour to elucidate it in some way this morning. I would like to say, if I might digress for a moment, that I believe this morning the Lord drew near to my soul and favoured me with a solemn, savoury view by faith of the perfection, beauty and glory of this righteousness. So attractive was it to me that my soul was, as it were, melted within me. I felt to be covered by it, embraced in it, and saw such perfection in it that I felt that, as united to the Lord Jesus, I was perfect even as He is perfect. O how wonderful it is to get any view, any revealing, any manifestation to our souls of the Lord Jesus in what He is, in His Person, blood and righteousness. Well, it brings one nearer to heaven, makes the things of earth fade away, divine realities attractive, the things of God the one thing needful. They rise above all secondary things and become the chief object and desire of our hearts. It is a great thing to have a living religion, a secret religion, to be favoured at any time with some communion with God in Christ, to have our rocky, stony hearts broken. You know there is a reality in religion. Though perhaps we do not feel much about it, and for the most part are very distant from it, yet there is a sweet reality in it which rises above, and in the nature of it is sweeter than even the sweetest things in this life. What an honour God confers upon a poor mortal, does He not, by these remarkable and wonderful emanations and manifestations of His love which He is pleased to reveal and make known to His people. It is, indeed, a glorious gospel, a full gospel, a free grace gospel.

The Apostle, writing here, declares that, 'Therein,' (that is in the gospel) 'is the righteousness of God revealed from faith to faith'. In the first place then, there is to be considered the righteousness of God, and how and in what way it may be said to be revealed to faith, or from faith to faith. The righteousness of God! Then it is divine; not the righteousness of a creature, not man's righteousness, not something, though perhaps great, that has been accomplished by a creature, but a divine righteousness, the righteousness of God. In the first place we might say that the righteousness of God intends that perfection of His nature, His righteous character, His divine attributes. The righteousness of God is revealed both in the law and in the gospel. It is revealed in the law in the condemnation of sinners, and revealed in the gospel in the salvation of sinners; yet it is one righteousness, the righteousness of God, and as pure and perfect in the gospel as it is in the law. The salvation of sinners in every point and particular harmonizes with the divine attributes, and there is no violation of the divine perfection and justice of God in salvation. The righteousness of God is then first (though not as here intended), those divine perfections which are in God Himself; the character, the righteousness and the justice and glory of God as revealed in His holy law. He is essentially righteous, He is righteousness itself, righteousness underived. Righteousness in God is not a conformity to a law, but the Law is a reflection of that righteousness which is in His very nature. He must be righteous; perfection in God has ever been and must be. The righteousness of God!

Now this is revealed and made known in the law in all the

precepts of it, in the claims of it, in the requirements of it, in the justice of it and the spirituality of it. God is just and righteous in all that He requires in the moral law, which is a revelation of His justice and righteousness. This law is spiritual; it penetrates into the very heart of a man, it dissects, separates, brings him under condemnation, sets his sins before him. It is a solemn reality to be brought under condemnation, to have 'the sentence of death in ourselves, that we should not trust in ourselves, but in God' alone. If we have any knowledge of God's righteousness as seen and revealed in His law, it will always bring condemnation when we feel the application of that law and have any view of Christ. God is eternally righteous, perfectly righteous in all His thoughts, words, actions, decrees, works, manifestations and purposes. He must be. He is the Fountain of righteousness, and He has created man, did create man, the first man Adam, under that law, giving him power and a will and ability to keep it. Adam had what we term a free will; he was made pure, upright, righteous as before God; but he was mutable, he was a creature; he was not, in a gospel sense, a spiritual man before he fell, but he was a righteous man as created, pure and upright as created in the image of God. He stood in a covenant of works before he fell, not in a covenant of grace. Before he fell he could not worship God as a sinner saved by grace by the merits of His Son, though he could worship Him purely as his Creator and his God upon the grounds of works; but when that covenant was broken, the image of God was defaced in him. By reason of that terrible fall, there was a separation; the covenant was broken and he became a lost, guilty creature. Now we stand under that law of righteousness. The law of God still stands, and the righteousness of God is in that law as much now as in the day when He created Adam in innocence; and though we have no inherent power to render obedience to it, we are not absolved from its claim because of that inability. God made man upright, and the righteousness and justice of God, as in that law revealed, still claims from us that rectitude, righteousness and perfection in heart and life as from the first man Adam. The righteousness of God, then, may be said to be there.

But the righteousness of God, as here implied and intended in the gospel, is the righteousness of Christ; not that righteousness that is in God absolutely considered; not the righteousness of bare omnipotence *but* a righteousness which has been procured, wrought out and provided. It is not the righteousness of Christ in that He Himself is a righteous Person in respect of His divine Person and human nature, but the righteousness of God here really implies both the active and passive obedience of Jesus Christ. It is the righteousness of God because Christ is God and a divine Person always, though a human Person in respect to humanity combined with the Godhead, one Person; therefore, it is the righteousness of God, the righteousness of the God-Man, the Mediator who stands between absolute Justice and a guilty creature; the righteousness of the Christ of God. Inasmuch as it is revealed and made known in the gospel, it implies first His active obedience. The active obedience of Christ consists in His doing the will of God. He says in prophecy in the Psalms, 'Lo, I come . . . to do Thy will . . . Thy law is within My heart'. He came with that word set in His heart, so to speak, with a determination, and He was straitened, we read, until He had been baptized with that baptism. It was the will of God that He should suffer. Now the active obedience of Christ consists in the performance by Him of all that God required Him to do. It embraces the whole estate of His humiliation from the manger to the cross, all His life, His works, His miracles. He was 'made under the law', and His active obedience consisted in a perfect conformity to it throughout His whole life from His birth to His death upon Calvary. There was never once the slightest deviation from a perfect conformity to the divine law of God; a perfect obedience was rendered by the incarnate Son of God to every precept, not only in outward action but in every thought and in every word. Yea, He 'magnified the law and made it honourable', and every part of that work His Father commissioned Him to do, He accomplished. His active obedience really consists, then, in that full and perfect obedience to the law of God as a Substitute, and this is the righteousness of the Christ of God, the righteousness of God. Now, my friends, it is a great thing really to get any perception of this in experience. We sometimes feel our sins and mourn over them, perhaps, a little, when we have grace enough to do it. We may have had some application of the law to us, felt the terrors of it in our conscience, some of us, trembled under its condemning power, felt and feared we should go to hell, and seemed very near to it sometimes. Now it is very great to see that law fulfilled and magnified in the Person of the incarnate Son of God, in His active obedience. He came with a purpose, and that purpose was to magnify the law of God. All the requirements of the divine perfections of Deity were met in the Person of the Son of God, and the law was honoured by Him and fulfilled in every word by His perfect and active obedience.

In the second place the righteousness of God, of Christ, is revealed in the gospel not only as the righteousness of His active obedience to the law, but of His passive obedience. It was not enough really that He should conform to it Himself. A conformity to the law in His life was not sufficient, but the will of God concerning Him was this, that He should bear the penalty, endure the curse, suffer the curse in His own soul. Now this is the passive obedience of Jesus Christ. He gave His back to the smiters, submitted Himself without resentment to mocking, scourging, buffeting, spitting and reproach, and was brought even to death. Freely and willingly did He offer Himself as a Sacrifice to wash away the guilt of His Church, and this is His passive obedience, His righteousness, the righteousness that He wrought, procured and provided. Now when we view Him in those agonizing sufferings in Gethsemane's garden, when we look upon Him as dying upon Calvary's cross, we see in Him that passive obedience to the will of His Father. In the garden, when under the intensity of those sufferings, He said in prayer, 'O My Father, if it be possible, let this cup pass from Me: nevertheless not as I will, but as Thou wilt'. Here was the subjection, the willingness, the passiveness, the passive nature of His obedience to the will of His Father. I know, my friends, it is very difficult for us in any way to conceive, even in a faint degree, the intensity of those sufferings. 'What He endured no tongue can tell', but we have to consider this, that the wrath of God, the just wrath of God against sin, was there poured out upon Him so that His soul sank into deep mire where there was no standing, and we have to view Him as a Man there. Though a divine Person, He suffered as a Man, and He seemed, as it were, left to a severe test, tested to the very utmost of His capacity and power. If He had not been a divine Person, if there had not been a union of the divine Person with human nature, it would seem that He could never have stood that awful test. Yet He was submissive in the trial; there was the Will of God always before Him: 'Not My Will, but Thine be done.' Now we have to consider this, that what you would suffer, what I should suffer in hell, if we were sent there, was endured in that curse that Christ endured when He stood as the sinner's Surety. Now if sometimes your sins are as much as you feel you can bear, what must that intolerable load of sin have been to Him, when the sins of millions of men were imputed to Him and He stood in the place of guilty men? Yet this was His passive obedience: 'He is brought as a lamb to the slaughter: and as a sheep before her shearers is dumb, so He openeth not His mouth.' He was passive in those intensified sufferings which He endured as the sinner's Surety; and this is the righteousness of God as revealed in the gospel. What grace! What love! What condescension! What mercy to sinners, guilty people, lawbreakers! A righteousness provided, a complete righteousness.

> ''Tis Jehovah's own providing,
> Wove by everlasting love.'

Watts says, speaking of this righteousness:

> 'And, lest the shadow of a spot
> Should on my soul be found,
> He took the robe the Saviour wrought
> And cast it all around.'

It is a perfect righteousness, the righteousness of God. It must be perfect; it is God's righteousness, and there can be no imperfection in Him, no flaw anywhere. It is a robe without a seam, no weak spot, sufficient, perfect, glorious; a righteousness that is covered with divine glory; imputed righteousness. Bold shall we stand, then, in that great day.

> 'Bold shall I stand in that great day,
> For who aught to my charge shall lay,
> While through Thy blood absolved I am
> From sin's tremendous curse and shame?'

The righteousness of God!

This righteousness is revealed. It is not a righteousness that He has wrought or has in possession in Himself, to be kept there with no emanations of it. No, it is a righteousness revealed, revealed I might say in two places. First in the gospel; the righteousness of God, of Christ, is revealed there. His righteousness, His work, His active, His passive obedience may be said to be the sum, fullness and substance of the gospel. Take Christ out of the gospel and it is no gospel. Why, there is nothing left for a guilty creature. Christ shines in the gospel as naturally as the sun shines in the firmament of heaven, and the glory of God shines in Him with a divine, heavenly lustre. The righteousness of God is revealed in the gospel; yes, and the poor creature may sometimes, notwithstanding all his sins, see the righteousness of Christ in the gospel and feel a hope in his soul. May we not say sometimes,

> 'No more, my God, I boast no more
> Of all the duties I have done?'

We place our entire hope in the righteousness of Christ. It is all we need for heaven; it provides a fitness, it gives a fitness. It is revealed thus in the gospel. But there is another place where it is revealed, and that is in the heart of a believer. It comes there. How is it revealed there? By the Holy Ghost, the Spirit of God, Who takes of the things of Christ and shows them to poor people, reveals this righteousness in them. It is seen by faith; faith receives it and puts it on. It is a great thing, my friends, to get any discovery of this, any view of this righteousness in our own cases. If we look at our works we are condemned because there is sin in them; though they may be good in themselves as before men, and, flowing from grace, evangelically wrought, they are acceptable before God, yet there is no merit in them. The Apostle Paul was made willing to renounce all that he valued, even his very best, and count it but dung and dross that he might 'win Christ, and be found in Him'. He wanted a better righteousness than that he once valued, not his own righteousness which was of the law, but the righteousness of God which is by faith. We can face death with that righteousness; with that righteousness covering us we can enter the swellings of Jordan, appear before God and meet Him as a Friend. You need no better, we can have no better; a righteousness not of works but of grace, a glorious righteousness, a wedding dress, when we shall be presented before God without 'spot, or wrinkle or any such thing'. 'The righteousness of God revealed'; therefore it cannot be acquired. It is not something that you can attain to; it is nothing you can manufacture. No, we cannot go up into the heavens to bring it down, or into the depths to bring it up, but it is just that word which is brought into the heart. The righteousness of Christ is that robe which will cover a poor, guilty sinner when he comes to stand before God.

It is said to be 'revealed from faith to faith: as it is written, The just shall live by faith'. It would appear that the better way to take the meaning of this, 'From faith to faith', is to consider it as meaning varying degrees of faith. Faith is one in respect of the nature of it, but there are degrees of faith in the divine operations of it in the hearts of the Lord's people. There is what we might term a cleaving faith and an appropriating faith. Now according to the degree in which this righteousness is revealed, faith receives it. There may be faith in a believing heart where there is a conviction and a need felt that one must have a righteousness better than his own. There may be some discovery made of the suitableness of Christ's righteousness, of the beauty of it, of the glory of it, some discovery, some opening up of it. Then there is a cleaving to it, which implies some manifestation of it, some revelation of it in a way that shall bring the subject of the revelation to cleave to it. It is received by faith. Now it is 'from faith to faith'; from faith in the desire to faith in the possession, from faith in a real sense of need of it felt, to faith in a solid resting upon it as the only hope, to faith in a gracious receiving of it in sweet experience, a sense of being covered in it. It is 'revealed from faith to faith' according to the degree of faith. There may be a weak faith; there may be a strong faith. It seems to imply a growth in grace, growing in a knowledge of this according to the revelation and manifestation of it.

Now apply yourself to your own case. Could you come here and say you have seen a divine beauty in that righteousness? seen a glory in it as wrought by Christ and perfected by Him? As for your own interest in it, that is another matter. Yet you see an attraction, a beauty, a glory in it. Well, it is revealed to faith. There is faith in the heart to see what is needed, to see the sufficiency of it, but it is 'revealed from faith to faith'; that is, according to the measure of teaching. As you travel along and further discoveries of it are given, faith begins to lay hold of it and you begin to trust in it, lose your own natural covering, your rags, till brought perhaps by gracious leading to place your dependence in it and to renounce all besides. 'From faith to faith.' Then perhaps a day may come when you may be brought to feel you stand complete in it and covered by it, so that God may look upon you in Christ as covered by His righteousness, complete, forgiven and justified, and standing before God, as though you had never committed a sin. The righteousness of Christ both pardons and justifies the guilty creature, and makes him fit, and prepares him for heaven. 'From faith to faith'; from faith in some gracious apprehension of it to faith in a sweet appropriation of it.

'As it is written, The just shall live *by* faith'; not live *upon* faith. Faith is not to be the food of a believer. No, he is not to live upon his faith, trust in it, rest upon it; no, but to live by faith upon Christ. All spiritual living, then, as before God, is really by faith, and by faith in Christ. A true believer will, as he is exercised, eat the flesh of Christ and drink His blood by faith, and live upon Him. Christ becomes All in All; All in All in desire, and in the Lord's time, in possession. The just is not a person just in himself. There is a right sense of justice as between man and man, and the exercise of justice; but this is in relation to God, where no man can be truly just except by virtue of his union with the Son of God, and by standing in Him in His righteousness. Then he is just, and such a person will live by faith, live upon Christ by faith, live a life of faith upon Him Who loved him and gave Himself to atone for his sins.

THE BANQUETING HOUSE

10 March 1935

> 'He brought me to the banqueting house, and His banner over me was love.' (S. of S. 2:4)

It is not because I feel in my own soul in the enjoyment of what is here described that I have read it before you as a text this evening, but rather because of my great desire for it, and of my felt need of it, and because this afternoon it was certainly very attractive to me, with, I believe, a desire that I might be brought into some experience of it; and I would desire it, not only for myself, but for you here present, both collectively and individually.

This morning I made an attempt to speak a little of the beauty of the Church in relation to her standing in Christ; but my words seemed, according to my own feelings, but like an empty sound; they seemed to fall short of the point altogether; and although it is not often that I take another subject in the evening, I did not feel I could take it up again. Perhaps it was lack of faith, I do not know, but having some feeling towards this word, I have read it before you, and will endeavour, with the Lord's help and light, to make some remarks upon it.

You know it is not easy to stand before an assembly and speak of the things of God, a dying man before dying fellow-mortals, of matters that concern their eternal state. I would desire to be clear of the blood of all of you, and to stand here, in the presence of God, and to speak those things He has given me to speak, and be as His mouthpiece, if so He might honour me; for we have to speak what He gives us, sometimes shaken all to pieces before a service, then greatly distressed afterwards, sometimes helped, and when helped, not always safe with that help to use it rightly.

The Lord is good to His people; we have proved Him to be a good God. Surely we can say, 'He hath not dealt with us after our sins, nor rewarded us according to our iniquities'. Many times He has come to us over our sins; they have not always kept Him from us. He has come to us in our times of need, in our distresses and afflictions, and favoured us with that good wine of the kingdom of His grace. There is a sacred, holy intimacy existing between Christ and His Church, an intimacy which consists in communion, and which in itself is sacred and holy. Sometimes it would seem that when we venture to read this Song, or take a verse of it for a text, we need to take the shoes from off our feet, for it is holy ground indeed.

We have two parties speaking in this Song, Christ and His Church, the Shepherd and His sheep, the Bridegroom and His bride, the Lover and His spouse. In those various titles, Christ is spoken of, His graces are set forth, His beauties are loved; the Church, her beauties, her grace, her alliance to Him, her affection to Him, and His affection for her. 'Oh! My dove, He says, that art in the cleft of the rock, let Me hear thy voice, let Me see thy countenance, for sweet is thy voice, and thy countenance is comely.' It seems almost incredible that anything in a poor sinner could be a sweet sound to the Lord Jesus, but it is so. There is a beauty in the Church's standing and relationship to Him as the Bridegroom of the chosen bride. Yes! He says that He greatly desires to see her beauty. He is her Lord, her King. The Church here speaking in the second chapter so describes Him, as the Rose of Sharon, the Lily of the Valley; 'As the Apple Tree among the trees of the wood, so is my Beloved among the sons. I sat down under His shadow with great delight, and His fruit was sweet to my taste.' Admiration for Christ! He is above all others, as the Apple Tree among the trees of the wood, more to be desired than all beside. 'The Desire of all nations.' He is the desire of His people. 'He is the chiefest among ten thousand and the altogether lovely.' We can never think too much of Him, never exalt Him too much. He is infinitely worthy of infinitely more honour than can ever be conferred upon Him by sinful mortals. He is as the Apple Tree among the trees of the wood; would we not lay our crowns at His feet and crown Him Lord of all, sit down under the shadow of His cross with sweet delight? I delighted and sat down and His fruit was sweet to my taste. And the Church here expresses what He did. 'He brought me',—Christ her Lover,—'He brought me to the banqueting house, and His banner over me was love.' I would like to notice this in some particulars.

What does it mean? It may perhaps seem too great for us to rise to, and yet it is not, really; it really consists in the gracious emanations of His love and grace towards His people, whereby He feeds, sustains, and nourishes them, as a shepherd does his flock. Why does He bring her? He brings her because He loves her. 'I have loved thee with an everlasting love, therefore with loving-kindness have I drawn thee.' If we enquire as to why He does this, why He brings her to His banqueting house, we shall find the cause entirely in Himself, because He loved her from eternity. She was given to Him in covenant; He became her Bridegroom, and the Church became His bride. There is a marriage relationship. He loved her in eternity before she came into being, and foresaw all that would be in relation to her fall, and interposed in the divine council of peace to be her Surety, and her Saviour.

'He saw me ruined in the fall,
Yet loved me notwithstanding all,
He saved me from my lost estate,
His loving-kindness, O! how great!'

Perhaps we can hardly apply that to our own cases, and yet are there not times when we feel some sense of interest in His love? Can you not look back to the way He has brought you along, and see and realize in some point, that He has regenerated you, instructed and led you in the paths of peace and righteousness? It is because He loved you. Eternal love was the cause, the reason why He brought His Church, and does bring her, to Himself. How does He do it? How does He bring His people? He brings them by the drawing, alluring power of His grace. He does not drive them. He draws them by the cords of His love. People are not driven to heaven, they are drawn by His resistless grace.

'Jesus draws the chosen race,
By His sweet resistless grace.'

Effectual calling overcomes all their objections, brings them down, gives a sense of need, shows them their poverty, their sense of sin, and draws them to Himself, makes Himself known unto them, and by a sense of their guilty condition they are constrained by sheer necessity, to come to Him for mercy and salvation. And that is how He does it, draws them by His love, allures them, brings them into the wilderness, speaks comfortably unto them, and draws them to Himself. 'Comfort ye, comfort ye, My people, saith your God. Speak ye comfortably to Jerusalem, and cry unto her, that her warfare is accomplished, her iniquity is pardoned, for she hath received of the Lord's hand double for all her sins.' So He brings her by His grace and love to Himself. He is her Head, her King, her Prophet, her Priest, all and in all. 'He brought me.' See what it implies. It means that you cannot come yourself, in your own strength, inherent power, wisdom, or choice. No! You cannot make up your mind to come, and come of your own free choice. He must give you the heart, the desire, and bring you in. So He will. He brings the helpless sinner in, into the covenant, into the banqueting house. 'He *brought* me.' Notwithstanding all your weakness, sin, poverty, and ruin, He brings you in. 'He brought me to the banqueting house.'

What is this banqueting house? It is not Christ Himself exactly, because He is defined as the Person who brings her in, and yet we might say that Christ brings His people to Himself. Yes! All they have and receive in a way of mercy and grace, they receive from Him, and He brings them to Himself to receive it. But the banqueting house seems more particularly to set forth the gospel of His grace. It may, perhaps, be said to be the Scriptures, the Word of divine truth, where the gospel is set forth, where it is revealed and made known and held forth to poor sinners. He brings His people there. Well! Has He never brought us there? Has there not been a word, a place, a time, some circumstance, where He brought us to search the Scriptures? You were in real need at some time, you searched the Scriptures for some comfort for your soul, for some encouragement, perhaps prayed over them, and did not the Lord give you something? Has He not sometimes given you an encouraging word, a promise, a lift, a token? He made the Scriptures to you as the banqueting house, the house of wine, the house and the place where He has fed you with the bread of life, and given you that which has sustained and nourished your soul. 'He brought me to the banqueting house.' He invites them to come and gives them the strength to follow that invitation. 'Ho! every one that thirsteth, come ye to the waters, and he that hath no money, come ye, buy and eat; yea! come buy wine and milk without money and without price.' If you go into a shop to buy something, you must have the money, unless you purchase on credit: you must have the money to pay for it; but you may come to the Scriptures as a poor beggar, in bankruptcy, and the Lord gives you something. I might say that you will not get it until you are bankrupt, and oh! what a place to come to, my friends. When you have nothing to pay He frankly forgives, and surely that is being brought into the banqueting house; when a poor sinner, with his load of guilt and debt, comes to Christ, to the cross, and having nothing whatever to offer, no righteousness, no goodness, no good works, not a leg to stand upon, as we speak, just receives a free pardon.

We might just say, too, that the banqueting house is where the blessed provisions are, all of which are found in the gospel of His grace. Forgiveness, righteousness, justification, sanctification, redemption, all the blessings of the everlasting gospel of God's pure, free, grace, are in the banqueting house; that is where they all are, all in Christ, and you may come for them, He brings you, you are compelled to come. 'He brought me to the banqueting house.' But may we not go a step further? may we not say that the banqueting house may be in His public courts? Does He not meet with His people there sometimes? Has He not appointed the public means of divine grace for this purpose? He will feed you there. Perhaps you get your case traced out confirmingly. The Lord meets you in that, and you receive a token, a lift; something touches your heart, perhaps, draws you out after Christ, revives, strengthens, and nourishes. Today the ministry appears to be used more particularly for establishing than for quickening and ingathering, but the preached gospel is for the strengthening of Christ's kingdom and the ingathering of poor sinners in great numbers. Now the Lord does not seem to use it so much in that way, but for the edification of His people. Said Christ to Peter, 'Feed My sheep, feed My lambs'; and that is one end of the ministry to feed the sheep of Christ, instrumentally.

A minister, even the best, has no inherent power in himself, he is but an instrument, and a feeble one at that. If the Lord uses one in the public means of grace to feed His sheep, it is a blessing and an honour. Does He not sometimes make His public courts, the gates of Zion, the house of God, as a banqueting house? Have not your souls sometimes, in years gone by, been fed in this place? Has not the Lord dealt out to you by means of the ministry, the bread by which your soul has been strengthened? Some of us can say, it has been a place where He has met with us, confirmed us, instructed us, and fed us. 'He brought me to the banqueting house.' You are not left out are you? Not entirely? You have had some of those holy operations in your soul sometimes. Well! you say, 'I feel just now to be quite barren, destitute, hard and unfeeling, and seem to have no religion at all.' What can you do then? You have no strength, you cannot come? Why, you need the Lord to come to you. We need Him to come to us when we cannot come to Him. 'He brought me.' He must do it. And He does it by His Spirit's divine operations in the soul. Has there not been a time, perhaps in your house, at your work, perhaps alone in secret in meditation, in private prayer, in reading the Scriptures, or in public worship, when the Lord has met with you, and condescended to break through the dark clouds that have seemed to spread, and shed abroad His love in your soul? Could you not say there has been such a time? I believe there has. You say, 'I do not know much', no, it may be so, but still there are those seasons when He draws His people by the allurements of grace and love, to Himself. 'He brought me to the banqueting house, and His banner over me was love.'

A banner may represent several things. Sometimes it is an emblem of war. A banner is at the head of an army, as they go forth into battle. It is an emblem of loyalty. A banner is waved over an army sometimes to show they are loyal to the flag. Sometimes it is an emblem of security and strength; but here it is an emblem of love. 'His banner over me was love.' This in respect of the Church was eternal love; it never had a beginning in time; He loved her from everlasting, with everlasting kindness. 'I have loved thee with an everlasting love', and this is the banner that is waved, that is spread over His bride, His spouse, His Church, His love. Why, there would not be very much in religion without love; on the part of God it is all love. This is the banner which waves majestically and gloriously over every member of His mystical body. Everlasting love, in all His dealings, love towards them in eternity, in separating them, giving them the grace of life, in all the mighty work of the Lord Jesus, in coming down to earth and redeeming them, in laying down His life to save them from eternal death, in enduring Himself that just punishment which He suffered and endured for their sakes. It was love that brought Him from heaven to the cross, love to sinners lost, love to man's lost race. And what about our love? Do we ever wave that banner? I believe it is Toplady who says,

> 'Loved of my God, for Him again
> With love intense I'd burn,
> Chosen of Him ere time began,
> I'd choose Him in return.'

O! it is a great thing to feel a little love to Jesus Christ, and when that is the case, then you are in the banqueting house. There is the banner of love over you, love has brought you in, love gives you there that wine, the good wine of the kingdom.

I have sometimes heard it said that the religion of Jesus Christ is a religion of love, and though perhaps, that may be but very little believed and realized, it is a blessed truth. It is all love. 'His banner over me was love', and this not only in respect of His eternal purposes of love towards His people, but in all His dealings with them. He makes no mistake, love comes into it all. That which is best for them in their trials, their afflictions, and woes, and sufferings, His love comes into it all. I have loved thee therefore have I chastened thee. 'Whom the Lord loveth He chasteneth, and scourgeth every son whom He receiveth.' Have you not sometimes seen His love in His chastenings? Have not those seasons when you have been in the deepest trial, been sometimes the seasons when you have had that peculiar sense of His love? It does not mean that He loves us if He does not chasten us. He chastens because He loves us too much to allow us to have our own way, and to walk our own ways. Love is in all His discipline, all His teaching, those divine instructions of the soul, those inward teachings and communications. 'I was brought low and He helped me.' 'Return unto thy rest Oh! my soul, for the Lord hath dealt bountifully with thee.' Sometimes in those seasons of chastening, the Lord makes His love particularly manifest, gives an evidence of the Spirit of adoption, breathes it into the soul, speaks His love into the heart, waves the banner, so to speak, of His sovereign love over the believer. It covers him all his life through. 'He brought me to the banqueting house, and His banner over me was love.' The union is very sacred. He is an elder Brother born for adversity.

Well! it is a mercy for us if we have any personal experience of the love of Christ. It is too great to express in words, it is best known, best felt. There may not seem to be much love in some things, in respect of God's dealings which are very mysterious and sometimes very afflicting, and yet at the same time, there is love in all His dispensations. Love comes into it, and it is realized more or less as the Lord makes it manifest. The love of His heart toward His people as expressed in the gospel of John, is very particular. The love that He bears toward His people is infinite, and when there is any return of that love to Him burning in the heart, it is acceptable in His sight. The beauty that He desires to see is the beauty of love, love in the heart of the believer to Him. He is their Lord and King. We have but little love, our hearts for the most part are cold and faint. We languish, faint, and seem to die sometimes. We have but little love, how poor it is, how cold it is, and yet at the same time, there is sometimes a little love flowing out to Him. What will produce love in the heart of a believer? A view of Christ. If He is seen by faith showing Himself through the lattice, looking forth at the windows, the renewed heart goes out towards Him, in the exercise of faith and love. They commune together. 'His banner over me was love', even in bringing me down by a sense of sin. A sight of His law, that separating experience that the people of God have, is all flowing from His everlasting love. Love brings them out from the world, gives them a heart to seek Him. Love sustains them in all their pilgrimage, love brings them to the end of their days, and love takes them to heaven; and the everlasting enjoyment of that love will be their delightful occupation in everlasting glory, to love Him and be with Him, without a veil between. To see Him as He is there in immediate vision, to drink in full draughts of that eternal love, and to worship Him without sin, even the very being of sin, this is love.

> 'What is love? My soul would answer
>   Nought deserves the endearing name
> But the God of love, the Saviour,
>   Whose dear heart's a constant flame.'

If only we could perceive what His love has done and what it is doing, in our souls even now, we should go forth toward Him in the influence of love more than we do. 'He brought me to the banqueting house, and His banner over me was love.' I should be glad to enter into an experience like this again. I know what it is, I believe, to be brought to His table and to dine, as it were, with the King of kings, and feel His sweet love in my soul a little; but you know we do change so, that sometimes the most clear things seem to be hidden and covered, and the devil comes and says there was nothing real in it after all. What then? Why, we need Him to come again, and make it over again, and give us another token, another ray of light, and another evidence of that love, that we may be brought into the banqueting house.

'He brought me to the banqueting house, and His banner over me was love.'

Amen.

THE WORK OF THE SPIRIT OF TRUTH

9 June 1935

'Howbeit when He, the Spirit of truth, is come, He will guide you into all truth; for He shall not speak of Himself; but whatsoever He shall hear, that shall He speak; and He will shew you things to come. He shall glorify Me; for He shall receive of Mine, and shall shew it unto you.' (John 16: 13, 14)

THE speaker here is the incarnate Son of God, speaking to His troubled disciples, shortly before He left them and entered upon that great work of redemption in which He offered Himself as the one sacrifice for the sins of His people. He is here speaking to them words of comfort and consolation, in respect of His own departure, and of the various afflictions and sufferings that they should be called upon to endure, as Apostles and preachers of the gospel committed to their trust. And He is here referring to the coming of the Spirit, in some places termed the Comforter, the Holy Ghost, the Spirit of truth. Christ speaks of Him as a divine person, not merely as an influence, though He is indeed an influence and a mighty one; but He is a person, a person in the Trinity, and He is God, and when Christ speaks of Him here as promised, He speaks of Him as such. Howbeit when *He* the Spirit of truth is come, not *it*, as though it should be something inferior; but when He, a person, the Spirit of truth, is come, He will guide you into all truth. There is some very sacred reading in these few chapters, evidently words that Christ spake to His disciples under very sacred and peculiarly painful conditions. In many ways it would seem that their minds were very dark; they could not seem to understand His meaning, when He spoke of leaving them and that they should not see Him, and then again that they should see Him; it all appeared so very mysterious to them. Even after the great work was accomplished and Christ rose from the dead, they were apparently very ignorant with regard to His mission, and what was to be accomplished by it. There is a sacred intimacy here. Christ, the Son of God, here speaks to them personally and intimately, and when we can read these chapters in any measure under the light and influence of the Spirit of God, it does seem to bring us into the very light, sacredness, beauty, and essence of the gospel. We might perhaps say that in some parts of these chapters, we have the very essence of the gospel in the words of Christ spoken to His disciples, immediately before He suffered. He speaks of the Holy Spirit here as a Spirit of truth. 'Howbeit,' that is notwithstanding what I have previously told you of things in part, not fully. He says, I have not told you all, there are several things that I might have told you, but ye cannot bear them now. There were certain things which Christ withheld from them at that time, because as it would appear, it would be so painful and distressing to them, that they would be unbearable. Yet, notwithstanding this He says, 'When He, the Spirit of truth is come, He will guide you into all truth'.

I would like then in the first place, just to treat upon this point, the Spirit of truth, and why He is termed such by Christ. He speaks of Him as I have previously stated, as a person, and I would here assert before you, that I believe the Holy Ghost to be a divine person, truly and properly God, as much as the Father and the Son, and essential to our salvation as much as the Father and the Son. As there can be no life and no heaven without Christ, and without His redeeming work, neither can there be without the Holy Ghost. In His part in the counsel of peace, and in the covenant of grace, and in salvation, in the application of those blessings that Christ is exalted to give, He is essential. He is, moreover, the object of worship. We as sinners, may pray to Him as God, invoke His help, pray for His teaching, for His gracious operations, His guidance, His power. We may pray to Him in the name of Christ, as much as the Father. All real prayer is addressed to the Trinity, because God is one God, but every prayer must be presented in the name of Christ, who by His obedience and death, has opened the channel of mercy for sinners, and without whose obedience, no prayer can be accepted. He is the Spirit of truth because He is the dictator of the Holy Scriptures. Holy men of old spake as they were moved by the Holy Ghost, and when we read the

Scriptures, and can believe them to be verbally and plenarily inspired, we may read them with a holy confidence, believing them to be the very words of God Himself, wherein His will is revealed to men. All things necessary for us to know concerning God, His perfections, His will, the destiny of man, heaven, hell, the gospel, the person of Christ, all is here revealed. Men, sinful men, in themselves, yet being sanctified by the Spirit of God, holy men, wrote them; they were moved by the Spirit of God, inspired. The words they wrote, were, as it were, breathed into their minds, and they wrote the Scriptures, not themselves, independently, but the Holy Ghost wrote the Scriptures, by them, instrumentally. Therefore when we read the Scriptures, we read them as the Word of God, not as the word of man. There is no book like it, no other book to be compared to it. It is an infallible book, and as we can believe, the men who translated it into our own language, did translate it under the gracious teaching of the Holy Spirit in their souls.

We can safely say that, generally speaking, the Authorised Version of the Scriptures, the translation we now have in our hands is true, in all vital and in all substantial points, to the original Scriptures which were written immediately by the inspiration of the Holy Ghost. Our translation, as we have it, contains no error, notwithstanding all the difficulties necessarily attending the translation from one language into another. Therefore we have cause to bless God for the Scriptures, and for this, that they are the Scriptures of truth, and they were written by the Spirit of truth. In this particular we may say, that He is the Spirit of truth, the light of truth, and the Scriptures as we have them derive their power, their authority, their life, their saving efficacy, because they are the Scriptures of truth, and were dictated and written by the immediate inspiration of the Holy Ghost Himself.

He is, however, the Spirit of truth as distinct from the letter of truth. The Apostle in drawing the distinction, from the two opposing points, speaks thus, 'The letter killeth, but the Spirit giveth life'. Therefore we may draw this contrast between the letter and the Spirit. The letter in that sense, as spoken of, is but the form without the power, although the letter there spoken of possibly may also refer to the Old Testament dispensation, the legal dispensation, and the letter of the law, which can but bring condemnation in its application to the conscience. But we may define it like this as well, that the Spirit is the Spirit of truth, because He has the power of truth. All efficacy, life, and true power felt in a believing heart is because of this, because He is the Spirit of truth. He is the Spirit of truth in this sense, because He applies the truth to the consciences of His people. All gracious teaching that is given by the Holy Ghost, will always be uniform with the written Word. There will never be confusion there. I do agree that a gracious person may sometimes feel and realize a sweet anointing of the Spirit upon his heart, feel a spirit of prayer, a spirit of access, a spirit of sweet humility, which may all be by the Holy Spirit's teaching without any words in that sense actually applied. But the point is this, that the Holy Spirit in all His influences, breathings, operations, and divine teachings, will always confirm the Scriptures, and will always be uniform with them, and will bring the subject to them. He is the Spirit of truth, because He reveals to the heart and conscience of the Lord's people, the spiritual meaning of the Scriptures. I do not know whether you have felt it sometimes, but there are occasions, when in reading we may suddenly feel a divine light in our souls upon the words that we read: they may seem to be suddenly and almost unexpectedly opened to us, and there is a depth and spiritual meaning in the words we read at that time, particularly made known to us, which perhaps in the same light, and the same sense, we have never received before. What is that? It is the Spirit of truth graciously applying the spiritual meaning of the Word to the heart and conscience. This may sometimes be in respect of Christ. When we read the Scriptures, we may see Christ by faith in the Scriptures, and that in a particular way, in the form of a manifestation of Him, which may draw out our affections to Him in the exercise of worship, and this is by the spirit of worship. 'Howbeit, when He the Spirit of truth is come.' The only right way of knowing truth, is by the Spirit of truth. Here we may know the Scriptures in their depth, their hidden meaning, their divine revelation. We can sometimes observe the mind of God, seek His will and do it. The Word of God is sometimes a light to our path and a lamp to our feet. Therefore we may say that all true application of the

Scriptures, whether it be in the form of a promise, a reproof, a light, something to guide us, it is always by the Spirit of truth. He reveals truth, and reveals Christ Who is the truth.

Here Christ speaks of Him and His coming. 'When He the Spirit of truth is come, He will guide you into all truth'; not just merely for one portion perhaps, alone, and leave you entirely ignorant of any other part, but He will guide you into all truth, that is, all truth that is necessary for our salvation. 'When He is come.' Here particularly Christ refers to His coming upon the day of Pentecost. The disciples were enjoined by Christ to remain at Jerusalem until they were endued with power from on high. And we have an account of that remarkable time in the second chapter of Acts, when the Holy Ghost was poured out in an extraordinary manner, when His gifts were upon the Apostles, and Peter being full of the Holy Ghost preached his first gospel sermon. There was the coming of the Holy Ghost, though He may have been said to have come before, because even in Old Testament saints, the Holy Ghost, with regard to their knowledge of the truth and teaching, was in them. But He was to come in a more manifest way, and this coming was upon the day of Pentecost, when He descended upon the Apostles, and they were endued with power from on high. He comes to all His people; He comes and takes up His abode in their hearts. He comes as He is here promised as the Comforter, to comfort them in all their tribulations and afflictions, and in all the inward crucifixion that a believer sustains. All true religion really consists in the indwelling of the Holy Ghost. 'Know ye not that your bodies are the temple of the Holy Ghost, and ye are not your own? Ye are bought with a price, therefore glorify God in your body and in your spirit which are His.'

There is His coming then, in His gracious operations, in His quickening influence, in His application of all truth, to the heart and conscience of His people. It is a mercy if it can be said that the Holy Ghost has come to any of us. We can have no true knowledge of God, no power with regard to the exercise of it in prayer, no right teaching, no manifestation of Christ, without the coming of the Holy Ghost. But He comes to abide. 'He shall abide with you for ever, even the Spirit of truth, Whom the world cannot receive.' He does not come and then change his mind through some disappointment, and leave again. When He comes He comes to remain. He shall guide you into all truth. He comes too, as the Spirit of adoption. The Spirit beareth witness with our spirit that we are the children of God. And this is a very sweet coming when He comes in His gracious operations, and makes Christ known, and breathes that inward witness in the heart, confirming one, and bringing one to a point in experience with regard to his standing. When He is come 'He will guide you into all truth'. It seems really to suggest this, that there is a growth in grace, a growing in the knowledge and understanding by the inward teaching of the Spirit of truth. He shall guide you into all truth. And He does this in the first place by leading His people into a knowledge of the truth, and that particularly with respect to a knowledge of themselves. All have sinned and come short of the glory of God, and it is a knowledge of this that the Spirit of truth leads His people, guides His people, into. It is not, possibly, very pleasant to us sometimes, to have discovered to us the corruptions of our nature, the enmity of our hearts, and the condition in which we are by the fall, but it is necessary.

The Spirit of truth does this, He wounds, He kills, He slays, before He heals and makes alive. He guides us into a knowledge of the truth, our lost condition by the fall, our ruined condition. It is not very pleasant to self, and to flesh and blood, to feel that we are hopelessly lost in ourselves, but it is so. By the fall of our first parents, and by our own sins, we, in our own state and persons, are utterly lost, dead in trespasses and in sins, and it is a knowledge of this, that the Spirit of truth guides His people into. But He guides them into the truth of the gospel, the way of salvation, the way of escape, the refuge that there is for sinners. He guides them into this.

Some of us can remember the time when, like the publican, we had to pray, and we have to still, 'God be merciful to me a sinner', and a true knowledge of this is by the Spirit of truth. He gives that sense of sin, applies the law to the conscience, condemns the sinner, and brings him in lost, shows him that it is utterly impossible for him to meet the claims of divine justice, and brings him down to a sense of his own utter helplessness and ruin. 'The soul that sinneth it shall die.' But He does not leave him there to despair, He gives to such an one a spirit of confession, and opens to such an one, a way of mercy, and a way of escape from deserved wrath. When He comes He will guide you into all truth. He guides His people into the truth of the Person of Christ. I have sometimes said here before, and I would like to repeat it, that it is a great thing, in soul experience, to be brought to realise in some measure the value and necessity of a knowledge of Christ. I believe that we can never really enter into the saving power of the gospel, unless in some degree Christ is revealed in our souls. But when He is seen by faith in His suitableness, grace, and glory, and in His power as the Intercessor of His people, His presence in heaven clothed in our nature, when He is seen in these things, then the spirit goes after Him, in the exercise of prayer and faith and hope. And this is by the Spirit of truth. He guides His people into a knowledge of the truth of Christ's divine Person, that He was the eternal Son of God, of His human nature, and how He took that nature, in the fullness of time, into union with His divine Person.

He guides them into all truth. He guides a convinced sinner into this truth, that his sins are pardonable. When condemnation is really felt in the conscience, one may feel that it is almost impossible, in his own case, for forgiveness ever to reach him, but the Spirit of truth makes known that the atonement of Christ is sufficient, all-sufficient, and, moreover, that,

'The vilest sinner out of hell,
Who lives to feel his need,
Is welcome to the throne of grace,
The Saviour's blood to plead.'

And it is a truth worth knowing. When one really feels the burden of sin, and the guilt of it on the conscience, it is a truth good to be known that there is a sufficiency in the blood of Christ to cleanse him from all his sin and guilt, and to present him without spot before God. The Spirit of truth leads one into a knowledge of this: 'If we confess our sins, He is faithful and just to forgive us our sins, and to cleanse us from all unrighteousness.' Sometimes it would seem like this, that a great part of the experience of an exercised child of God, consists in seeking for pardon. Oh! if my load of guilt were gone, if I could but feel in my own case, that my sins were washed away! There is that living desire born, as it were, in the very soul of a gracious person exercised before God, to know his own personal interest in the love and blood of Jesus Christ; and the Spirit of truth guides him into that knowledge, not only into the knowledge of the sufficiency, the invaluable worth of the atoning blood of Christ, but also into a knowledge of the forgiveness of sins, by the application of that blood to his own heart and conscience. When we get that in some experience of it, then we have a true rest, and He guides His people into this. He guides, or He leads them, into a knowledge of the righteousness of Christ. It is one thing to talk about the righteousness when we feel our own filthy rags, but it is another thing to feel that it is our righteousness. When a poor black wretch feels, by a sweet discovery to him of Christ's righteousness, his rags taken away, and his standing complete in Christ, he finds his heaven upon earth, and the Spirit guides him to this. Yes! He brings that righteousness, and He clothes the sinner with it.

'He will guide you into all truth.' He guides His people into this truth, that there is a sustaining power in the gospel to support the Lord's people in their times of affliction. When we have to pass, as some do, through deep waters, heavy trials, trials of a peculiar nature, is there not some leading in this, in respect of the power of truth to support you in those trials? Have you not seen the tree cast into the waters, and the bitter waters made sweet? Was there ever such sweetness in truth, as when perhaps, in circumstances, things have been bitter? Has the Lord not come into some spot in your life, and made His truth precious, and sustained and supported and kept you from sinking? The Spirit of truth leads His people into this truth, that there is a solid foundation, a resting place, a sufficiency in God Himself, and in the gospel, for all that they may need for time and eternity. He leads them into the truth that all things will work together for their good. All things are linked together. Trials and afflictions in themselves, may sometimes seem to do us much harm, but in the issue, under God's gracious purpose, in the exercise of this dispensation, He makes them work together for our good, and this is a truth good to be known.

He will guide you, or lead you into all truth, for He shall not speak of Himself. That is to say, He shall not speak independently. When the Spirit speaks, it is God that speaks by Him; He never speaks, as it were, alone, or in opposition, or in contradistinction to the mind of the Father or the Son. Seeing that God speaks to His people by His Spirit, it is God Himself who speaks. It is not the Spirit speaking one thing, and God intending another, it is God who speaks. He shall not speak of Himself. He shall not speak in opposition, or independently, but He shall speak in full agreement with the Father and the Son. And it implies this more particularly, that He shall speak, not of Himself, but Christ. That is His peculiar office. 'He shall glorify Me, for He shall receive of Mine, and shall shew it unto you.' It will be our mercy if we can enter through the grace of God, into the vital nature of real religion, and it can only be this way, by the indwelling, habitation, teaching, and leading, of the Holy Ghost. I would desire to bless God for the Holy Ghost, and pray for a Holy Ghost religion; and I would desire that I might be led by His teaching into the truth, in the nature of it, and into the efficacy of it, that I may know it in my own soul, and that you, as a congregation, may know it also. 'He shall guide you into all truth.'

THE LORD'S SUPPER

6 October 1935

> 'And He took bread, and gave thanks, and brake it, and gave unto them, saying, "This is My body which is given for you; this do in remembrance of Me". Likewise also the cup after supper, saying, "This cup is the New Testament in My blood, which is shed for you".' (Luke 22: 19, 20)

IT has been the goodwill of God to leave upon record to be observed by His believing followers two sacred ordinances. An ordinance is a rite which is established by a divine authority, to be observed by a divine command. These two ordinances are believers' baptism and the Lord's Supper. The first ordinance we observed here last Wednesday evening, when one was enabled, by God's grace, to follow Him in gospel obedience. There is a sacred beauty in that divine ordinance, signifying and setting forth, as it does, the suffering, dying, and rising again of our blessed Redeemer. How sweet it is when with a true understanding of its signification, and a right apprehension of its meaning, His humble followers are enabled to walk in such a way of obedience to His command.

> 'View the rite with understanding,
> Jesus' grave before you lies;
> Be interred at His commanding,
> After His example rise.'

That is the ordinance of baptism, water baptism, an ordinance which has the peculiar and distinct sanction of the eternal Trinity.

The second ordinance is the Lord's Supper. It is generally so termed in Scripture, first, because He instituted it Himself immediately after and following the last Passover, when His disciples were gathered with Him there in that upper room; then He instituted this sacred ordinance. The Lord's Supper it is, and it is so named because believers at that sacred feast, when they observe it rightly, are enabled by precious faith to eat His flesh and drink His blood. It is termed the Lord's Table because He has Himself provided that feast, and does presence Himself with His people in it. Some of the Lord's people have been graciously favoured with His peculiar presence at His Table; others have not been so favoured. But we may say this, that it is a season of peculiar sacredness and solemnity when the Lord's body is discerned by faith, and there is some measure of fellowship, even if it be in sacred love felt in the heart for that infinite love that He has manifested towards His people in laying down His life to atone for their sins. Christ is the Author of this ordinance; we have, therefore, authority and example. He Himself instituted it; He was once baptized, and once He partook of the Lord's Supper, thus He was what we might essentially call a Strict Baptist; that is to say, that He was baptized before He partook of the Lord's Supper. So, from that standpoint we have a scriptural guide, as well as from the analogy of Scripture, to insist upon this, that those who commune with us must first follow Him in the ordinance of believers' baptism.

There is a sacred glory in this ordinance in view of this consideration, that the blessed Son of God Himself, *Himself*, took the bread first, and did break that bread, and gave it to His disciples in commemoration of His own precious death. Likewise also He took the wine and poured it out, and said, 'Drink ye all of it; this is the New Testament in My blood which is shed for many'. Here in this verse that I have read Christ speaks of His own body as being given. 'This is My body which is given for you.' This was particularly sweet to me in considering this evening's service. If we could only contemplate this profound mystery, and the amazing condescension of our blessed Lord, we should truly be humbled. He gave His own body; He gave it freely, freely and willingly. He gave it for guilty men with His soul full of love toward them, and in a holy determination, if I might use that word rightly, effectually to save them from eternal punishment and death. Just for a moment, if we can, let us view Him there in that upper room, breaking the bread, and speaking to those few disciples with Him, 'This is My body, this represents My body, which is given for you'. How remarkable is that word that we sometimes sing,

> 'He groaned, He bled, He died for you,
> What more, ye saints, could Jesus do?'

But just think of this gift. We, if we valued a friend highly, might dispose to make him or her a valuable gift; but He gave His own life, His own body. Christ was what we might term in all reverence, 'a free grace gift'; we can never purchase Him, merit Him, or buy Him. He must be given, and He *is* given. He is given to beggars, He is given to bankrupts, to sinners who know and feel that they have nothing to give. This is the amazing glory of the gospel of distinguishing grace. Paul, in the Corinthians, speaking of this ordinance, the Lord's Supper (which he declares he had received from the Lord), says, 'This is My body which is broken for you'. Not only was it given, but it was given at what I might term the expense of awful suffering; broken as well as given. Would it not melt our hearts if for a few moments we could see Him by precious faith upon Calvary, His body bruised, torn, broken, and lacerated, remembering at the same time that it was pure, holy, harmless and undefiled, and this for His enemies, traitors, lost men, people who hated Him? We might, perhaps, do much for a friend whom we loved, but what would we do for an enemy? Christ died for enemies, that is in themselves in their natural state, lost in enmity and ruin. I would like to clear that point. The body of Jesus Christ was both *given* and *broken*, and it implies really just this, that He freely submitted Himself to the most excruciating pain, not only physically, but to soul agony, spiritual suffering, which consisted in the curse falling upon Him, and the outpourings of penal wrath which brought Him down to the dust of death.

But I would like to notice this point, the particular time when He instituted this ordinance, when death, that terrible death, was immediately before Him and He knew it. Yet we find Him saying in respect of the Passover, the last Passover that He Himself celebrated, 'With desire have I desired to eat this Passover with you before I suffer'. There was a holy desire in Him to come even to such a place of suffering. He says, 'I have a baptism to be baptised with, and how am I straitened until it be accomplished.' What condescending grace, poor sinner, is it not, when we consider that He had such love, such thought, such care for His people, as to institute this ordinance just before He entered upon His sufferings, remembering them in His infinite love, that they should remember Him in sweet obedience to His will in observing it according to His command.

But there is another point in relation to the time. It was the same night in which He was betrayed. The Apostle Paul in speaking of this says, 'The same night in which He was betrayed He took bread', and there is a very solemn consideration here, because that betraying person was there present. Whether he actually partook of the Passover or the Lord's Supper does not appear to be clear; I should very much question if he did, but he was there at the Passover when this ordinance was instituted—a betraying Judas. Yet it was seen that the love of Jesus even in such a scene as that, and under such conditions, in the presence, so to speak, even of an enemy, remembered His followers, and instituted an ordinance for them to observe. 'The same night in which He was betrayed He took bread.'

Now if I have grace and light I would like to speak a little upon the various points which this ordinance signifies, in relation to the body of Christ. We read that first in the order of observance He took bread, He gave thanks, He blessed it, He brake it, and gave it to His disciples. It is all symbolical, and we may say this, that the taking of the bread shows forth His condescending grace in taking our nature upon Him. As the bread represents His body, so He did take our nature and came down to this earth in a state of humiliation. God sent Him forth. 'Forasmuch then as the children are partakers of flesh and blood, He also Himself likewise took part of the same, that He might destroy death, and him that hath the power of death, that is the devil.' He took our body, a pure body, a real body, not an aerial substance; a true, real, flesh-and-blood body, was the body of Jesus Christ. And as the administrator takes the bread in the ordinance, so Christ condescended to assume human flesh, and took up our nature into union with His divine Person; and this is an amazing and blessed doctrine which is a constant source of comfort and strength and joy to His people. Some of you, possibly, have been favoured with a view by faith, as we speak, of the human nature of the Lord Jesus Christ; I hope, I believe, I have had such a view. I had it on one occasion at least by this word, in a sweet application to my soul

> 'Is this the Man? 'Tis He, 'Tis He,
> 'Tis Jesus God's dear Son
> Wrapped in humanity to die
> For crimes that I had done.'

It is very sacred, and sweetly humbling to a believer to have any discovery to his faith of the true humanity of the Lord Jesus Christ. 'He took the bread.' We read that He 'drew them with the cords of a Man, with bands of love', and I do believe this, that when by the Holy Spirit's light and teaching we are favoured with a view of the human nature of the Lord Jesus it will always draw us to Him. I believe that it will draw us in the exercise of true worship, because when we worship we must worship God in the Person of Jesus Christ.

Not only did He take the bread, but He gave thanks, He blessed it; that is to say, He sanctified it. It is, so to speak, setting it apart for a particular use. The bread is to be reserved for a particular purpose, not to be commonly used or broken, but to be sacredly used. He gave thanks for that bread, and when we come to think of it, it really implies, does it not, that He gave thanks to His Father in respect of His own human nature in which He had sent Him; and may not we give thanks? The human nature of Christ was in the mind of God, in eternity decreed, and in the fullness of time he came, 'made of a woman made under the law, to redeem them that are under the law, that they might receive the adoption of sons'. But the human nature, the body of Christ, was, so to speak, sanctified and set apart in the will of God for a particular purpose; He was set apart to be an offering for sin, an expiatory offering, to atone for the sins of His people. This was the price that was to be paid to divine justice. Justice, so to speak, claimed His whole body, His life, His blood, and that price was freely, willingly, and voluntarily paid.

'He gave thanks.' Where do we come in, poor guilty people? Have not we cause (if Christ Himself gave thanks to His Father in respect of His body which He was to lay down for His people's sake) to give thanks that He was willing to die an accursed death, for it was an accursed death, that we might live? Should we not be filled with gratitude for such a display of condescending grace? 'He gave thanks, He brake it'; this was the order observed here. Here we come again to His sacred body, which was broken. The breaking of His body may set forth more particularly the intensity of His sufferings. Not a bone of Him was broken, not a bone! When the soldiers came to see if they were already dead, we find that they brake the legs of the two thieves, but the holy body of Jesus was between; they passed, so to speak, from one to the other and brake their legs, but the sacred body of Jesus was there, and not a bone of Him was broken, 'that the Scripture might be fulfilled'. This, in a mystical way, seems to set forth the unity of the Church; not one bone was broken, not one member shall be lost, not even the meanest or weakest; not one shall be lost. But His body was broken, bruised, lacerated, and torn. We might say that His body was broken in the garden of Gethsemane under that intolerable weight of suffering, when, under the weight of imputed sin, He was pressed hard down. There He trod the winepress alone, and of the people there was none with Him. At the same time, the whole of the ransomed Church of God was with Him, mystically suffering with Him; but in regard to the penal anger of offended justice He stood alone. 'He trod the winepress alone, and of the people there was none with Him.'

The breaking of His body is more clearly set forth in His suffering upon the cross. He suffered also in the judgment hall, in the mocking, scourging, and ill treatment that He there received in a physical way, but it would seem to me that the breaking of His body may be more set forth by the awful weight of sin laid upon Him, which brought Him to death. His body was torn by avenging justice, exacting from Him full and complete satisfaction. The hell that we deserved was endured by Him there; He took our hell and gave us His heaven. His body was broken, but not only was it broken, it was distributed. The bread is distributed. Take, eat; take it, receive it. Each member communicating in Church fellowship receives a piece of that bread, and what does that seem to signify but this, that the virtue of the saving efficacy of the sufferings and death of Jesus Christ is given to every believer, set forth in the receiving of that bread? Moreover, there is this, there is the receiving by precious faith a crucified Christ. You see that point in particular when we, discerning the Lord's body in the holy ordinance of the Lord's Supper, receive by precious faith a once-crucified Christ, and we do thereby profess to believe that our hopes for heaven are founded upon His infinite merit and nothing else. Not only that, Christ speaks in John's gospel very decisively of this great doctrine; 'Except ye eat the flesh of the Son of God and drink His blood, ye have no life in you'. And when we observe in a public way this sacred ordinance properly, we do so living upon Christ by faith. I know that we may not always sensibly enjoy the unction of that life in our souls, but we do so professedly, we put our entire dependence upon Him for salvation. Not only so, receiving and eating the bread is really this, it is receiving in a sweet experience the fruits of His sufferings in holy fellowship. 'He took bread and gave thanks and brake it, and gave unto them, saying, This is My body which is broken for you.'

Then we have the manner in which we are to observe it in our hearts and minds—in remembrance of Him. When we celebrate the Lord's Supper we are always to do it in remembrance of the death of Christ. Our faith is to concentrate upon those sufferings, and we are in some sacred manner to humble ourselves before Him and pray that we may receive the benefits of His vicarious death. This is discerning the Lord's body, observing this ordinance in memory of His death. Have you ever seen your dying Lord here? Whenever you have been solemnly engaged at the Lord's Table, have you ever seen Him bleed for you, and been enabled by precious faith to feel in your own soul that His body was broken for you?

'Likewise also the cup after supper, saying, This cup is the New Testament in My blood which is shed for you.' The cup is a holy symbol of His precious death; the wine shows forth His blood. Now this wine is first poured out; it must be poured out in order that we may receive it; so the blood of Christ was, in a sense, poured out. 'He poured out His soul unto death', that is, He freely submitted Himself to it. When the soldier pierced His side, we read that there came forth blood and water. This blood does indeed show forth the freeness of His love in dying for lost people, it does show forth that infinite love He manifested in laying down His life. 'Drink ye all of it.' That does not mean all the wine, but each one is to drink of it, you are all to drink of it, every one; not one is to be left aside in this. Therefore, all the members of His mystical Church are to receive in their consciences the healing virtue of His death, and His blood that was to atone for their guilt. And we are to receive this ordinance to show forth our love to Him. He instituted it to show His love to us; we are to observe it to show our love to Him, and well we might sometimes sing

> 'His yoke is soft and mild,
> For love is all He asks.'

Is He not worthy of our obedience?

This wine is spoken of as the New Testament. In Matthew we read 'This is the New Testament in My blood which is shed for many for the remission of sins'. That is to say that it is by the shedding of this blood that the covenant of free grace is sealed and ratified. The blessings of that everlasting covenant can never efficaciously reach us apart from the shedding of that blood, therefore it is termed the blood of the covenant, or, the blood of the testament. Christ covenanted with His Father to die, and the shedding of His blood is the seal, the ratification, of that holy covenant. Now then, it is by virtue of the satisfaction given to justice, the full price paid, that we receive every free-grace blessing in our souls. Regeneration, adoption, forgiveness, justification, all come by the precious blood of the once-crucified Man. I believe I saw my heaven there one night, and felt I could cast my soul and body upon the merits of a precious Redeemer. I have no other hope now, neither do I desire any; it is sufficient.

> 'The blood of Christ, a precious blood
> Cleanses from all sin, doubt it not;
> And reconciles the soul to God
> From every folly, every fault.'

What love He has manifested to us! He says, moreover, that He will not drink of the fruit of the vine from henceforth until He drinks it new in His Father's kingdom. He only partook once of this ordinance, not again; but He will drink of that wine again when He sees with Him in glory all the purchase of His blood.

Then in a new way, and in a new manner, will He drink of the fruit of that vine in seeing the glorious and blessed effect of His own sufferings, in the presence there in heaven of countless thousands of ransomed souls.

Amen.

THE COVENANT MADE WITH US

5 April 1936

'Although my house be not so with God; yet He hath made with me an everlasting covenant, ordered in all things, and sure; for this is all my salvation, and all my desire, although He make it not to grow.' (2 Sam. 23: 5)

LAST Wednesday evening I made some few remarks in regard to this verse, and this morning again spoke, as far as the Lord gave me some measure of understanding, of this profound, glorious mystery and covenant of grace as it is in Christ. It was made with Him, and in it He by covenant agreement stands as the Head of His elect, chosen in eternity by His Father and given to Him, and as their Mediator, Surety and Testator. The Lord Jesus Christ is all this and much more beside in the covenant of electing grace. The covenant of grace is the main bulwark of the gospel, so to speak, and is so essentially, in relation to the security and the salvation of the saints of God, so that if it were possible for any one condition of this covenant to be broken, we should all everlastingly perish and spend an eternity in perdition. But, bless His Name, it is ordered in all things and sure and can never be broken. It does not stand upon any conditions in man, but it is ordered in all things and sure. And there is so much glory, if it could but be perceived and entered into, in this blessed covenant, that if a minister had grace and understanding enough to preach about it for a whole year, it would be as fresh and as attractive on the last Sunday in December, as it would be on the first Sunday in January. Yes, there is an infinite fullness, a treasury of grace, a divine attraction, an everlasting strength in this covenant.

But I should like to proceed this evening if I am helped, to speak a little as to how this covenant is made with men. I know I mentioned it briefly last Wednesday evening, but I would just reaffirm a statement that I made then, and that is that this covenant can never be said to be made with man except in the way of a testament; not upon conditions, but as a covenant of free grace and as a covenant of promise. Now David personally had that covenant made with him, hence he could speak here affirmatively and confidently, and say, 'Although my house be not so with God, yet hath He made with *me* . . .'. A wonderful point that. 'Yet hath He made with *me*.' He believed that God had made a covenant with His Church, but he had a gracious assurance that he was embraced therein. 'He hath made with me an everlasting covenant'; and although God made with him a covenant of royalty in relation to his seed and the kingdom of Israel, yet this covenant goes beyond all earthly things. It is not merely a covenant of royalty, it is a covenant of grace, an everlasting covenant. Now this covenant can be said to be made with men, that is, it is made with or on behalf of all the chosen seed. 'I have made a covenant with My Chosen, I have sworn unto David My servant . . .' Now this covenant is made first with the Church of Christ, in view of their relation to Christ and union to Him; as it was made with Him their Head, so it is made with the body in Him, but with this difference, that Jesus stands an accountable Person, for all His children, and stands as their Surety, answering for all legal claims that may be brought to bear upon them. Yes. So that as He is our elder Brother born for adversity, the Head of the Church, His body, the covenant is made with His people in Him. Yes, and this brings this blessed truth to light, that all the blessings which Christ procured as the Testator of this covenant for His people are theirs. Therefore we may say that he 'hath blessed us with all spiritual blessings in heavenly places in Christ'. In view of this then, we can say, 'All things are yours, whether Paul or Apollos or Cephas . . . all are yours; and ye are Christ's, and Christ is God's'. Believers are joint heirs, heirs of God and joint heirs with Christ, and this not independently, but by virtue of the indissoluble union in which the Church stands in Christ. Therefore what He is, He is for His people, and all that He possesses as heir of the blessings of this covenant, is theirs. You will receive what the Lord gives you; every place that you put your foot upon is yours, but all the blessings are for the comfort and salvation of the Church. Therefore the covenant is made with them, but it is made in this sense, it is made with them in the gracious application of those blessings which are procured for the Church by Christ's death, it is made with them in that way, with every living vessel of mercy.

Now then, when the Holy Ghost is pleased, when He condescends to apply to you, to convey to your soul any divine blessing, when He may be pleased to seal home upon your conscience a sense of His love, He makes a covenant with you. In every word that He speaks to His people savingly, in that word He makes a covenant with them. 'I have made a covenant with My chosen.' Hence, in that chapter which I read in Isaiah, there is the invitation, 'Incline your ear, and come unto Me, hear and your soul shall live, and I will make an everlasting covenant with you, even the sure mercies of David'. But it is a very close point really; we may perhaps be wrongly impressed in our minds in regard to some things; we may think we have received things from the Lord, when perhaps we have not, but this stands sure, when the Lord does really come and shed His love abroad in a poor sinner's heart, He makes heaven secure to that sinner, and binds Himself by His Word, which cannot be broken, to take him there. In that sense He makes with him an everlasting covenant. He makes it with him by applying the blessings of it to his soul, makes it with him by sprinkling His own blood upon his conscience, makes it with him by sealing his conscience with regard to his interest in His love. In the sealing of the Spirit, in the witness of the Spirit, in the sprinkling of the blood, a covenant is made with His people. And He makes a covenant or testament with them in a gracious promise sometimes. If the Lord promises to take you to heaven, you will be there when His time comes, as sure as He gives you the promise. You have never known Him to break one yet. We may have thought sometimes He gave us a promise, and have had to prove in a furnace that it was not from the Lord; but if He does give you a promise, He will stand firm to it, whatever it may have reference to, either in this life or to the salvation of our souls. Yes, it is ordered in all things. Now when the Lord draws near to a poor, self-condemned sinner, and seals pardon home to his conscience, when He says, I have loved you, you are My child, He makes a covenant. He makes a covenant with that sinner, and He will never change His mind, never say, Oh! I wish I had never had anything to do with such an one: He loves their persons though He hates their sins, and may chasten them for them, yet His love remains as warm as it was in eternity when the covenant was made, and knows no change. Hence, He is Jesus Christ, the same yesterday, and today, and for ever.

It is a great thing, is it not, to have a covenant made with us? How condescending it is on the part of God to draw near to a poor sinner and make a covenant with him. Has the Lord ever come to some of us in trouble, in affliction, in a time of sorrow and distress, and shed abroad a touch of His love in our hearts, spoken a kind promise to us, a promise which has enabled us to be still, a promise which has enabled us at that time to cast our burden upon Him; has He ever done that? If so, He has made a covenant with you, has made a covenant to you in this, that whatever promise He may have given, He will fulfil to the very last shred. Yet hath He made with me an everlasting covenant, and this covenant is ordered in all things. Not some things made quite sure about and some other things precarious, some things left to chance. No, it is ordered in all things; every condition of that covenant is made positively sure. It is ordered in all things then, for the glory of the eternal Trinity; the glory of God is in that covenant that He has made with Christ, and His Church in Him—His glory. And the glory of God is revealed in what that covenant implies and means in the coming forth in the fulness of time of the Lord Jesus Christ, and of His glory as revealed in all the covenant transactions which were necessary in order to fulfil its obligations. The glory of God is in its formation; the glory of God is in the terms embodied in it; and the glory of God will be in the final issue, the glory of the Trinity; the glory of the Father in choosing, the glory of the Son in dying, and the glory of the Spirit in applying. But it is ordered in all things, it is ordered in all things for the sure and certain salvation of the whole Church of God; it is ordered in all things in that. There can be no point overlooked; nothing can be left undone; everything must be carried out to the last detail. This was so in the case of the Lord Jesus Christ. Yes, all that justice required of Him in a way of obedience and punishment was answered; this was accomplished by Him as the Surety of His Church and people. It was ordered in all things as to the time when it should be, yes, ordered in all things, everything timed, timed in eternity. Yes, His going forth is prepared as the morning; yes, everything is timed in this covenant. Therefore when the fullness of time was come, God sent forth His Son made of a woman, His birth was timed, His death was timed, and all between; and everything that you receive is timed, all timed in the covenant ordered in all things.

Yes, and it is ordered in all things with regard to the certain provision of every needful blessing to the Church in this time state. Has the Lord failed you yet? Has He not brought you hitherto, perhaps to the surprise of yourself? Have you not to speak well of Him? Has He not come to you when you have needed Him? Has He left you in times of affliction and sorrow? No! You have to say, He has been a good God to me; I have treated Him basely, but He has supplied my need. He has come to me and blessed me, I believe, many times. Some of you can say that. So, you see, it is ordered in all things; everything concerning the Church was ordered of God and appointed of Him. Every trial that you must have and I must have, all the changing vicissitudes in this time state, were all ordered by Him, and all ordered well; all the deliverances, those times when He should come and make that covenant with you, everything ordered as to time. This comes into our life's history, into every circumstance of life in this changing scene, therefore it is ordered in all things and sure. It is ordered in all things and sure, sure in relation to its foundation. 'Nevertheless, the foundation of God standeth sure, having this seal, The Lord knoweth them that are His.' It is a great thing to have a sure foundation for a building, and the foundation of the Church was laid in covenant, and laid sure. God laid His own Son in covenant, to be the foundation of the Church, upon which it should be built. 'I lay in Zion for a foundation a stone, a tried stone, a precious corner stone, a sure foundation.' It will stand all right; it will stand all the floods and storms of time; nothing can sweep the foundation away, neither could it sweep away a brick placed upon it either. The whole superstructure stands as firm as the foundation. And this shall be in the last day, when the topstone shall be brought forth 'with shoutings, crying Grace, grace unto it'. It is ordered in all things and sure also in regard to its plan, eternally designed of God, and a plan which was foreseen by Him in all its accuracy. When an architect makes a plan for a building, he can see the building in his mind's eye, as though it were already built; he has the plan of it, the design, in his mind, and he can draw the plan accurately, as though the building were completed. So it is in this covenant. It is sure in regard to its plan, perfectly accurate, every one enrolled in it known to Him, and no possibility of one being lost. It is said in regard to the Church, that though she might be 'tossed with tempest and not comforted', yet the promise is, 'I will lay thy stones with fair colours, and lay thy foundations with sapphires. And I will make thy windows of agates, and thy gates of carbuncles, and all thy borders of pleasant stones.' So that it is all sure and according to plan, and it is just as sure in its promises, just as sure. The Lord never makes a promise that He cannot fulfil. No, the promise in His own mind is already fulfilled, for with Him there is no time, He knows the end of a thing from the beginning; it is ordered in all things and sure. Therefore, I should believe that here, for a tried saint of God, there is some ground of consolation. If, when beset with sin, and beclouded, as we sometimes are, with unbelief, oppressed by temptations, and distress, we can cast our eyes this way and behold the covenant of electing grace, see that covenant standing firm and sure in Christ, there is strength here. Yes, it remains the same, it does not depend upon our frames and our feelings, does it? When we have a good frame, as we speak, when the Lord is near to us, I would say, and we have some sweetness in our souls in meditating upon heavenly things, we can take a delight in this, in meditating upon those divine realities, and have some hope in our souls that we have an interest in them; but at other times everything seems so beclouded, things seem so dark. They are all covered, not lost, you know, but they are covered over, you cannot see them, they are hidden, and we question whether we know anything at all, but still that doesn't alter the covenant. No!

> 'Though with no sweet enjoyments blest,
> This covenant stands the same.'

It doesn't rest upon anything in us, no, not even the best experience it is possible for a creature to have, it doesn't rest upon that. At the same time, it is a very great mercy to possess an experience. It is a great mercy to have in our souls any real hope that God has made a covenant with us. It is a great thing really to be brought down to know that we are lost, guilty, ruined creatures, and to be brought to the footstool of divine mercy, and to have the way of salvation opened, and opened for us, to feel the healing balm of Jesus' blood upon our conscience; a very great mercy. The covenant is made with us then, but it does not stand upon that as a foundation. No! it stands upon Christ. He is the foundation of that covenant, therefore it is ordered in all things and sure. It is in the hands of a competent person, one who, having undertaken to answer all obligations on behalf of His people, will honour those obligations.

'For this is all my salvation and all my desire.' We might imagine the Psalmist here, favoured with a very special view of this blessed covenant being made with him, and seeing everything provided there for him, making his heaven secure; therefore he could say, 'This is all my salvation'. And so it is, for there is no salvation apart from it, there is no salvation apart from this covenant; salvation is in it; it is all the salvation of a sinner; all his salvation hangs upon it, all rests upon it. 'This is all my salvation.' Now if the Lord is pleased to bring this point home to us, and to open up the beauty of it to us, we can say the same as David here, we can say, 'This is all my salvation'. What does that covenant mean? It means that Jesus Christ came to die for sinners, it is really a covenant of free grace, a covenant wherein and whereby saving blessings flow to lost sinners. And when a poor creature is brought by the Holy Spirit by faith to Calvary, and can see there to his soul's peace and joy, Jesus bleeding for him, Jesus dying according to covenant agreement, he can say, '*This* is all my salvation'. It is all in a precious Christ, all embraced in that wonderful work that He accomplished on Calvary's tree, all my salvation. And it means this, it means that all the blessings of salvation are in that covenant. There is no saving blessing for a poor sinner outside the covenant of free grace, not one.

'Out of Christ, Almighty power,
Can do nothing but devour.'

But in this covenant all blessings which are essential for the salvation of the Church are firm and sure, it is ordered in all things and sure, and this is all our salvation. It is all our redemption; by it the Church was purchased, bought, brought back, delivered, and secured, and entitled to everlasting bliss and glory. 'All my salvation.' Every blessing of salvation is in it. Is it the forgiveness of our sins? Here it is. Is it the justification of our persons? Here it is. Is it eternal life? The promise of it is here, for it is the covenant of life, the covenant of peace, the covenant of promise; it is all this. It is a full salvation, because a full Christ is in it. A full salvation. The Lord doesn't do things by halves, no, His salvation is a salvation worthy of God. Yes, a perfect salvation, an eternal redemption.

'And all my desire.' What is your desire? If you live before God, your desire will be this, to read your name there: your desire will be to know that your name is enrolled in that covenant ordered in all things. Some of us can say, can we not?

> 'When I can read my title clear,
> To mansions in the skies,
> I *will* bid farewell to every fear,
> And wipe my weeping eyes?'

This is all our desire, to know our interest in a precious Christ, to know that those blessings that are treasured up in Him are ours. It is our desire to receive them, to have an application of them to our souls, this is all our desire. Could you rise to a point in experience and say, This is *all* my desire? Does it come before and above all earthly things? Is it more to you than all time things? Should we presume, some of us here, if we were to say, in so far as we hope we know ourselves, and the value of an immortal soul,

> 'I could from all things parted be,
> But never, never, Lord, from Thee.'?

This is all my desire to know that I am bound up in the bundle of life with the Lord my God. Nothing compares with this, nothing stands upon the same footing, many things have their importance, but this is paramount; this rises above all other things, everything is subordinate to this. 'This is all my desire.' Some things we can afford to leave, we shall have to leave everything very soon; but this is something everlasting, abiding, it is all my desire. Could we say that, it is our one desire to have Christ revealed in us as having fulfilled all the terms of that covenant for us, as having made our salvation sure in that covenant? It is so with some people; I believe it is with some here, I hope and believe sometimes it is with me, it is all my desire. And, you know, when we come to die, nothing will avail us but this, having a covenant made with us; it will be the one thing needful then, and if we are alive in our souls, it will be our one desire to know that we stand right for eternity. How unspeakably awful it will be to die a lost creature, to be irrevocably and eternally lost; how ineffably awful! But here is a covenant made, firm, sure, and abiding, and every condition honoured, and it will be our mercy to be found in it.

'Although He make it not to grow.' The covenant itself can never grow, the covenant was made a complete covenant. As far as it is in God, in the Trinity, it can never expand, never be more than it is, because it is complete. There is no imperfection in this covenant, but it may expand in us. It may grow in respect of our understanding of it, and our interest in it, and our standing upon the foundation of it. It would seem here, that in a literal sense, David did not see that grow with regard to his family, and his temporal kingdom; but a poor saint of God may have to say at times, It doesn't seem to grow in me. I do not seem to grow in regard to my knowledge of it, or my interest in it, yet it is all my desire, although He make it not to grow. And there may be sometimes a suspension of its blessing in the case of a child of God, a withholding, so that one may say, I do not seem to make any advance in anything; I seem to be losing ground, going backward. Yet the covenant is firm, although He make it not to grow. At the same time there are seasons when it expands in the soul, when there is a sweet opening up of it by the Holy Spirit; then it expands in us, not in God. This covenant then, is a covenant that can never break. 'Although my house be not so with God, yet He hath made with me an everlasting covenant, ordered in all things and sure, for this is all my salvation and all my desire, although He make it not to grow.'

Amen.

'HE LEARNED OBEDIENCE'

17 October 1937

> 'Though He were a Son, yet learned He obedience by the things which He suffered; And being made perfect, He became the Author of eternal salvation unto all them that obey Him.' (Heb. 5: 8, 9)

IN this wonderful epistle the apostle holds forth in a remarkable way the Person of the Son of God. This was ever the main scope of his ministry; it was the one desire of his heart to exalt the Redeemer, to lift Him up. And in my feeble way I can say the same; it is my desire to preach Christ because I hope and believe, if I am not deceived, I have loved Him, and have felt the holy sufficiency of His precious merit and death to save my soul from eternal destruction. There can be no subject so attractive, so sweet, so divine, so heavenly, as the subject of the glorious Person of the Son of God. In this epistle the apostle declares Him to be such. He opens with admirable language, language which I may say has a wonderful attraction in my soul. He brings to light the glorious Person of the Son of God; He is, He was the Son of God; not only the Son of God, but God. Quoting from Psalm 45, in chapter 1, he says, 'Thy throne, O God, is for ever and ever'. Here is the eternal Son; not a Son by office, but a Son by nature, the only-begotten Son of the Father! A wonderful, an amazing truth, an attractive one too, to an enlightened sinner. But not only is He held forth as God, as the Son of God, but He is a Man, a Man! a real Man! O, what gospel there is in that word. 'But this Man after He had made one sacrifice for sins for ever, sat down at the right hand of God.'

> 'A Man there is, a real Man,
> With wounds still gaping wide.'

But He declares Him to be the Sin-bearer. 'So Christ was once offered to bear the sins of many.' Of many. Of a countless number to men, but a number known to God, and known from eternity too, because they were chosen by Him and chosen to salvation. Therefore 'the foundation of God standeth sure, having this seal, The Lord knoweth them that are His'. He shines as a Man, He shines as God, He shines before the eyes of His people as a glorious, attractive, blessed, holy, eternal Person, very God, very Man!

The main scope of the apostle in the epistle is to set Him forth as a Priest. A Priest, the great High Priest of the Church, called of God to be a Priest; not taking the honour upon Himself, but 'Called of God an High Priest for ever after the order of Melchisedec'. It is in this particular relationship and office we have now to consider Him. In the verse I have read the apostle speaks of Christ as being the Son of God. 'Though He were a Son, yet learned He obedience by the things which He suffered.' And this is the word which was so attractive to me yesterday, because it brings to light the amazing condescension of the Son of God. 'Though He were a Son' yet He became a Servant. He became a Servant; He never became a Son, He was that from everlasting. 'In the beginning was the Word, and the Word was with God, and the Word was God.' There is His eternal Deity; there in the same verse is His eternal Sonship; there also is His distinct personality. He was a Son (as before mentioned), not by office, but the Son of God from eternity in His divine nature. A mystery agreed, but an essential doctrine. But this is the point; 'though He were a Son, yet learned He obedience'. In order to do this, He must assume the office of a Servant which He did, He became His Father's Servant. 'Behold! My Servant, Whom I uphold, Mine elect, in Whom My soul delighteth.' He became a Servant; and for what purpose did He become thus the Surety of His Church? In order that He might effectually rescue, ransom, redeem, save, pardon, justify, and glorify her to an endless eternity; and for this, to this end and purpose, He became a Servant. He was a Son; there is His honour, His glory, His majesty. He is the 'brightness of His Father's glory, the express image of His Person'; what the Father was in relation to those divine perfections of Deity, the Son was, the express likeness. But O, we see Him as a Man, a Servant. 'We see Jesus Who was made a little lower than the angels.' O, He descended, He came down below, beneath angelic creation;

unfallen angels do not stand in need of the gospel, they need no Redeemer; unfallen angels cannot penetrate the amazing mystery of incarnate Deity, of redemption, of a lost state, and of a saved one. He came down. 'Though He were a Son.' Here we see His eternal glory, the glory that He had from the foundation of the world, being ever the delight of His Father, brought up with Him before the mountains were brought forth; but the amazing wonder of divine love appears in His condescension.

> 'But lo! He leaves those heavenly forms,
> The Word descends, and dwells in clay.'

That was very sweet to me when I was looking it up last night.

> 'The Word descends and dwells in clay,
> That He may hold converse with worms,
> Dressed in such feeble flesh as they.'

'Though He were a Son' He deigned to come down and condescended to men of low estate, to be dressed in feeble flesh. The eternal Son was veiled in the flesh of humanity. He did not take upon Him the nature of angels; greater love by far than that was revealed in the Person of Emmanuel; He took on Him the seed of Abraham.

> 'He laid His glory by,
> And wrapped Him in our clay.'

O my friends, it is wonderful to apprehend that in any measure. You *must* be a saved soul if you feel your affections drawn to incarnate Deity, you *must be* a saved soul for that.

'He learned obedience.' What does that mean? It means that He rendered obedience to the Will of His Father. He learned obedience, not in the sense that we learn things; there is no implication of the infirmity of ignorance here. We learn things often through making mistakes. Sometimes you say, 'I made a mistake at such a time, and from that I learned a lesson'. Thus we poor, blind creatures learn by experience and by suffering too, sometimes; but Jesus learned obedience, not in that sense; He learned it in a way of passing through it, by passing through that valley of suffering in order that He might be perfected, not as a Son but as a Priest. You see, He could not be the High Priest of His Church without first offering the sacrifice, and He could offer no sacrifice but that of Himself; therefore He must first pass through the fires of temptation, of conflict, of tribulation, sorrow, anguish, bitterness, suffering, agony, and death itself, in order that He might be perfected as the great High Priest of His Church. 'He learned obedience.' You see, unless the Lord Jesus had passed through what He did, endured and suffered what He did, He could never be a sympathising High Priest, could He? But now He is, because He is perfected. 'He learned obedience by the things which He suffered.' Having suffered, He is able to succour His suffering members. There is the beauty of this doctrine; He is able not only to save to the uttermost, but to succour every tempted soul, every tempted soul.

> 'Touched with a sympathy within
> He knows our feeble frame,
> He knows what sore temptations mean,
> For He has felt the same.'

How can this be? How *can* it be? Only because He, as the Captain of our salvation, was made 'perfect through sufferings'. Not that there was any imperfection in Him—God forbid the thought! His eternal Deity was absolute purity, essentially so; His humanity was none the less pure; but He was made perfect as a Priest, which He could not be without first passing through untold, ineffable, inexpressible suffering. There is something peculiar to the sufferings of Christ which cannot be with anyone else. What is that? He suffered—a sinless Person for guilty men; He suffered, the Just for the unjust; He suffered—Himself a sinless Man. He suffered—a holy Man, for guilty, fallen traitors, for wretches who deserve the just judgments of God, and the outpouring of His wrath. He suffered—the Just for the unjust. That cannot be said of anyone else. His Church, His bride, may fill up that which is behind of the afflictions of Christ, but His poor members suffer as sinners, that is to say, as being sinners in the sight of God. When I say that, I mean, that when we suffer in a way of fellowship with the Lord Jesus Christ, fellowship in suffering, we suffer not as sinless creatures, but as being the guilty party. What is more, our suffering is produced by a view by living faith of the agonies of the Redeemer; but His sufferings were personal sufferings, the sufferings of a sinless Man, and they were peculiar to Himself, never experienced by anyone else.

'He learned obedience.' Obedience to what? Obedience to the will of His Father, that was what He learned. Aye! And it was a painful learning too, not as I have before said, as an ignorant person learns lessons. He knew what the will of God was, but He obeyed that will; He learned obedience and He learned it by suffering. The obedience of Jesus here then, is the obedience to the will of God. And what was the will of God? Why, it was that He should take our nature upon Him, that was the will of God. The will of God was that He should become the righteousness of His people. The will of God was that He should suffer the penalty of the law for their sins; all this is embodied in the will of God concerning Christ. And did He not know? He did. He knew perfectly what the will of God was in relation to His whole estate of humiliation, suffering, and death. And not only did He know what the will of His Father was in eternity, but He willingly consented thereto, willingly and freely volunteered, so to express it, in covenant agreement with His Father, to become the Surety of His lost, afflicted, ruined, Church—that is, as the Lord saw she would be in the fall. He knew that, and He knew what it meant, knew what it meant to Himself, knew what the cost would be. O, but He never drew back! He undertook, and He carried it through to perfection, and in that respect and sense, He learned obedience. He did not say when He came down to this earth in His suffering humanity 'I never thought it would have cost me this, or I would never have come'. Rather do we not in the depths of His agony, find Him passive in the hands of His Father, subjecting Himself to the will of His Father? He learned obedience to the will of God by the things which He suffered. And what were the things which He suffered? Notice the apostle says *the things* which He suffered, not by *the thing* which He suffered. The one main thing He suffered was the death of the cross, but He suffered many, many other things beside that. 'The things which He suffered.' And what were they? Why, they were manifold, they followed Him, so to speak, throughout His whole life. He suffered by poverty. 'Foxes have holes, and the birds of the air have nests, but the Son of Man hath not where to lay His head.' We should not think much of it if we had nowhere to go, except to a lodging-house or a workhouse. But He suffered by poverty; no great estate had He in this world; His kingdom was not of it. When tribute was to be paid to Caesar, a miracle must be wrought, and the coin must come from the fish's mouth. He suffered the scorn of men; they reviled, they scorned, they hated Him. He suffered the malice of His enemies, and some of them were filled with the most malicious intentions and designs against Him. They sought many times to take His life, and yet He never did any harm to them. He only came (observe that word rightly) to save lost men, and yet their hearts were filled with the most awful, malicious enmity. A sinless man, none the less, who never uttered a wrong word, or put one in the wrong place, or conceived a wrong thought in His mind; but He suffered, although a pure Man, and His human nature was united to the divine nature. As a Man He suffered, He was not immune from those terrible onslaughts of men against Him—far from it. We can never conceive what He must have felt, the bitterness of soul He must have felt when some of those things were brought against Him. He suffered the blasphemies of men. O, the blasphemous utterances they propounded against Him! He was holy, harmless, undefiled, separate from sinners, and yet allowing lepers to come to Him. They blasphemed and He suffered that, and He suffered the rejection of men too. 'He came unto His own, and His own received Him not', but His sufferings reached their awful crisis towards the close of His career in this sinful world, when as related of Him He said in prayer, 'Father, the hour is come, glorify Thy Son, that Thy Son also may glorify Thee'. His sufferings reached their crisis, so to speak; then they deepened. What were the blasphemies of men, the scorn of men, the malicious intentions of His enemies to take His life, compared to the wrath of offended justice, the outpouring of that wrath upon Him? 'Awake, O, sword against My Shepherd, against the Man that is My Fellow, saith the Lord of Hosts. Smite the Shepherd.' What were the schemes of men against His character and honour compared to the awful onslaught of vindictive justice which vented itself upon His holy humanity?

'That wrath would have kindled a hell
Of never-abating despair,
In millions of creatures, which fell
On Jesus, and spent itself there.'

Those were His sufferings; He suffered in the garden, He suffered on the cross.

Now we might, I know, go more fully into this subject, but I have just mentioned it to you to show that by these things He learned obedience. They were necessary, that is to say they were all necessary for Him in order that He might be perfected, made perfect as a Priest, a great High Priest. 'He learned obedience by the things which He suffered.' Why did He suffer them, poor sinner? Why did He suffer them? Answer that question in your own conscience. If you feel there the sting of sin and the bitterness of guilt, why did He suffer them? He suffered them vicariously, He suffered them for your sakes, if indeed you are among that number destined to inherit eternal glory as trophies of redeeming grace. He suffered, the Just for the unjust, endured your hell, that you might freely receive heaven and enter into it. He learned obedience, and that obedience had to be in every particular. If there had been one flaw in any part of His life, in the slightest degree, the whole of His suffering would have been rendered invalid. The obedience must be a perfect obedience, and it was a perfect obedience, but He had to learn it bitterly. He suffered even the treachery of His friends; Judas, professing friendship and discipleship, betrayed Him into the hands of His enemies; Peter, professing, and having too, such love to his Lord, at that critical moment swore to the women 'I know not the Man'. But these sufferings were necessary that in all the things which His people suffer they suffer as members of His mystical body, the scorn of men, some poverty sometimes, the treachery of professed friends, and the malice of the enemies of truth; the hatred of the world too, they suffer in some sense, in conformity to the blessed Redeemer. But in all your sufferings, in all my sufferings, we may view Him, may we not, a sympathizing High Priest. Your path is painful, your trials are heavy, your conflicts are sharp; but His way was darker, much darker than ours, His way was rougher, much rougher than mine.

'Did Christ, my Lord, suffer, and shall I repine?'

We do repine, at least we have done so; but may the Lord graciously help you, my beloved brethren, to view this Priest. He learned obedience; He had something to go through for it, that is, He experienced by passing through all that was necessary in order to perfect the will of God concerning Him in it, and that He might be the Captain of our salvation by the things which He suffered.

May the Lord give us some mutual, sweet, sacred opening up of this blessed truth in our souls; it will support us in our trials; it will comfort us in our sorrows; it will produce that relief in our spirits which nothing but some discovery of the Lord Jesus in His humiliation can; it will make us willing to walk the path He has designed for us.

THE PERFECTING OF THE THINGS WHICH CONCERN US

1 June 1938

'The Lord will perfect that which concerneth me: Thy mercy, O Lord, endureth for ever: forsake not the work of Thine own hands.' (Psalm 138: 8)

WHATEVER our state or condition before God here this evening may be, this must be said of all of us without exception—we are passing mortal creatures, here upon this earth for a short time, soon to enter eternity, and our eternal destiny is in the hands of God, known to Him alone. 'The Lord knoweth them that are His.' Every heart is fully open to His view; every exercise is known to Him clearly and fully; every concern, every trial that may be pressing upon us, every weight, everything temporal and spiritual is fully known unto God and open to His view. If we are true pilgrims we are journeying. This world is not our rest; it is no abiding place. 'This is not your rest; it is polluted.' 'Here we have no continuing city', but what a mercy if it can be said, 'We seek one to come', if we are journeying toward a heavenly country, that 'city which hath foundations, whose builder and maker is God'; if we have Canaan's heavenly land in view and faith whereby we may hope and believe that we shall one day be there to see the King in His beauty, and realise that for which now we humbly hope; to see the fullest anticipations of faith realized; to enter into the inheritance reserved for every overcomer, and to receive the victory from Christ and to give thanks for ever 'unto Him Who loved us and washed us from our sins in His own blood'.

'The Lord will perfect that which concerneth me.' All our trials, afflictions, sorrows, tribulations, life and death, are in the hands of Christ. 'All my times are in Thy hand.' And though the way to life and peace and happiness and heaven is attended with much difficulty, obstruction, opposition, sorrow, pain and suffering, yet God will surely honour His own promise and He hath said, 'I will never leave thee nor forsake thee'. In this remarkable Psalm the Psalmist bestirs himself to a grateful and gracious remembrance of former mercies, and acknowledges the goodness of God to him therein, in former trials and deliverances. 'In the day when I cried Thou answeredst me.' What a mercy if we can look back to an answer to prayer in our lives; to have an answer locked up there; to look back upon a spot or place of which we can say, 'He blessed me there, He answered my prayer at such a time, delivered me and wrought for me'. This Psalm, too, is an expression of confidence that God would be with him still; that He who had brought him hitherto, would help him all his journey through; that He would not leave him to fall at last; that the work He had begun and was carrying on would be performed, completed, perfected. 'The Lord will perfect that which concerneth me.' What was it, mainly speaking, that concerned David? Was it not that God would be with him, sanctify his trials to him, sustain him in them, bring him through them, bring him through all and glorify Himself in his eternal salvation? Was not that the main thing? Do we not hear him saying earlier, 'Say unto my soul, I AM Thy salvation'? and later, 'The Lord is my salvation'? 'The Lord will perfect that which concerneth me.'

Now we might consider, I believe profitably, this word as it may apply to our individual cases. There is an individuality in this word, 'The Lord will perfect that which concerneth *me*', *my* case. My case, your case, your matters, the Lord is above them, has control over them, has ordered them, and will perfect them. That is, He will complete His own work, ripen and fulfil His own appointments and engagements. He will leave nothing undone.

> 'The work which His goodness began,
> The arm of His strength will complete.'

'That which concerneth *me*.' There are some things which the Lord's people have in common; all, more or less, are concerned in the same things. There is what I might term a united concern and there is also an individual concern. Generally speaking, as it has respect to spiritual things, we may say that we are all concerned in the same things, if our souls have been made alive before God. What is the concern of a living soul? May it not be summed up in one word—salvation? Is not that the one concern? Isn't it the chief point, the one point, to have a personal interest in those everlasting blessings which are promised to the Church of God, to be blessed with all spiritual blessings in heavenly places in Christ? Surely it is. It rises above everything else really. As the things of eternity outweigh the things of time, so the things of the soul are paramount in importance. When we say that the salvation of the soul is the main thing which concerns us unitedly, as hoping we fear God, may we not say that there are things which flow out from that? There are many things, because the spiritual state or exercise of a child of God may vary greatly; he is not always on the mount of rejoicing; far from it. Neither is he always in the depths of woe and darkness. No, he rises and he falls in this respect, has to go in and out to find pasture. Therefore if we consider, in passing, the variety of states or experiences of the Lord's people, we may say they have their different concerns, though they all lead up to the same thing. One may say, 'My chief concern is to know I am right with God'. Often such a one may be saying,

> ''Tis a point I long to know,
> (Oft it causes anxious thought),
> Do I love the Lord or no?
> Am I His or am I not?'

Is there this language in thine heart, art thou seeking this? constantly crying before the Lord with such a case and enquiry? O, it is a mercy if it be so, for surely the Lord will perfect that which concerneth you; that is to say, if this is your concern, your burden, trial, exercise, need, to have your standing made clear, to receive your title to heaven, to feel the sweetness of sonship, to realise the spirit of adoption, then press your case, for none ever waited in vain for this great thing. The Lord will perfect that which concerneth you. Is there not encouragement here? Although some, it may be, are long walking in darkness, and others may be fainting because the Lord is long silent, and others may be greatly discouraged because they seem to make no progress—in fact, they may appear, as it were, to be going backward—still this is true, the Lord will perfect that which concerneth you. If He has begun that work in thy soul, He hasn't begun it to leave it, to change His mind, and take another course. 'He which hath begun a good work in you will perform it until the day of Jesus Christ.'

Another may say, 'The thing which concerns me is the forgiveness of my sins. My sins lie as a burden upon my conscience. I feel guilt there pressing me down, and I have condemnation within, the sentence of death. I feel God is against me, the Lord is against me.' You may feel to some point the terrors of a broken law and may fear the terrible issue of sin in everlasting punishment; and what is your desire or your concern? Is it not to receive forgiveness, to have that burden removed, taken away, to have peace in your conscience, to have peace with God, to have all your sins washed away in the Redeemer's blood? Well, the Lord will perfect that; that is to say, He will, in His own time, hear your prayer, thus bring peace and forgiveness home to the heart, and enable you to rejoice in His salvation.

Another may say 'I am not where I once was. I am not in the comfort, sweetness and joy of the gospel I was in formerly. I have to say,

> 'O where is now that glowing love
> That marked our union with the Lord?'

'O, that it were with me as in days past!' Well, we might do well, perhaps, to enquire why this change is. Has there been a departing from the Lord in heart affection? Have other things taken His place? consequently has there been a leaving of your first love? Is it a backsliding condition? Do you have to say sometimes, 'Search me, O God, and know my heart: try me and know my thoughts, and see if there be any wicked way in me, and lead me in the way everlasting?' The Lord will perfect that, if there is a desire and a cry to be restored. If your language is, 'Restore unto me the joy of Thy salvation', will not the Lord perfect that? There is much in common, is there not, in these things, with the living family of God? They are travelling in the same way to heaven. They have one hope, one object, and in these things they walk together as those that are agreed. They are enabled at times to edify one another, to encourage each other in the way, and to believe, as the Psalmist here, that the Lord would perfect that which concerned him. It is a comfort if we can rightly perceive this; if we can lay hold of the faithfulness of God, believe that He will not forsake the work of His own hands.

In temporal things there may perhaps be even a greater variety. No one has exactly, perhaps, the same trial, disappointment, loss, sorrow, affliction as another. Your trial may press upon you heavily and you may have much darkness therein, and you are not able to perceive the purpose of God and the issue of things, what they will be. As enabled, lay hold of this, 'The Lord will perfect that which concerneth me'. He may not bring you out of the trial in just the way you anticipate. 'The Lord hath His way in the whirlwind and in the storm, and the clouds are the dust of His feet'; but He will perfect His own work. He may seem to us sometimes to work crosshandedly, to bring a death upon things, almost to go against His own Word. Even the prophet Jeremiah said, 'Wilt Thou be altogether unto me as a liar and as waters that fail?' But if indeed we are brought at times to doubt and question even the wisdom of God in some dispensations, (for they are beyond our understanding), yet He will perfect that which concerneth us. He is too wise to err, too good to be unkind. Surely no trial can be laid upon one without a divine purpose therein. Is not the hand of God in every providence, to fulfil His own will and to perfect His people thereby? Will He not make all things work for their good and for His glory by them? Are not our times in His hand? O, then receive this kind word, 'The Lord will perfect that which concerneth me'. Is He not able even to make our own failures, mistakes and sins work for our good? A good old Scottish divine, I believe, said this,

> 'Sin for my good must work and win,
> But 'tis not good for me to sin.'

Cannot the Lord bring good out of evil? Has He not a ruling hand in all these things, dark though they appear to us? 'Shall there be evil in a city and the Lord hath not done it?' 'The Lord will perfect that which concerneth me.' Your trial is yours, but it is God's as well; it came from Him. 'Affliction cometh not forth of the dust, neither doth trouble spring out of the ground.' Observe the hand of a divine Providence, and if you do I believe you will observe too the lovingkindness of the Lord.

Another may say, 'The thing which concerns me is unanswered prayer'. We have tried to pray for certain things and these things remain unanswered. But then, how much may there not be in the secret will of God? Has He disposed to make everything plain to us? Would we not rather subject ourselves to His divine will, even in our petitions and say, 'Thy will be done'? Are we warranted to look for answers to all our prayers? Would it be good for us that everything were granted us? And yet at the same time the Lord has said, 'Seek, and ye shall find'. But the Lord deals in infinite wisdom with His people, and in regard to their prayers as pertaining to the things of this life, will deal with them according to the counsel of His own will. There is a sweet harmony, I feel, between the immutable decrees of Jehovah and the appointment of prayer. We read in the 102nd Psalm that the Lord will favour Zion at the set time. 'The time to favour her, yea, the set time, is come', and at that set time, just then, we have that word which follows, 'He will regard the prayer of the destitute, and not despise their prayer'. The prayers of saints and the decrees of Jehovah do not clash, if indeed the Lord has wrought that prayer in the heart of one of His own children.

Another may say, 'The thing that concerns me is the promise unfulfilled'. Has there been an intimation of something? Have you reason to believe that the Lord has spoken? Is there something lying upon your heart causing heavy exercise? Is there something there that Satan at times attempts to play hard upon, to bring you under the cloud of fear and despondency, to distrust a wise and gracious God, to shake your confidence in Him? 'Hath He said, and shall He not do it?' We need, do we not? a right spirit of self-examination in regard to this. If the Lord gives a promise, as He does sometimes to His people, He does not often give the date when the promise shall be fulfilled. Have not some of His children had long to wait for the fulfilment of His promise? Have they not been hard pressed to wait upon God to see the fulfilment of some things? In such a case as this have you not often had to pray, 'Lord, remember the word unto Thy servant, upon which Thou hast caused me to hope'. It seems sometimes as though the Lord had forgotten, as though He had 'forgotten to be gracious,' as though He had 'in anger shut up His tender mercies'. A silent God and a roaring devil hard press a poor tribulated saint down to the ground, and he may feel he will surely fall a prey to infidelity in the issue and prove no better than an atheist; and yet, notwithstanding all this, surely 'the Lord will perfect that which concerneth me'. How good if we can lay hold of this and look, as it were, beyond the misty cloud; and though we may fear as we enter the cloud, may not faith look beyond and hear the voice of Jesus and believe that the cloud will disperse and nought will be seen save Jesus only? Consider this word: 'The Lord will perfect'—that is, He will ripen, He will complete—'that which concerneth me'.

'Thy mercy, O Lord, endureth for ever.' This is a plain statement, but a very far-reaching one. I should doubt if anyone believed it more firmly than David did, for he makes mention of it a good many times, and in the 136th Psalm, at the close of every verse, he says 'His mercy endureth for ever'. This is a comfort, is it not, in this path of fear and tribulation? The mercy of God, everlasting mercy, divine mercy, enduring mercy. What is mercy? Why, it is the free favour of God to sinners; the happy release of law-breakers from the just claims of justice; the free exercise of divine compassion to miserable creatures who deserve the just judgments of God, and that for ever. O, sweet mercy! 'The mercy of God is from everlasting to everlasting upon them that fear Him.' The mercy of God is both general and special. It is general both with respect to the human creation and the lower grade of animal life. 'The Lord is good to all: and His tender mercies are over all His works.' Daily we partake of the mercy of God. By His mercy we breathe without pain; by His mercy we enjoy the daily comforts of this life. By His mercy we are sustained in the use of our faculties. By His mercy all our needs are supplied. This is general, even to the rebellious and profane, to God-dishonouring and God-denying men. But O, the special mercy of God! This is particular to those who believe, reserved for the election of grace, for those appointed to eternal life, to inherit glory. These partake of the mercy of God, and such are sometimes favoured with a little holy meditation thereon, too. The mercy of God is free. O, how free!

'Mercy never can be bought;
Grace is free; and all's the Lamb's.'

No price is asked for this, or we could never receive it. No equivalent can be paid to purchase it; mercy cannot be bought or it would cease to be mercy at once. No claim have we upon God for this. It flows freely; and it flows freely to the most undeserving, who are steeped in iniquity and sin, and who would despise it of themselves, but who are brought painfully and profitably to perceive their need of it, and to pray for it too. O, the freeness of divine mercy!

Mercy is sovereign, too. 'I will have mercy on whom I will have mercy.' O, how solemn this is! It divides the world into two classes. 'Jacob have I loved, but Esau have I hated'; the one receiving mercy freely, equally undeserving with the other, and the other left to his own choice, alas! But O, though the mercy of God is sovereign, it is free to any sensible creature who truly realizes the need of it.

'Mercy is welcome news indeed,
To those that guilty stand;
Wretches that feel what help they need,
Will bless the helping hand.'

Wonderful mercy is the mercy of a triune God. This mercy is pure, holy mercy; mercy flowing to poor creatures corrupted through sin, without any taint of imperfection in it; holy mercy; mercy which harmonizes with the attributes of the divine majesty of heaven. The mercy of God never tarnishes His justice. Both may be perceived at Calvary. There justice and mercy meet, righteousness and truth.

Mercy! It is the mercy of the Trinity. The cause, the first cause, is in God the Father; from Him it flows freely. He is a God Who delighteth in mercy. This is His own declaration of Himself, abounding in mercy and truth. The Redeemer is the channel through which this mercy flows. It flows through His cross and by virtue of His sacrifice, and it is dispensed by the Spirit of God Who applies it to the wounded conscience. This mercy, free mercy, is received, and it endures! That is, it is everlasting, not given for a time. Mercy is eternal mercy in God; it is one of the divine perfections of Jehovah. He was ever merciful; as He was ever just, omniscient, immutable, gracious, so He was ever merciful. It endures. This is so sweet. Acts of mercy may be done by creatures, by men, and may be greatly admired, but they may cease. Now the mercy of God abides, endures, notwithstanding what there may be in the creature to provoke the withdrawal of that mercy. It endures for ever. What a blessing this is, to be sure! There is something very sweet to me in this enduring; as though the Psalmist would say, 'Lord, there is much in me to try Thy patience, to provoke Thee to turn from me, to have no further favourable dealings with me, and yet Thy mercy endures'. God remains the same in His mercy, and this will not make us treat sin cheaply or be disposed to test, as it were, the mercy of God by sinning; but rather it will often make us say

> 'Take away the love of sinning;
> Alpha and Omega be.'

'His mercy endureth for ever.' Yes, we hope in it here, but we shall glory in it there. The hope of a poor sinner saved by grace here is in the mercy, the free mercy of God; but there in the heavenly state, when sin will be a thing of the past, we shall glory everlastingly in the free, abundant mercy of a triune Jehovah, flowing through Emmanuel, God with us, seated at the right hand of the majesty on high.

'Forsake not the work of Thine own hands.' The Psalmist, after speaking with a measure of confidence, seems to conclude with a prayer; 'Forsake not the work of Thine own hands'. I would be disposed to think that the Psalmist believed that the Lord would not forsake the work of His own hands. He had confidence that God would fulfil His Word, and I believe that we may profitably pray for those things which we believe the Lord will accomplish. We know that He will do His will in heaven and in earth, but that is no deterrent to a poor sinner's saying, with regard to his own case and his own trial, 'Lord, Thy will be done; forsake not the work of Thine own hands'. What are the works of God here? Substantially I should say they are the manifold operations of the Spirit in the soul, the work of God there. Truly they embrace all His works in providence, everything pertaining to this world, nations, kingdoms and men, and the standing of the Church and all things; but there is the individual work, the work within your heart and my heart, and for this we pray, 'Lord, forsake it not'. The fruits of the Spirit, such as faith, hope and love, subjection to the will of God, obedience to the precepts of the gospel, and so on, which flow from the principle of love to the Redeemer; and all the works of God, the handiworks of our heavenly Father; for these may we not pray, 'Forsake not the work of Thine own hands'. 'Lord, let Thy Will be done in me; bring me through, perfect the work of grace, sustain me in this world, bring me honourably through, leave me not.' See how this blends with the Lord's own promise to His people. Here is a poor sinner saying, 'Lord, forsake not the work of Thine own hands. Leave me not neither forsake me'; and here is the Lord saying, 'I will not leave thee; I will not fail thee; I will not forsake thee'. So they blend together; the prayer and the promise dovetail together; and all this is the handiwork of God, a gracious work here, to issue in everlasting glory.

Amen.

'OPEN THY MOUTH WIDE'

25 June 1939

'I am the Lord thy God, which brought thee out of the land of Egypt: open thy mouth wide, and I will fill it.' (Ps. 81: 10)

Do you hear that, poor, sensibly guilty, seeking, hungry soul? I say, do you hear that word?—'I AM the Lord thy God, which brought thee out of the land of Egypt.' If so, do you believe that word? Do you believe it has an application to your case? Has God brought you out of that Egypt? or are you still in the house of bondage? If God has brought you out of Egypt and you are still in the wilderness, listen to this word and receive it, believe it and act upon it: 'I AM the Lord thy God . . . open thy mouth wide and I will fill it.' God never deceives people; what He says He will do, He does. 'Open thy mouth wide'; it shall not be in vain. Has God ever been unfaithful to His Word? 'I will fill it.' Is not this a condescending promise of God to poor sinners who have been delivered from their Egyptian bondage? Is it not an invitation of heavenly attraction? 'Open thy mouth wide, and I will fill it.'

This Psalm is one of exhortation, an exhortation to praise God, to acknowledge former deliverances and to wait upon Him in the exercise of faith. It appears to be a Psalm that used to be sung upon certain festival occasions, very probably at the feast of tabernacles, and also at other feasts at a time when the solemn praises and worship of God were publicly observed, and when musical instruments were used, the timbrel, the harp, the psaltery, the trumpet. Reference is made to the appointment or ordination of these festival occasions, the feasts. 'This He ordained in Joseph for a testimony, when he went out through the land of Egypt.' Later in the Psalm we may observe that if, when the voice of God was heard, obedience had been rendered to His injunctions it would have been well with them; God would soon have subdued their enemies and favoured them in every way. But by the Psalm we may notice that the case was otherwise. 'But My people would not hearken to My voice; and Israel would none of Me. So I gave them up unto their own hearts' lust: and they walked in their own counsels. Oh, that My people had hearkened unto Me, and Israel had walked in My ways!' But it would seem now that the Lord God of Israel is speaking; He is speaking to His dear people: 'I brought them forth out of the land of Egypt.' A close connection is here to be observed with the preface to the ten commandments in Exodus 20. 'I AM the Lord thy God, which have brought thee out of the land of Egypt, out of the house of bondage. Thou shalt have no other gods before Me.' I AM the only God to be worshipped. 'Thou shalt worship the Lord thy God and Him only shalt thou serve.' Here God is speaking to them. He reminds Israel of what He wrought for them. 'This He ordained in Joseph for a testimony, when he went out through the land of Egypt: where I heard a language that I understood not.' We are not to understand by this that there was something taking place in Egypt that the Lord could not understand, so to speak, but rather something that He approved not, or, He had regard to the cries and groans of His own people there. Therefore He 'removed his shoulder from the burden: his hands were delivered from the pots'. He seems, so to speak, for a moment to take them back to Egypt: See what I did for you there; I delivered you from the burden, the oppression, the bondage, your hands from the pots (or baskets that they used to bear or carry the bricks). You called unto Me there, in your trouble you called upon Me. The Lord heard their groans, their cries there; He went down, raised up and commanded Moses to go unto them and bring them forth. 'Thou calledst in trouble, and I delivered thee; I answered thee in the secret place of thunder.' After they came out of Egypt they soon came into difficulties, where destruction threatened them. 'I answered thee in the secret place of thunder.' Evidently that word had respect to the remarkable deliverance God wrought for them at the Red Sea, where we read that He troubled the hosts of the Egyptians; and we may gather that, on that occasion there were mighty thunderings from heaven. 'I answered thee there. I proved thee at the waters of Meribah'—the waters of strife. When thou didst murmur against Me, I proved thee; I withheld the water for a time from thee, and thou didst murmur and saidst, 'Is the Lord among us or not?' But the Lord gave them water from the rock. Now He says in view of these things, 'Hear, O My people, and I will testify unto thee: O Israel, if thou wilt hearken unto Me; There shall no strange god be in thee; neither shalt thou worship any strange god. I AM the Lord thy God.' We may notice how this conforms to the command and the law for worship: 'I AM the Lord thy God; . . . thou shalt have no other gods before Me'; worship Me. Who is this? This is Jehovah, Being of Beings, the Majesty of heaven, the eternal, glorious God—'thy God.' This was true in a national sense of His people with whom He made covenant. Is it true of us in a spiritual sense? Ah! some might have to say, I could not claim that relationship. Yet the Lord says concerning all who are brought out of Egypt, 'I AM the Lord thy God'; I delivered thee, I heard thy groanings, I answered thee in the secret place of thunder, proved thee at Meribah; 'I AM the Lord thy God, which brought thee out of the land of Egypt.' He reminds them of His power, of what He had done for them, and later of their base ingratitude notwithstanding, and the consequences that attended their departures from Him. While God will ever be mindful of His covenant, yet we read, 'If his children forsake My law, and walk not in My judgments; If they break My statutes, and keep not My commandments, then will I visit their transgression with the rod, and their iniquity with stripes. Nevertheless My lovingkindness will I not utterly take from him, nor suffer My faithfulness to fail. My covenant will I not break, nor alter the thing that is gone out of My lips.'

The next point here is the land of Egypt, the place from which we are brought out. What does that mean? or to what may the land of Egypt, in a spiritual sense, refer? Does it not seem to mean the world?—that place which the people of God are brought out from by regenerating grace. The land of Egypt seems typical of three things. It is typical of the bondage of the world which holds the natural man; he is in a state of bondage to it. He is a man of the world, and the world has a power over him from which he cannot deliver himself, nor has he any wish to do so. Man in an unregenerate state is as a slave to this world; he is in the world that lieth in wickedness—the land of Egypt. I think that the land of Egypt is typical of the state the people of God are in before they are called by grace. God's people are His people ever, in covenant with Him from eternity, but they are the subjects of the fall, and the history of Israel as journeying through the wilderness seems to set forth in many respects the pilgrimage journey of the children of God. But we are in Egypt by nature; we are in the world and are slaves to it. Not only so; the land of Egypt seems to represent the darkness of sin. Those Egyptians were idolaters, they were in the darkness of idolatry. They had no knowledge of the true God, and sin has a power over men by nature. The Apostle Paul referring, in the epistle to the Romans, chapter 6, to the people of God in their delivered state, says, 'Sin shall not have dominion over you: for ye are not under the law, but under grace.' But sin has dominion over man by nature. He is in the land of Egypt, and there he will remain until effectual, invincible grace delivers him and brings him out from the darkness of sin. But it seems also somewhat descriptive of the wickedness of the human heart. Those Egyptians were a wicked, idolatrous people, and although Israel, when in that state of bondage, were the people of God, yet at the same time the place and the condition of things there is descriptive of those prevailing iniquities that abound in the heart of man. The heart is said to be, 'Deceitful above all things and desperately wicked.' The land of Egypt typifies man's natural state, then, the world from which he is delivered by effectual grace, by God, 'the God of all grace'. 'I AM the Lord thy God, which brought thee out of the land of Egypt.'

Is this true of us? Has that deliverance been effected in our experience? Some here may be in Egypt, still under the dominion of sin, following the dictates of their own heart and mind, having no inward conflict with regard to their own state and case before God. We may perhaps in one sense speak of Egypt in relation to a child of God, as descriptive of the bondage he may be brought into under the law which oppresses him, but that is not a proper view. The taskmasters who oppressed the children of Israel in the land of Egypt were wicked men, and though some speak of those taskmasters who exacted of the children of Israel more than they could do, as descriptive of the law, I think it can hardly so be in a proper sense; but rather may we not notice that sin is a hard master and exacts more of us than we can give? We can never give satisfaction, though we may serve sin. But still there is a point there: God's people know something of legal bondage, bondage under the law which holds them and exacts from them more than they can give. They cannot obey its terms, and grace delivers them. They are delivered from the law by the body of Christ that they should bring forth fruit unto God.

But this is the point here: I brought thee out of Egypt, therefore, seeing I have done this, 'Open thy mouth wide'. 'Hear, O My people, and I will testify unto thee'; listen to My words, 'Open thy mouth wide, and I will fill it'. This is, of course, a figurative expression, 'Open thy mouth wide'. It does not infer that a person is to make a great noise; it has respect to no outward ostentation; there is no need to shout in order to make the God of heaven hear our voice. It does not refer to a loud cry in a literal sense, but is a figurative expression which suggests the approach to God of a sinner saved by grace, in the exercise of true faith, to ask for great things. One hymnwriter expresses it:

> 'Thou art coming to a King;
> Large petitions with thee bring;
> For His grace and power are such,
> None can ever ask too much.'

This is as a direction to open our mouths wide; it therefore has relation to the exercise of prayer, the approach of a sinner to God. But several things may be implied. It implies worship, certainly: 'Open thy mouth wide' in worship; that is, let God be the only Object of your worship. 'I AM the Lord thy God which brought thee out of the land of Egypt, out of the house of bondage. Thou shalt have no other gods before Me.' 'There shall no strange god be in thee; neither shalt thou worship any strange god.' 'Open thy mouth wide'; as though the Lord should say, I have in Myself all you need, so that there is no occasion or necessity to seek supplies from any other quarter. Serve Me, worship Me; I AM thy Deliverer. I proved thee at Meribah, answered thee in the secret place of thunder; worship Me. Now to open our mouths wide in this sense is to approach the Majesty of heaven through and by Christ, to ask in humble worship and prayer for great things. To open the mouth wide is not only to open it in worship (though it must be in worship every time; every approach of a sinner to God must be in worship; He is to be adored, honoured, revered in the heart; He is to be the one, only Object); but it is to approach Him in the boldness of faith. 'Let us . . . come boldly unto the Throne of Grace, that we may obtain mercy, and find grace to help in time of need.' This is a great point. The Lord Jesus said to His disciples, 'Whatsoever ye shall ask in prayer, believing, ye shall receive'. It is the boldness that a quickened sinner is at times favoured to exercise at the Throne of God's Grace. This is opening the mouth wide. It implies a godly importunity; that the Spirit of God, in helping one's infirmity may give one, Jacob-like, to say, 'I will not let thee go, except Thou bless me'. This is opening the mouth wide. You see, it infers an importunity; not just simply coming with your case and going away satisfied almost with the form of coming, but a spiritual importunity at the Mercy Seat is here intended. 'Open thy mouth wide.' It is sweet when faith in a poor sinner enables him thus to wait upon God. O, it is! It will be usually in meekness, reverence, humility, repentance and love. You hear the voice of God, it may be, as your Father, saying, 'I AM the Lord thy God', all-sufficient; even as He said to Abram, 'I AM the Almighty God; walk before Me, and be thou perfect'. Come to Me, come to Me! Come boldly. 'Open thy mouth wide'; do not be afraid to ask. Sometimes there is a reserve in a child of God. There is a certain thing, perhaps, you want the Lord to do for you, but it seems too great. It may appear, with regard to some particular matter, almost like presumption to ask God to do the thing for you. 'Open thy mouth wide.' 'Is anything too hard for the Lord?' Does not the Lord say in Jeremiah, 'Is there anything too hard for Me?' Therefore, believing this, a poor, weak sinner may, for Christ's sake, approach omnipotence and open his mouth wide. Nothing is too great, nothing is too small here. Open thy mouth wide to infinity, immensity; think of the treasury of divine grace there, the exhaustless store; think of the words, the promise, 'My God shall supply all your need according to His riches in glory by Christ Jesus'. Therefore 'Open thy mouth wide'. Is it presumptuous? Not if the opening of the mouth is in faith. No, it is the boldness of faith.

'Lord, I cannot let Thee go
Till a blessing Thou bestow.'

Opening the mouth wide is also expressive of peculiar liberty in a sinner, of a gracious, holy familiarity that is sometimes given when you feel as though the Lord brings you into His immediate presence in Christ, and O, the sweetness of praying! the sacredness of praying! The liberty you have given you in pleading with the Lord for your own case, your soul, matters in providence or family maybe, or business, anything, in the home life or whatever it may be! Now and again the Lord's people are favoured with a peculiar liberty in prayer, and when that liberty, that access, is given, then they can ask for great things. Ask Him. You can believe that He is able to do exceeding abundantly above all you can ask or think, therefore, 'Open thy mouth wide'. You have not to go to a God with limitations. No, there is no limitation to His power, neither is there any limitation to His willingness. All things, of course, must be consistent with His righteous character and the decree of His own will; but, whatever you need, poor sinner, does not the Lord say, 'I will yet for this be enquired of by the house of Israel, to do it for them'. Take that to the Lord; say, Lord, you said this. He will receive that. Put Him in remembrance. He says, 'Let us plead together: declare thou, that thou mayest be justified'. If the Lord allows you to argue with Him—understand the word rightly; Job said he would fill his mouth with arguments;—if the Lord allows you to argue with Him, 'Put Him in remembrance'. A reserve may arise there from unbelief. 'Open thy mouth wide'; will the Lord resent that? No, God will fill it, He says.

To open the mouth wide is also representative of putting our trust and delight in the Lord. 'Trust in the Lord, and do good; so shalt thou dwell in the land, and verily thou shalt be fed. Delight thyself also in the Lord; and He shall give thee the desires of thine heart.' Therefore, 'open thy mouth wide'. To open thy mouth wide is to believe the Lord can do that thing for you; to give Him the honour that belongs to Him as able to do exceeding abundantly. Also joined with this is the grace of trust, trusting in Him. Let the Lord manage matters for you. When you can put your case into the hand of God, then you will 'handle matters wisely'. 'Open thy mouth wide.' I believe that Hannah, in her distress, was favoured to do that when she went into the tabernacle in her great sorrow of heart, and was misjudged by Eli who concluded that she had taken too much wine, and reproved her therefor; but Hannah said, 'I am a woman of a sorrowful spirit: I have drunk neither wine nor strong drink, but have poured out my soul before the Lord'. Have you ever been in a case like that? It may have been something in your circumstances. It was something Hannah wanted, and she poured out her soul for it, and got it too. She opened her mouth wide, and God will honour that in a sinner. Never put a limitation to the Lord. The case of the centurion is very much to the point here: his servant was lying sick, and he went to Christ and told Him, and the Lord said, 'I will come and heal him'. But the centurion said, 'Lord, I am not worthy that Thou shouldest come under my roof: but speak the Word only and my servant shall be healed'. He opened his mouth wide there. Was he reproved for that? No, he was commended. Why, said the Lord, 'I have not found so great faith, no, not in Israel'. He opened his mouth. The case of the leper, too, bears upon this. That man, that poor leper—we read in one place he was 'full of leprosy'. Very descriptive that; he was full of it. Have you ever felt like that? he had not one or two symptoms of the leprosy coming, but he was, 'full of leprosy'. A certain leper came to Him and said, 'Lord, if Thou wilt, Thou canst make me clean'. He did not say, Lord, I wonder if you have power to do it; but he said, 'Lord, if Thou wilt, Thou canst make me clean'. I am full of leprosy. The thing was done suddenly; the Lord said, 'I will; be thou clean'. He opened his mouth wide too; and if you and I, feeling as we may at times, our leprosy, are enabled thus to go to Christ, saying, 'Lord, if Thou wilt, Thou canst make me clean', will that prayer be denied? No, it cannot be. If that petition is thus put in faith in the sufficiency of Christ to wash a poor, black piece of hell, He can do it. 'I will; be thou clean'. He opened his mouth.

When Herod put James to death by the edge of the sword, and apprehended Peter and put him in prison, there did not appear to be very much hope. He was put into the prison with four quaternions of soldiers to keep a close guard upon him, to be brought forth in the morning. But what do we read? 'Prayer was made without ceasing of the Church unto God for him.' And what happened? The prison doors of the first and second wards opened, and Peter was miraculously delivered and came to the house where the people were praying. They had opened their mouths wide; but when prayer was answered they could not believe it; they could not believe that Peter was there; they told the damsel who went to the door that she must be mad. They opened their mouths wide. Have you ever been favoured to wrestle with God and open your mouth? Yet when the Lord has answered your prayer you have been confounded; you could not believe it; it was more than you could receive.

'I will fill it.' What a word this is! 'I will fill it.' He is able to fill it. He will fill it with His own goodness. 'He satisfieth the longing soul, and filleth the hungry soul with goodness', Psalm 107 has it. That mouth that is opened in prayer and faith shall be satisfied with good things. What good things? The good things of the gospel. It is something more than all you want on your table for lunch; the good things of the gospel. 'I will fill it.' O what a field is here! But one may say, What about my guilt, wretchedness, ruin, and hardness, and a cluster of other things, almost enough to sink one to despair? 'Open thy mouth wide.' The gospel utterly forbids despair. 'Open thy mouth wide, and I will fill it.'

Amen.

REDEEMING THE TIME

2 July 1939

'Redeeming the time, because the days are evil.' (Eph. 5: 16)

It is because I feel my personal need of this timely admonition that I have read it before you this morning, and I doubt not those of you who are in some measure taught by the Spirit and grace of God will feel to be of the same mind. Time is flying swiftly and rapidly away. We are filling up the brief, short span of this our mortal life. Life is short, necessarily so, as a consequence of sin, and it may well be said that we know not what a day may bring forth. This is particularly true in these grievous, evil days in which we are living, when men's hearts are failing them for fear. We are more or less in a tension of grave apprehension of what may come upon us in the near future, and we do well to be prayerfully concerned in relation to the signs of the times and the things that are now transpiring in the earth. Doubtless we are in the last times and are probably under the seventh and last vial, when the closing predictions of Holy Scripture pertaining to events and developments in this world will come to pass. We do not wish to be indifferent to the things that are taking place; but the saints of God have this comfort—their times are in the hand of God. All our times are in His hand, and when faith is given to appreciate this rightly it will afford a measure of consolation and rest to the spirit. Even in troublous times, midst gathering clouds and threatening storms, a child of God blessed with living faith may take refuge in the faithful word and promise God has given to His people. It is well for us, then, as enabled, to apprehend what God has said and to enter into our chambers: 'Come, My people, enter thou into thy chambers, and shut thy doors about thee: hide thyself, as it were, for a little moment, until the indignation be overpast.' We are not immune from natural fear, yet we may be favoured to hear the Lord speaking to us, saying, 'Fear not!' as He did to His beloved servant Daniel: 'Fear not: . . . be strong, yea, be strong'; and when the Lord said that, Daniel said, 'I was strengthened'. When the Lord speaks the divine word to a sinner, there is power in that word. Therefore, though there is indeed much to give rise to natural fear, to make the hearts of men and the hearts of God's people too, tremble, yet we are not without a Refuge—blessed be God! He declares Himself to be the Refuge of His people: 'The eternal God is thy Refuge, and underneath are the everlasting arms.'

The word I have felt led to read is preceptive and has relation to time and the redemption of time: 'Redeeming the time'; and the reason, 'Because the days are evil'. The word or term 'time' seems to suggest a limitation, a certain limited duration or period. If we take away all limitations and boundaries we launch forth as it were, into a boundless expanse. There are, in a sense, two things, time and eternity, here. Time must necessarily have certain limitations, else the word has no application. It means a limited period; take away those limitations and we have eternity. Eternity, though it embraces time, stretches immeasurably and incomprehensibly beyond it. Eternity is something we cannot understand, and it is not intended that we should. No beginning, no ending, has eternity. Time necessarily involves a commencement and a conclusion, a beginning and an ending. In just observing one or two points here before passing on, we may say that time, as so termed, has respect to the duration of the world. God has fixed that time to a moment, undoubtedly. It is a time known only to Him; it is not given to us to know the times and seasons, the brief days, years or centuries before 'the heavens shall be rolled together as a scroll', and 'the elements shall melt with fervent heat'; before there will be that one great conflagration, and the earth shall be burnt up, and the angel shall appear from heaven with the open book in his hand, with a voice as a lion roaring and declaring the Word of God, saying that time shall be no longer. But there is a duration, a time fixed for the earth to stand, from the creation to the end, to 'the restitution of all things', and the word, as in Scripture, refers to that period.

Time has also respect to our own particular lives, the number of our days which again are in the secret will of God—wisely so.

'So teach us to number our days, that we may apply our hearts unto wisdom.' The Apostle in another place says, 'This I say, brethren, the time is short'. Our life is said to be but a vapour, a span, a flash. Soon the place that knows us now will know us no more for ever. We must soon depart into an unseen world. We cannot lift the veil now, but Holy Scripture declares that we must appear before the judgment seat of Christ and must be adjudged either to eternal life or death for ever and ever, Amen. When we consider this, we do well to make close and solemn inspection of our own case before God, as to how and where we stand. It has been said that he who has a soul to save has not a moment to lose. He who has Christ and heaven to win cannot afford one idle moment. Life is necessarily uncertain; we know not how soon the message may come and our eternal destiny, perhaps now not clearly defined to us, be surely manifest. Well is it then to pray from our hearts,

> 'Prepare me, gracious God,
> To stand before Thy face;
> Thy Spirit must the work perform,
> For it is all of grace.'

The Scriptures speak of the Lord's time and our time. When the brethren of the Lord Jesus wanted Him to go into Judea, apparently for some ulterior motive, He reproved them and said, 'My time is not yet come: but your time is alway ready'. We are often ready to fix our own time in which to do this or that thing, but the Lord says, 'My time is not yet'. It is seldom possible that our time and the Lord's time in certain things are the same. While we might be anxious to move in certain things, the Lord would say, 'Wait upon Me; your time is now, My time is not yet; wait upon Me'. There is, too, 'an appointed time to man upon earth'. Job said that all the days of his appointed time would he wait till his change came; by which we gather that he was willing to submit those matters into the hand of God subjectively and passively, not knowing how many days were allotted to him. But there is a time appointed of the Lord to fulfil His purposes. We believe that all things are in the hand of God; we believe He has an appointed time fixed to fulfil His secret, His eternal decrees. This may be in relation to all events in divine providence pertaining to us individually and collectively. 'The vision is yet for an appointed time, but at the end it shall speak, and not lie; though it tarry, wait for it; because it will surely come, it will not tarry'. The will of God, now secret, in due course becomes the revealed will, when His purposes are made known, when He performs the things appointed for us.

The particular point for consideration here is the redemption of time: 'Redeeming the time'. We know that we are in time, that it is swiftly passing away, that we shall very, very soon merge into an endless eternity in comparison with which time, even the duration of the whole world, is like a fleeting spark; but when we consider this and the word here before us, what are we to do? How can we redeem the time in these evil days? In one sense we cannot redeem past time; we cannot recall one day of our lives and live that day over again. A day spent is a day gone, a day gone into eternity, so to speak. The way or manner in which that day was spent, the state of our hearts, lives, motives, actions, all drop back into the past; we can never live yesterday or the past week over again. Every day is as a new day, to live as a new life. We cannot recall a moment, and it is truly impossible to go back to youth and infancy and live a life over again. In that respect therefore we cannot redeem the time. But in the sense in which the word is here intended, I believe we may to some point redeem the time, even in relation to former days. To redeem is to buy up the opportunity; to improve, to make the best possible use of our time. But how can we do this in relation to time that is past? I suggest three ways. First, we may, to some point, redeem time past by a prayerful examination of the way in which our former lives have been spent, in confession, and in humbling ourselves before God. In the scriptures we have many instances of redeeming the time; and if we take two striking ones from Nehemiah 9 and Daniel 9, part of which we read, we may see the best possible way in which we may redeem the time as pertaining to the past. The only right way in this particular is to humble ourselves before God in a deep confession of our sins, which may bring a measure of grief and sorrow and contrition of heart in the remembrance of them. Nehemiah and other good men called the people together, proclaimed a fast, and made a public confession of sin for their former iniquities; and

Nehemiah went through their history, rehearsing the goodness of God, and their wickedness, calling them to confession and repentance; so 'redeeming the time'. Good Daniel, too, a 'man greatly beloved', was led very blessedly into this on behalf of his people in their captivity; he was led to confess and mourn before God the desolation of the Sanctuary, the sins of the princes, nobles and rulers, and to wait humbly upon God for His mercy; and that seemed to be the turning point of their captivity. We see Daniel's confession and prayer for the Lord's return and deliverance, and the answer to it in the people's deliverance by God's providence; and after returning to their own land and in some measure restoring the waste places and building the wall and the temple in troublous times, we see them acknowledging the hand of God and worshipping Him, yet still making confession of their sins. So one good way of redeeming the time in relation to past days of our life is in confession of sin. Confession, confession, confession! Mercy, mercy, mercy! 'Redeeming the time.'

Then again, we may redeem the time by seeking unto God that we may learn some profitable lessons through our former mistakes and what we may have suffered consequently; that is another profitable way of redeeming the time. Some of us may look back with sorrow upon a misspent life; the spirit perhaps in which we have been in our trials, the impatience we have manifested and the rebellion that has risen up in our hearts against God when the hand of affliction has been upon us; the hard thoughts we have had of God, and the disposition of our poor, depraved nature to do this or that thing. Some of us may have taken steps, perhaps, in something, in our own strength, or by the determination of our own will brought ourselves into difficulties, in former days. I doubt if anyone can look back upon his life as now spent and say, I have nothing to regret in regard to anything I have said, any step I have taken, or my deportment and walk before God and His people; nothing to regret! Shall we not have to say, O Lord, how I have fallen! How I have sinned! How foolish I have been here and there! Well, if by this reflection profitable lessons have been learned of the depravity of our nature and heart, then we may redeem the time and seek that, by God's grace and help, we may live nearer to

Him than we have done. We may learn lessons by past experience, may we not?

Then again, another way of redeeming the time with regard to former days is in reviewing the goodness of God to us and the way He has led us. 'Thou shalt remember all the way the Lord thy God led thee these forty years in the wilderness.' Look back upon it, friends, look back upon it! What will it do for you? It may do two things; it may fill your heart with the goodness of God to unworthy you, and humble your heart under a sense of your own backslidings and failures. But O, notwithstanding that, some of you, when you look back, have to say, The Lord has been good to me. Goodness and mercy have followed me all the days of my life. When I have departed from Him He has laid His hand upon me, and though I have indeed been chastened, yet in love He has brought me back again to His feet. O, how good He has been! That is redeeming the time! If you feel your heart softened a little by the goodness of God to you in former days, then pay your vows, give thanks unto His Name at the remembrance of His holiness, for it is of His mercies we are not consumed. I should be disposed to say that every child of God could look back upon his life and say, Lord, how unworthy am I of such manifested goodness! Not only have some of you seen the hand of God in His providential dealings with you, but O how good He has been to your soul! He has not left you to fill up the measure of your iniquity in hardness of heart and enmity, to die and be lost for ever. No! Then can you not say, I will 'abundantly utter the memory of Thy great goodness'? His goodness is great. Ah! what can be more humbling than this? When we are favoured so to look back we abase ourselves. O yes! and admire the patience and longsuffering mercy of God unto us, notwithstanding all our provocations. 'Redeeming the time.' Thus, in those three particular ways, to some point at least, the Lord's people, as exercised towards Him, may redeem the time.

How can we redeem the time in relation to present and future days? I believe that we may do it by seeking prayerfully unto God, committing our cause unto Him, and praying that we may grow in grace and in a deeper knowledge of Himself. A good way of redeeming the time! Do you have often to mourn your lack of light, of knowledge, of revelation, of grace? Seek unto Him; the

Apostle desires that he might 'know Him and the power of His resurrection'; and when, in the exercise of faith given, we can wait upon God for a clearer, deeper knowledge of His mind and will, that we may understand what the will of the Lord is and thus be not unwise, we are redeeming the time; that is, we are making the best possible use of it. Remember what I said at the beginning: an old divine said, If we have a soul to save we have not a moment to lose; and one way of redeeming the time now is to seek unto God, confess former departures and failures, and apply diligently unto Him for growth in grace, a deeper knowledge of His mind and will in our experience. How profitable this must be, must it not? and if we bring it down to this one point we can say this sums it up, 'Jesus reveal Thyself to me'. O to know more of a precious Christ, to have Him formed in our hearts the hope of glory, to have a blessed assurance that we are 'heirs of God, and joint-heirs with Christ'. 'Redeeming the time!'

Not only so, but we may redeem the time by a close, diligent, prayerful searching and reading of the Scripture, and in praying for a deeper understanding of the meaning of the Holy Ghost there; a good way of redeeming the time! Hart has said with regard to reading the Scripture, 'Join prayer with each inspection'. Prayerful reading of the Word of God when opportunity offers is a good way of redeeming the time. It is, in short, making the best use of the short, fleeting spark of time allotted to us here in this world. Not only so, but a gracious attendance upon the Word and ordinances of truth and the means of grace is a good way of redeeming the time; not simply to put in so many attendances and then to gather to yourself a kind of satisfaction that you have not missed any service where you could possibly avoid doing so, but in a prayerful, a gracious attendance upon the means of grace, in seeking the face of God, in coming hungry, desiring food for your soul, in seeking confirmation in the matters that pertain to your soul's standing before God, in some spiritual edification or reproof, as it may be. With the Psalmist there was a holy delight in this. 'One thing have I desired of the Lord, that will I seek after; that I may dwell in the house of the Lord all the days of my life, to behold the beauty of the Lord, and to enquire in His temple.' It is good for us when, being hungry for God, we look forward in sweet anticipation to assembling with the saints of God and meeting with them now, desiring, hoping that God may speak to our souls in a way of heavenly instruction. O what a mercy to be lively in the things of God. 'Redeeming the time.'

Why? Why all this? 'Because the days are evil.' What is the reason or cause why the days are evil? The only answer we can give is this,

> 'O thou hideous monster sin,
> What a curse hast thou brought in!
> All creation groans through thee,
> Pregnant cause of misery.'

There is the answer to that query, why are the days evil? In one respect we might say that the days have been evil ever since sin entered into the world, from the first transgression onward. They were good days when Adam, in sinless innocence, walked in communion and fellowship with God; but by the subtlety of the wicked serpent our first parents fell, and they and we fell on evil days, and evil they have been too. We see the increasing tide and flood of iniquity covering the earth, and the visitation of divine judgement in a mighty deluge sweeping away that wicked generation. Evil days! So we might go right through, but I must close by observing that the present days are evil days. For that reason in particular I offer this timely injunction, 'Redeeming the time'. The days are evil, they are exceedingly portentous, and those things predicted by Paul to Timothy concerning the last days are exceedingly prevalent today. 'Men shall be lovers of pleasures more than lovers of God.' Evil days are seen in the world's mad rush for pleasure, the woeful desecration of the Lord's day, the deserting of the public means of grace, dishonouring God; modernistic teaching in schools, poisoning the minds of the young with pernicious errors, so that the future generation is, as it were, growing up under the cloud of evil, atheism, infidelity and all wickedness. Mercifully there are exceptions; but generally speaking we see the rising tide of evil, sin, wickedness, and the approaching judgements of God. The lack of union, the strife, contention and other things, even among professing bodies in religion, are all signs of evil days. Let us therefore, by God's grace, redeem the time; that is, apply ourselves secretly and publicly to seek God, implore His divine mercy, His needed help, His divine direction, His forgiving grace, His sustaining power to keep us, to help us to live, to direct us; redeem the time that we may live to His glory and, when His appointed time comes, be taken home, where there shall be no sin.

Amen.

THE REDEEMED OF THE LORD

22 November 1942

'Let the redeemed of the Lord say so, whom He hath redeemed from the hand of the enemy.' (Ps. 107: 2)

I had not anticipated taking this subject this afternoon; in fact, since the close of this morning's service I have in my inner feelings been, as we speak, at the ends of the earth. I felt much disappointment on account, in my feelings, of a failure in speaking this morning and have been driven here and there, wondering and questioning what I should do for this afternoon. But it may be, and the Lord knows, that there is a purpose for good even in one's feeling of humiliation. We have to learn thereby our utter dependence upon Him; and a sense of shame, at times, is not the worst thing for us if it has the effect of humbling us before God and bringing us in a certain sense into the place described of the Lord's people in this Psalm when 'they fell down, and there was none to help'. Dependence is mortifying to our proud nature, but dependence upon God to a believer is at times sweet, because he realises there is no ground for despair on account of his own poverty, but He may apply himself continually and freely to that Fountain of all grace who can respond to and answer every need. Therefore in some of these inner things (and I pass through many things not known to you, my hearers and my people too) if in these inner exercises that I pass through (and that you pass through for you pass through things I do not know) we have grace really to observe these things I feel persuaded that we shall understand and perceive much of the lovingkindness of our God in them.

So I have been thinking again of this Psalm and have been trying to reap another fragment from it; and in reviewing it again there were three particular features in it which have impressed my mind. Firstly with regard to these redeemed ones we can say they had a good beginning. Why so? Because the Lord gathered them. They were not a people who made up their minds to be religious for certain purposes that might be advantageous to themselves, but they were dealt with by the merciful hand of God when they were lost and ruined in the fall of Adam, and would have been everlastingly lost but for His quickening grace. I like that word because it is expressive; He 'gathered them out of the lands, from the East, and from the West, from the North, and from the South.' So the Lord began with them, and if your religion is of God He began it with you! All real religion begins in God's coming to poor people in their helpless, ruined state. Whatever outward circumstances He may use, the new birth is divine, that is to say, it is from God. And furthermore, providentially we see how the Lord gathers His people from all parts of the world; doubtless He has them in the most unthought-of places. He gathers them 'out of the lands, from the East and from the West, from the North and from the South', and we believe He has gathered some who are here at this present time. It is a wonderful mercy to have a real religion. It is an amazing thing that, though the matters of eternity are of paramount importance, they are of the least concern to the majority of people, who pay but little heed to them, having much care and thought for material things for their bodies, but little care for their souls. Let us give good heed to the Word of Christ, 'What shall it profit a man if he shall gain the whole world, and lose his own soul?' What would the world be to us if we were lost eternally? It is safe to say that on a dying bed nothing but that precious provision of the gospel can give abiding and lasting comfort.

Secondly, these people who were thus gathered were brought forth in a right, though a trying and difficult, way. The Lord never designed that it should be otherwise with His people; they have to be pilgrims, often struggling against wind and tide, facing much opposition within, and sometimes without too, contending with crosshanded providences that weigh them down and press their minds and spirits, whereby the great adversary of souls will assail them and try to make them infidels if he could. But still, notwithstanding the vicissitudes of life and the changes through which these people pass, the Lord leads them forth by the right way. They are taken out of the wrong way and put into the right way and if the Lord had a hand in the beginning He will keep it up; He will never take up the case of a sinner and then drop it.

> 'Whom once He loves He never leaves
> But loves him to the end.'
> (Gadsby's 351)

'He which hath begun a good work in you will perform it until the day of Jesus Christ.'

But O what changes they had, what trials they suffered, what sins they committed, and what extremities they were driven to, sometimes reeling to and fro and staggering like a drunken man, sometimes at their wits' end. You may have been, and in all probability all the Lord's people are at times, at the end of their tether, as we say, and know not what to do; but it is then that the Lord appears. Several times it is reiterated in this Psalm that when they cried unto the Lord in their trouble He heard and saved them out of their distresses. Let us observe these things. It would seem, therefore, that the Lord's purpose in laying these trials upon His people is to bring them to this point and place, because evidently they did not cry before, but when 'He brought down their heart with labour'; when 'they fell down and there was none to help', when they went 'down to the sea in ships' doing 'business in great waters' then they saw His wonders. Then they cried unto the Lord in their trouble, and He was just the same every time. That is a mercy, is it not? It does not say, in the first instance they cried unto Him and He delivered them out of their distresses, and the second time decided to do it once more, and the third time would have no more patience with them. Where would you and I be if such were the case with us? Continued lovingkindness and exhaustless patience are needed with such creatures as we, for we are continually turning aside from Him. O what fools we are! 'Fools because of their transgression, and because of their iniquities, are afflicted.' They went away from Him, yet He would not leave them, but would bring them back again. He dealt with them in chastening, brought them down, and they cried unto Him and He forgave them again, pardoned them again, delivered them again.

Frequent deliverances! 'Many are the afflictions of the righteous; but the Lord delivereth him out of them all.' 'O that men would praise the Lord for His goodness, and for His wonderful works to the children of men!'

There is another point here, and that is thirdly, He brought them ultimately to their desired haven. They did not perish in the storm, did not go to the bottom of the sea in the tempest; though often doubtless you may fear you will ultimately, you never can if Jesus is the Pilot, for He goes before; all the storms are at His command. 'He bringeth them to their desired haven.' He brings these poor people there. Then it can be said that all their sorrows and cries will be turned into praises and their song, yea, their everlasting Alleluia, will be unto Him Who loved them and washed them from their sins in His own blood and hath made them kings and priests unto God and His Father; to Him be glory (and to no one else) world without end. 'So He bringeth them unto their desired haven.' So He began with them; He gathered them, He brought them on by a right way, and kept them in it, and ultimately brought them to the desired haven. O what a mercy to be in the hand of God thus. Let us then by His grace seek that wisdom whereby we may observe these things and understand the lovingkindness of the Lord. Doubtless there is much lovingkindness in the bitter things, that is, in the things that are bitter to us. But O, some of you would have turned things about if you could; you would have altered things; you would have straightened this or that crooked circumstance. How differently you would have had things if you could; but still the Lord is good, and He makes crooked things straight and rough places plain. Let us give thanks unto Him. Who are the people that could unite in this song? The redeemed of the Lord. Let them say so, let them sing the song. 'The righteous shall see it and rejoice: and all iniquity shall stop her mouth.' That seems to reveal to us the twofold fact that ultimately the righteous shall open their mouths in praise, and shall joy and rejoice in God's mercy in salvation; but all iniquity shall stop her mouth, shall be dumb with silence before this great God and His ways.

'Let the redeemed of the Lord say so.' This word redemption means, as we understand it, to buy again by paying a ransom price, or to deliver from some state and condition of slavery and bondage and servitude. The word is put before us in the Scripture in a typical way by the redemption of Israel from the land of Egypt. Truly that redemption was by the power of God alone by the hand of Moses His servant, who as the leader of His people in bringing them forth from their Egyptian captivity may be a type of Christ; also in respect of the slaying of the paschal lamb whereby the price of redemption is foreshadowed. It was God's ordinance and command that the lamb should be slain and should be eaten, and the blood sprinkled upon the lintel and two side posts of the houses. Thus the Lord redeemed His people from their bondage, brought them out with a mighty hand and with an outstretched arm. But that is only a type, a figure, and though an evidence of one of the many wonderful works of God to His people, falls into insignificance in comparison with the redemption by Christ of all His spiritual seed from eternal death, from the curse of a broken law and everlasting punishment, all of which they deserved on account of their manifold transgressions and breaches of God's righteous law. Yet He redeemed them. He redeemed His ancient people and delivered them; He brought them out, He led them through, and ultimately brought them into the promised land. Although this Psalm does not seem to apply to the children of Israel in respect to their deliverance from Egypt and wilderness wanderings as God's national people, so much as to His spiritual people, who are gathered in, not from a literal Egypt but from all parts North and South, East and West; yet He redeemed Israel and thereby foreshadowed that great and glorious redemption whereby the chosen seed, chosen from before the foundation of the world, were redeemed by the blood of Christ.

Let me look for a few brief moments at this redemption. First, in respect of the cause and reason of it. Where can we find this? In ourselves? The cause of it was never in us; the end of it is in us, because of our transgressions and sins. No hope could there ever be for us of deliverance, life, pardon, justification and heaven, apart from God Himself; but the end is in us. I feel persuaded of this great point that every object of this redemption will, in the Lord's dealing with him feel that end; will be pained by his own sin and guilt and yet will receive that forgiveness that flows from the wounds and merits of our blessed Emmanuel. O yes, but the cause of this is in God. It is in Himself, and it was there from everlasting, it flows from His free, eternal, everlasting love. It knows no other source, it can come no other way. The design and plan was in the decree and council of Jehovah before the world was. This is that 'river, the streams whereof shall make glad the City of God, the holy place of the tabernacles of the Most High'. It is amazing, is it not, to us sometimes that the Majesty of heaven should have looked with complacency in eternity upon poor sinful, guilty, ruined men, upon such insignificant mortals as we, and given us a place in the blessed Person of Christ in the decree of electing love. O friends, if that were so really, and if we are the objects of that love that was in the heart of God from everlasting toward His people, we shall surely need an eternity to praise Him for it, for it will indite in our hearts a song that we shall never tire of in eternity. But here we see the cause of this great and grand design and the plan of it in the council of the Trinity, Father Son and Holy Spirit. Each of the divine Persons in the Trinity has His part; and yet the work in respect of the design and fulfilment and the blessed effects of it are all in one blessed God, one God in three Persons, Father, Son and Spirit. As we have it revealed to us in the Scripture, we may believe that the part of the Father in this great transaction, was to elect and appoint His own Son to be the suffering Surety of His people. 'Behold My Servant whom I uphold, Mine Elect in whom My soul delighteth.' The Lord Jesus Christ was appointed in the decrees of the Father to be His Servant. He was ever a Son; but in the council of peace, in the covenant engagement essential to the salvation of the Church, He became a Servant. He did undertake to honourably and faithfully fulfil the will of God; He espoused the cause of His people. All this was committed into His hand by the eternal Father, and the part of the blessed Son of God, in love to man's lost race, was to condescend, in the fullness of time, to come down to this earth, as we speak in our language, though He was still in heaven in respect of His divine Person—to appear on this earth in human nature, to suffer and die, and pay the ransom price of man's redemption. This was the part of the Son. Moreover, it did not end there with His groans and death upon Calvary's cross, but He rose again and ascended into heaven as the Representative of all the redeemed of the Lord. O, I bless God for such a truth as that. I need a living Priest and I feel sure I have one in heaven; at least I know I am lost without one; that much I can avouch. But I have felt the strength of that word which Christ said to His disciples, 'Because I live, ye shall live also'. O blessed Christ, His life is our life. Then again we have the revelation to us by the Holy Ghost of the cause of this great and grand work of redemption. That appears to be His part in that profound and glorious mystery. He takes of the things of Jesus and shows them unto poor people. O what a sight it is! How it softens the heart; what worship it produces, how it makes you love Him, admire and adore Him. One hymnwriter got a little of that view when he said,

> 'I'd creep beside Him as a worm
> And see Him bleed for me.'
> (Gadsby's 950)

Now the Holy Spirit takes of these glorious mysteries and reveals them to faith. You say, I cannot understand them. No, that is perfectly true; I cannot understand them, but if the Holy Ghost reveals them to your faith you will receive them and love them and rejoice in them. O it is wonderful for a poor sinner to have an experience of the gospel in his heart. Yes!

> 'None but Jesus, none but Jesus,
> Can do helpless sinners good.'

Here then, we see the grand design and plan set in the eternal purposes and all fulfilled according to the will of God. But think of the ransom price that had to be paid for our redemption. What was that price? It was the heart's blood of the Saviour; nothing less would do. It was the price that had to be paid to deliver His spiritual Israel from the hands of the enemy, from that cruel, inveterate foe who held them in his power in their unregeneracy, who held us and would have held us now, had not the Lord mercifully delivered us from his hand—if He has done so—and we believe He has. But the ransom price the Saviour paid was paid to Justice, not to the devil; nothing had to be paid to Satan. The Lord's people are delivered from Satan's power but no compensation is there paid. The payment of the mighty debt was made into the hand of Justice who held us as prisoners under a broken law and an impending curse; and O, what a price, what a price it was! I feel that the Apostle Paul brings this point to light where writing to the Corinthians he says, 'He hath made Him to be sin for us, Who knew no sin; that we might be made the righteousness of God in Him'. Why, my friends, that is the gospel in two sentences—Christ made sin, and sinners made righteous by His obedience and blood-shedding, standing in their guilty place, suffering the curse they deserved, yea, enduring their hell that they might have His heaven. O what a price it was! Peter brings the same point to light. 'Forasmuch as ye know that ye were not redeemed with corruptible things, as silver and gold . . . but with the precious blood of Christ, as of a Lamb without blemish and without spot.' This is it! my friends, my spiritual hearers, this is it which nourishes faith, relieves in distress, gives birth to hope, inspires confidence, produces holy comfort, repentance, godly sorrow, faith and love. *You* get a sight of a bleeding Jesus and weep at His cross for a few moments; then it may be said you have a religion, a religion that will carry you to heaven ultimately. O yes! He paid the price great though it was. Here we have something that is beyond our conception. Yes, 'All we like sheep have gone astray; we have turned every one to his own way; and the Lord hath laid on Him the iniquity of us all.' O to see that wonderful exchange; the imputation of our sins to Christ and the imputation of His righteousness unto us. This is the gospel! 'Let the redeemed of the Lord say so.' Have you any hope in your heart that this mercy has come? 'Let the redeemed of the Lord say so.' Have you ground by past experience, by present feeling, in any measure to hope, to believe, that the price was paid to ransom your soul from the curse? Then say so! 'Let the redeemed of the Lord say so whom He hath redeemed from the hand of the enemy.' The Psalmist here would say 'If the Lord has done anything for you surely it is worth mentioning; why keep silence?' 'Let the redeemed of the Lord say so.' Speak of it. 'Then they that feared the Lord spake often one to another: and the Lord hearkened, and heard it, and a book of remembrance was written before Him for them that feared the Lord, and that thought upon His Name.' O how condescending was this!

But who are the objects of this redemption of Christ's? Why, poor sinners, poor sensible, needy sinners, the elect of God from all eternity; and none beside these elect ones are brought into the evidence of that election by the Spirit dealing with them in their personal cases, in their experience, in bringing them down, lifting them up, bringing them into trouble, bringing them out of it, into bondage, setting them free, bringing them to the Throne of Grace and opening their hearts in prayer, giving them to see deliverances, and enabling them to praise God for His goodness. 'O give thanks unto the Lord for He is good, for His mercy endureth for ever.' 'Let the redeemed of the Lord say so'; let them speak of the goodness of God, for they can. 'Those whom He hath redeemed from the hand of the enemy.' But O, some of you may say, 'Yes, that is very well for those who feel certain, who have had some deliverance, who can look back upon certain things with some measure of composure and can believe that the Lord has done this, and that, and has blessed them there.' Yes, it is; but you know even those people do not always feel able to speak; in fact for the most part it is very difficult. The Lord's people, it is true, vary much with respect to speaking of His dealings with them, but when the heart and lip is open and there is a little enlargement felt, and the goodness of the gospel flows out, then how acceptable it is! There seems to be no restriction here, does there?

'Let the redeemed of the Lord say so, whom He hath redeemed from the hand of the enemy.' But you say, 'I am not like that. I feel to be in such darkness, bondage, fear, doubt and uncertainty; everything is clouded over with me, I see not my signs.' Well, poor sinner, if that is your case, what can you do? Ask God to clear the clouds away, and if you have never had an evidence of His goodness in your felt sinful state, then wait on Him for it. Remember this word, 'They shall not be ashamed that wait for Me.' He is a good God to bad sinners. And it is sweet when there is a little light thrown upon the path, a little blessing felt in the heart, and a little sense of the goodness of God overcoming our reserve and constraining us to break out in praise to His Name for His mercy. O I wish many could! O how good it would be if the Lord were to bless His people up and down the land with a reviving, and to give them fresh things, give them such things as that they might delight to talk together of His goodness! We are living in dark days, but the truth remains, the gospel remains, let us be thankful for that. And if we feel dark, and distant, and cold, and weary, as these are here described, wandering in the wilderness in a solitary way, hungry and thirsty, our souls fainting within us; if we feel like that, then let us cry unto the Lord in our distress, for we have this word, 'This poor man cried, and the Lord heard him, and saved him out of all his troubles.' He will deliver you. He is a faithful God, for He has delivered, He doth deliver, and you can trust Him, that He will yet deliver.

'Who delivered us from so great a death, and doth deliver: in whom we trust that He will yet deliver us;'

'Let the redeemed of the Lord say so, whom He hath redeemed from the hand of the enemy.'

Amen.

ETERNAL LIFE GIVEN

20 November 1946

> 'My sheep hear My voice, and I known them, and they follow Me: And I give unto them eternal life; and they shall never perish, neither shall any man pluck them out of My hand.' (John 10: 27, 28)

SOME will remember that I discoursed briefly upon verse 27 on Sabbath evening, and spoke a little about the Shepherd and the sheep; and I do not purpose to go over that ground this evening in any detail, but to speak more particularly on verse 28. At the same time we have to perceive that the two verses are intimately connected, because the same Person is speaking, and speaking of, or about, the same people—the sheep—what He does for them, their eternal safety in Him and the fact that 'they shall never perish'. None are so wealthy as these sheep!

It is a wonderful mercy to be a sheep, a true sheep of Christ! There is a future before a sheep. 'I give unto them eternal life.' And if we lose that, friends, there is not much else worth having ultimately, is there? For to be without Christ, and to be without these blessings which He gives, is our greatest poverty. But if He be our Shepherd, we have 'All-and-in-all' through Him, and can never need another Shepherd.

'The LORD is my Shepherd, I shall not want.' There seems to be a definite tone about this, in respect of both the Shepherd and the sheep. The Lord says of His sheep, they are 'My sheep'. 'My sheep hear My voice.' Not these others—back in the verse before, to whom He speaks, 'But ye believe not'. Why not? 'Because ye are not of My sheep.' '*My sheep.*' This is what they do, they hear My voice and they follow Me. And the sheep are able to claim this blessed affinity with their Shepherd. 'The LORD is my Shepherd, I shall not want.'

Just very briefly in passing, may I reiterate what I said on the marks of a sheep? Some of us may feel very doubtful in ourselves, possibly, as to whether we have an interest here, whether we are really the sheep of Christ or not—where we stand. But there are here three definite marks of a sheep. Could we rise to that? One is that they believe Him. 'Ye believe not, because ye are not of My sheep.' This means that My sheep do believe. I like very much what Peter said in John 6, when some of those disciples went away, being offended with His doctrine. The Lord said to the twelve, 'Will ye also go away?' Then Simon Peter answered Him, 'Lord, to whom shall we go? Thou hast the words of eternal life.' Thou art our Shepherd. We have nowhere else to go but Thee. 'And we believe and are sure that Thou art that Christ, the Son of the living God.' I admit there is a distinction to be drawn in regard to this believing; that is to say, a sheep may believe in the Shepherd as to His qualities, may see in the Lord Jesus everything needful for himself, and may view, to a point, by faith, those perfections and qualities that shine in Him, in His office, and yet feel an element of doubt of himself, as to whether he is really a sheep, whether he really believes or not, as to his own case. That is, he may question whether the Lord is *his* Shepherd personally, may have to say, O if I could feel He is *my* Shepherd! Well, I believe I can say that if He is not your Shepherd, you would not see anything in Him, you would not see any attraction in Him, you would not want Him to be your Shepherd. There would be no following Him unless He is your Shepherd, because it is only His own sheep who do follow Him. At the same time you cannot rest happily as to your personal interest, by deductions. There must be a positive testimony of the truth in the heart, spoken and made known there by the Holy Spirit. It is never safe to rest on deductions in regard to truth. It is far better to wait on God for positive evidences of His favour and His mercy in a personal way. At the same time it is quite true that though there may be a cloud upon the heart, with respect to this personal interest, yet there would be no pressing after Him, no repentance, no good hope, no love flowing toward Him, no prayer, no affection, no seeking, unless He is your Jesus, for He is drawing it out of you. O these sheep believe Him. Could you say that? I believe that He is what He is, though I wish that I could believe that

He is my Jesus too. I believe Him to be a perfect Saviour. I believe His precious blood is the only atonement for sin. I believe His righteousness is the robe that covers His people. I believe He prevails in heaven for their cause, and I believe He will, one day, come again and claim His flock. Yes, then He will claim you!

Still, there is another particular feature of the sheep here, and that is they hear His voice. 'My sheep hear My voice.' Perhaps you say, I do not know whether I ever have. I believe you have if you are one of His sheep; in your experience, in some of your trials, sorrows, exercises, afflictions, seekings, in your soul you have heard that voice, 'a still, small voice' speaking in the heart; speaking, it may be, an invitation, a direction, a confirming word. The voice is in the Scripture, but the voice in the Scripture is also in the heart. It is not the letter of truth, but the power of truth. Yes! Can you go to a time when, in your distress and need, you felt the comforting, directing, inviting power of a word as applied to your case? 'My sheep hear My voice.'

'And I know them.' I know them; I know them perfectly; I knew them in the covenant of grace. I know every feature about them, I know every mark they bear, I know every desire they have. I know all their sinful propensities, I know how silly they are—silly sheep! Yet I know also their beauties, their attractions, their desires, their prayers, their pleadings—yes, 'I know them, and they follow Me'. This is a great mark; the sheep follow the Shepherd through the trackless desert. They cleave to Him as the children of Israel followed the cloud in the wilderness. These sheep follow the Shepherd. They are only happy when they are with Him, near to Him, hear His voice and are comforted by His words.

'And I give unto them eternal life.' O how can we comprehend what is involved in this? I have been rather struck by the fact that every thing in the gospel to a sinner, has to be given. It all *has* to be given; the Holy Spirit has to be given; He is a free gift to these poor sheep. 'If ye then, being evil, know how to give good gifts unto your children; how much more shall your heavenly Father give the Holy Spirit to them that ask Him?' He is a free gift. The Holy Spirit can never be purchased or claimed by us on account of anything in ourselves. He is freely given. All the mercy is on the Lord's side in His care for His flock, in His teaching, in His gifts. I give unto them these.

Is it life? That life must be given; it is nothing we can rise to, nothing we can purchase or manufacture of our own—it must be given. 'According as His divine power hath given unto us all things that pertain unto life and godliness.' It is a great place for us to be brought to, to realize that every covenant blessing must be given; freely given too. We shall never get to the cross with a penny; we must fall flat and accept what the Lord gives, with nothing to give Him in return but a grateful heart, for His wonderful mercy to such poor sinners; heaven can never be wages, though it will be a reward. It will be a free reward but it will never be wages; we can never buy it, we can never buy anything in grace, in this sense, for we have nothing to give. And yet this is our greatest mercy, for we should have no hope if we had to give an equivalent for what we receive. 'When they had nothing to pay, He frankly forgave them both.' And this life is given in His Son; it is the life of Jesus in us if He is our Shepherd. 'Because I live, ye shall live also.' But all has to be given, and all is freely given!

Is it repentance? That has to be given. Can you make yourself repent? Can you give yourself a soft heart? a humble spirit? We may think we are humble, and be as proud as we can be. But I do not know anything sweeter than true humility before the Lord; it breaks us, we fall into the dust, we feel to be but as worms—dust and ashes! Can we produce it of ourselves? Can we purchase it? No, it has to be given, and it is given, and given freely. 'For Christ hath God exalted with His right hand to . . . give repentance to Israel, and forgiveness of sins.' What a wonderful channel of mercy is here for a sinner! What a fullness! Heaven, as it were, opens itself to supply the need of a lost soul; an infinite fullness, shall I say, is at the hand of a coming sinner, open to him to receive, for

'The Lamb is exalted repentance to give.'

And yet to be unrepentant, hard, indifferent and unfeeling, is our sin. We can produce nothing gracious inherently. All has to be given.

Is it faith? That has to be given. There is nothing to boast of here; for though, indeed, the Scripture and the gospel speak so much of this faith; even if we had it but as a grain of mustard seed, we could shift a mountain with it; yet all has to be given. 'For by grace are ye saved, through faith; and that not of yourselves: it is the gift of God.' All has to be given. And yet it is this that is so sweet to faith because it is the work of faith to receive these things. All is freely given, short of hell. To Christ every blessing we owe.

> 'To Him every comfort I owe,
> Above what the fiends have in hell;
> And shall I not sing as I go,
> That Jesus does everything well?'

Can you believe He does? Can you look at your life and circumstances, disappointments, trials, crosses, losses, difficulties and changes, and say of them all, He hath done all things well? The sheep do! But they do not always say it. No, but these sheep have moments when they can commit all their concerns into the hand of the Shepherd, and leave them with Him as to the issue thereof. But He must give this faith, and He has it to give, too.

Is it grace? Grace to live, grace to bear our burdens, grace to walk, grace to speak, grace to honour Him, grace to follow Him, grace to walk in His ways, grace to glorify Him—He must give us this. He gave it to Paul when he suffered from a pricking thorn. He said, 'My grace is sufficient for thee'; and he said, Yes, Lord, so it is; for he said, 'Most gladly therefore will I glory in my infirmities'. All is freely given. And it is very sweet that it is so, because then there is no glorying in self, no taking the praise of anything to our poor flesh, but He has all the praise and all the glory too.

'I give unto My sheep eternal life.' I *give* it to them; they cannot buy it, for they have nothing to purchase it with. I give it to them. If a kind friend gave (we will say), a very poor person a nice house with pleasant rooms and nice furniture in a pleasant situation and everything he could desire; he *gave* it to him—he *gave* it to him—why, what admiration that would call forth from the receiver of such a bounty! But the Lord says, 'I give unto My sheep eternal life'. That is really worth more than all the property in the universe. If we possessed millions and lost this, we should be undone for ever; and yet he says, I give them this. I give unto them eternal life.

What do we understand by eternal life? It is more than we can understand! The issues of it are beyond our conceptions, and yet faith can believe it to be true. Paul speaks of it in the Epistle to The Romans, 'The wages of sin is death; but the gift of God is eternal life through Jesus Christ our Lord'. Eternal life stands as distinct from, or opposite to, eternal death! Eternal life is not merely an eternal existence—though it is that—but it is something immeasurably beyond that; it is not just a mere existence, dragging on through countless years in an eternal world. Eternal life is more than that. What is it? Eternal life is eternal deliverance; deliverance from sin, from death, from hell. It is eternal deliverance. Those who possess this life are free for ever from all tormenting conflicts that pertain to this poor world. Eternal life will be eternal love! For those who enter into it will be in the light of His countenance, in the enjoyment of it, to love Him there without anything to mar the happiness of that love. There our cup will run over; it will be 'waters to swim in, a river that could not be passed over'. It is sweet to feel a moment of this love here. Eternal life is eternal love.

Further, eternal life is eternal joy; and He says, I will give them this. He has it to give; in fact, He will be their joy. 'Whom have I in heaven but Thee? and there is none upon earth that I desire beside Thee.'

Eternal life will be eternal rest! A rest from conflict, temptation, sin, everything that mars the peace of a believer here. 'There remaineth therefore a rest to the people of God.' It is very sweet to feel the mind at rest here even if it be for a few hours, to feel a rest in your spirit; to be able to rest in Jesus. But that will be an eternal rest, for the former things will have passed away. This is eternal life, and He gives the sheep this. 'I give unto them eternal life.'

Eternal life will be eternal worship: 'Unto Him that loved us, and washed us from our sins in His own blood.' Sweet worship! The saints never weary there of that enjoyment. There is always an attraction that never fails.

Eternal life will be eternal conformity, for there we shall be like Him; we shall see Him as He is. We shall be like Him for

I think it must be said, that the risen bodies of the saints will be like unto the risen body of the Saviour; they shall see Him as He is and will be with Him. This is eternal life for the sheep and it is a gift. It is for the sheep. It is a mercy to be a sheep! How can the Lord give this great gift unto His sheep; how can it be? Why, it can be, because He Himself has redeemed them from the curse of a broken law. 'Christ hath redeemed us from the curse of the law, being made a curse for us.' He could not give eternal life if justice were not satisfied. But as we have been singing in the first hymn, stern justice is satisfied by the price He paid to purchase the flock. He bought them with His own heart's blood, therefore they are His property and He has a right to give them this. It is His to give.

'I give unto them eternal life, and they shall never perish.' They shall never perish. This does not mean that they will never fear they shall perish, for many poor, timid, fearful sheep do—the sheep of Christ do. In fact, I think it may be said, all, more or less, are subject to these fears, especially before the Lord graciously confirms them by some merciful token of His grace and love to their souls. There is a fear which hath torment; and this fear is felt too, where the conscience is convinced of sin, where a poor sinner is brought to feel what he deserves, and has to acknowledge it before God and has no excuse to make. He knows he has sinned and violated the divine law and has brought himself under this condemnation. But He says, 'They shall never perish'. 'There is therefore now no condemnation' to these sheep.

'I give unto them eternal life; and they shall never perish.' Not, they shall perish for a time and then be gathered up again. No, they shall never perish though they know they deserve to perish. I believe every one does. I believe the Lord brings these sheep to acknowledge Him to be just in His law, even should they perish. But they shall never perish. What is it to perish? To perish is the wages of sin; to perish is death—the eternal death of the soul. This is an awful consideration! Nothing can be compared to an interest in Jesus, to a good hope in His mercy—nothing can be compared to that. These sheep of Christ shall never perish. To perish is the second death. Death and hell shall be cast into the lake of fire that burneth with fire and brimstone.

O who can comprehend what the wrath of God shall be, in regard to the lost souls in perdition? To perish is not to be annihilated and cease to be; it is to be under the wrath of God under a broken law for ever. To perish will be to hear that voice, 'Depart . . . ye cursed, into everlasting fire, prepared for the devil and his angels'. To perish will be to have a worm at the conscience that will never die. 'For their worm shall not die, neither shall their fire be quenched.' O, how can I speak of this? And yet the Scriptures reveal it—very solemnly too; and we must not close our eyes to what is there revealed. The twofold destiny of men—eternal misery or eternal happiness; who can conceive the issue? And there will be no reprieve from that awful punishment. What a solemn consideration! O, to perish, to perish, will be unspeakably awful!

But the sheep here—they shall never perish, He says. A very confirming consideration this! They shall never perish. No; they may have been as near as it was possible to be, in their feelings, and have been almost sure they would perish, have practically given up under the darkness, bondage, fear, and torment. But they never have perished yet. There never has yet been one of the Lord's sheep perish for whom He paid the price.

'I give unto them eternal life, and they shall never perish.' O poor, trembling soul, take strength by this, cleave to Him, wait upon Him, seek His mercy, press your case, urge it on Him through all unfitness. A praying soul will never perish. A believing soul will never perish—a sheep will never perish. I give them this. You cannot buy it, but you may ask Him for it. Ask of Me, He says, 'Ask, and it shall be given you; seek, and ye shall find; knock, and it shall be opened unto you.' They shall never perish.

'Neither shall any man pluck them out of My hand.' This is their security in Him. Neither shall any man (though he may try, and they will try). No angel can do this; no devil can do this—not for a sheep! But O, the temptations, torments, assailments, the words that may be spoken, the voices, the conflict! Yes, but they are safe in the fold of Jesus; none shall pluck them out. No devil can pluck them out. 'I AM He that liveth, and was dead; and, behold, I AM alive for evermore, Amen; and have the keys of hell and of death.' No devil shall pluck them out of My hand; no false teacher shall pluck them out of My hand. They do a vast amount of harm by their heresies and pretences but they shall never pluck a sheep out—they are safe in this fold. They are in the covenant—they are safe there. If, as we read in Jeremiah's prophecy, if the ordinances of the day and of the night shall cease to be, then will I cast off Israel from being a seed to Me for ever (Jeremiah 33: 25 & 26). But has that happened? Have the ordinances of day and of night failed or gone into confusion? have they been cut off? No, they have continued unto this day; and so will these sheep, for they are safe in the fold of Jesus and shall never perish. No imposter, no false teacher shall pluck a sheep out of the fold—though they may many professors. Many have they turned aside by their heresies and plausible pretences, but never a sheep; not one sheep is lost, not one. No, no, nothing shall pluck them out of My hand.

This expresses their security in Himself. 'Out of My hand.' They shall not pluck them thence. By His hand we understand His power, and He says, 'All power is given unto Me in heaven and in earth', and it is this upholds a poor sinner; it is this power that holds him up; not a determination, not his natural determination, but this power that is in the hand of Christ. None shall pluck them thence. They are safe there. They are secure there; they are secured in His love because He has loved them with an everlasting love; none shall pluck them out of His hand. But O what fears often there may be, concerning this; the darkness, the storm, the wind; what fears often may be concerning our own safety. Yes, you may say, The sheep are safe—I do not question that—but it is, where do I stand? Well, that is the point. And yet there is much encouragement for those who feel doubtful of this. He can make it plain; He can turn darkness into light, make crooked things straight, and rough places plain.

But if you are a sheep you will be following Him. Follow His teaching; read it closely and ask Him to pour light upon it and enlighten you in your soul. Yes, you will follow His word, follow Him, cleave to Him through the wilderness. 'He led him about, He instructed him, He kept him as the apple of His eye.' Yes, there is no separation; the sheep will follow the Shepherd because they have confidence in Him and know His voice. Yes, and they know what He has to give; He has the food they need and He has also this gift of eternal life and they shall never perish. Sometimes you can feel that in your soul, and believe that it never will be. We have in Ps. 23 'Yea, though I walk through the valley of the shadow of death, I will fear no evil: for Thou art with me; Thy rod and Thy staff they comfort me.' The way is dark, is it not? but you must follow Him. The cross lies heavy, does it not? but you must follow Him. There are many briers and thorns in the way; yes, but you must follow Him. There are mountains ahead; yes, but you must follow Him. There is a deep valley; yes, but you must go into it. My sheep follow Me; no one else can provide for them; no one else has what they need. The shepherd understands them. Yes. 'I know My sheep and am known of Mine.' 'I lay down My life for the sheep.' It is the highest manifestation of His love toward His flock.

What a future is before these sheep!—eternal life! Conformity to Him, likeness, passing 'from glory to glory' into His presence; leaving earth for heaven, death for life, time for eternity. O what can be compared to this? May the Lord help us in His mercy to walk after Him and to listen for His voice—listen for it—listen for it! It speaks in your heart, that gentle whisper; it is such a quiet voice. O, one moment you may be in a turmoil, bewildered, torn this way and that but a word just drops in and there is a quietness and you can 'be still'. Is that not true? What voice is that? It is the voice of the Shepherd speaking to His sheep. Have you ever heard it? They know His voice; they know it to be the voice of the Shepherd. Could you tell that? You can tell it by the effect it has on your spirit. O may the Lord look upon us and number us among His true sheep and bestow this inestimable gift, that we may never perish, but experience that safety that belongs to those who are in His keeping.

Amen.

‘IT IS I; BE NOT AFRAID’

2 September 1951

‘But He saith unto them, It is I; be not afraid.’ (John 6: 20)

THE Lord Jesus spoke many confirming words to His disciples while with them in the days of His flesh, but never a confirming word without a need for that confirmation in their circumstances or their souls; neither will He speak to us unless we are in a place suited to the hearing of His voice. When that voice is heard, there will be an authority in it that surpasses every other voice that may be heard, and will bring, according to the need, a measure of gracious quietness and confidence into the heart, enabling one hearing that voice to ‘come up from the wilderness leaning upon her Beloved’.

In the first part of the chapter the Lord’s care for the temporal needs of the people is very observable. When ‘He went over the Sea of Galilee’ we read ‘A great multitude followed Him, . . . and He went up into a mountain, and there He sat with His disciples’; but the end of this chapter will show that the object or purpose of many who followed Him was painfully superficial; they ‘followed Him because they saw His miracles which He did on them that were diseased’; not because they were hungry for the Bread of Life, but because they received temporal benefit and were provided for. There were not many amongst that vast company who were like Peter when he said, ‘Lord, to whom shall we go? Thou hast the words of eternal life’. There were not many such followers, for we read a number became offended with His doctrine and ‘Many of His disciples went back, and walked no more with Him’. They were not offended with the miracles He wrought, not offended because they ‘did eat of the loaves, and were filled’; but it was the doctrine that offended them—doctrine! There is a great deal connected with a religious profession which has nothing whatever in it offensive to flesh and blood, but when it comes to the separating nature of truth, that is offensive to flesh and blood, and raises the spleen and enmity of human nature against that truth.

It is wonderful how the Lord provided for this vast multitude. Have you noticed what He said here? 'When Jesus then lifted up His eyes, and saw a great company come unto Him, He saith unto Philip, Whence shall we buy bread that these may eat?' Is there anywhere you can get some bread? Can you buy bread somewhere? Here are five thousand men beside women and children; can you buy bread anywhere? But 'this He said to prove him'; the Lord knew what He was going to do but He said this to prove him, and Philip did not just say, 'Lord, Thou art able to supply them', but he said, 'Two hundred pennyworth of bread is not sufficient for them, that every one of them may take a little' if we *could* get it, for this vast multitude. Then Andrew said, 'There is a lad here, which hath five barley loaves, and two small fishes': not a lad with five loaves and two fishes of a tremendous size, I have never seen fishes like them. No they were two small fishes, of no use at all, humanly speaking; but when the Lord disposes to manifest His power, He brings men to extremities and will show that nothing is too hard for Him. When they were all supplied, all had a sufficiency miraculously wrought for them, and beside that there were twelve baskets full of fragments gathered up. 'Is anything too hard for the Lord?' It matters not to Him how great the difficulty may be or how great the need, all sufficiency belongs to Him. Moreover, He has condescendingly assured His people that He will supply their need. 'My God shall supply all your need according to His riches in glory by Christ Jesus.' After this the people would have made Him a King for the miracle that He had wrought, but the Lord never sought earthly honour.

'He departed again into a mountain Himself alone. And when even was now come, His disciples went down unto the sea, and entered into a ship, and went over the sea toward Capernaum.' It seems in a way surprising that the Lord did not go with them, but He went up into a mountain to pray and was alone there. These disciples, we read in another gospel, were constrained to get into the ship—they were constrained, as though they were unwilling to venture upon this journey across the sea. But the Lord constrained them so that they had no reason to feel they were taking a wrong course. We may be in the way of the Lord's leading, but that does not infer immunity from trouble, storms, tribulation, opposition, and many difficulties. A Red Sea may come in the way of the Lord's leading; but if there is a Red Sea, it is because the Lord intends to divide it. Whatever comes in the way of His leadings is designed and intended for a purpose, to manifest His power in His people's deliverance. He constrained them. Has there ever been a time when you have felt, as it were, moved by the Lord under a gracious influence to take a certain step, and yet have found trouble in it? That does not mean it was a wrong step, although at times I know it can be so. It *can* be a wrong step; but there is a great difference between certain troubles that come in the way of the Lord's leading and teaching, to try and test our faith and grace, and those judgments which come to correct us for our folly and for running in wrong ways. All is designed for good in the Lord's purpose, but I believe there are times when, whatever trouble comes upon you to try your faith and grace, you can feel, notwithstanding all, that you are in the path or way that He would have you walk in; and that can bring a wonderful rest to the spirit, when it is felt to be so. He constrained them—and yet He did not go with them. Had He not a purpose in that? He let these disciples go into this ship alone, while He went up into the mountain to pray. How often it may be that Jesus can see us, does see us in our difficulties when we cannot see Him. So it was with these disciples. Many Scriptures can be confirming to the Lord's people, even in darkness. 'Who is among you . . . that walketh in darkness, and hath no light? let him trust in the Name of the Lord, and stay upon his God.'

Not only did they have to go alone but soon darkness came upon them and Jesus was not with them, 'was not come to them'. It is a great trial of faith to walk a dark path feelingly alone, but yet not alone really; darkness came upon them, and not only darkness but a great storm and a contrary wind. Everything seemed to go against them as against Jacob when he said, 'All these things are against me'. But what were the storm and the darkness and the wind to Christ? He permitted them. We cannot expect to get through this life without darkness and storms and contrary winds, for it is a path of tribulation that the Lord has designed for His children. It was a contrary wind, not a wind that blew the way they wanted to go; that would have been helpful to them; but it was a contrary wind, a struggle against wind and tide, and they became in great danger. This is how the Lord's people often prove things to be with them. How often there is a contrary wind, a wind blowing, as it were, in your face, hindering your progress and making it hard labour to move forward. A storm arose and the Lord was not with them. They were there a small company alone and yet His eye was watching them; though they did not see Him, He 'was not come to them'. It was a long time, apparently, before He did come; not in the first watch, as we read in Matthew, but in the fourth watch the Lord came to them, the last watch among the Jews, in the early morning. They seemed to have struggled in the storm a good part of the night before relief came, but the Lord is never before His time and never is behind. He will never be too late even if it is in the fourth watch. It may be some of you here are in the first, second, or third watch, and still Jesus has not come. The darkness continues; the storm rages; the contrary wind blows; danger appears on every hand; and still He does not come. He came in the fourth watch. It was not too late for them although probably they feared they would never survive that terrible night; but He came, walking on the sea, and drew nigh to the ship and they were afraid. Assuming it would be a spirit or some apparition, they were filled with fear. How often that may be the case with us! The very thing intended for our deliverance may fill us with apprehension. We fear sometimes where no fear is, and the Lord's children know that they are fearing creatures; hence the Lord has condescendingly given many 'Fear nots' in His Word to His people. In the beginning in Genesis the Lord said to Abram, 'Fear not, Abram, I am thy shield and thy exceeding great reward'. The Lord appeared to John in the Isle of Patmos and 'laid His right hand upon him, saying Fear not, I am the first and the last'. It is a wonderful thing to hear a 'Fear not' in your heart when you are tossed with the waves, when the night is dark, when there is a contrary wind, and you are filled with apprehension and fear. He said, 'It is I; be not afraid'. It is I. There is something very attractive here about the way it is expressed, It is I. The Person speaking is a great point. 'It is I, be not afraid.' It is I who have fed the multitude, It is I who have delivered you before. It is I; not I will get someone to help you or there is some possibility of the storm abating later, no, 'It is I, be not afraid'. Be not afraid.

The Lord frequently addressed His disciples in the first person. We hear His voice speaking in the first person in the Scriptures as in the Proverbs, 'I love them that love Me'. In the Song of Solomon he says 'I am the rose of Sharon, and the lily of the valleys'. 'I am come into My garden, My sister, My spouse.' It is I. 'I am Alpha and Omega, the first and the last.' Be not afraid. When the Lord will silence the fears of His people He will direct them to Himself, not to anything material or to some secondary matter, but He will direct their faith and confidence unto Himself. It is I; no less than Myself can suffice to work deliverance, to allay the storm or disperse your fears. 'It is I, be not afraid.' It is a great thing when a right view of the power and glory of His Person is given us; that would inspire our confidence more than all beside. It will bring a strength into your soul when you can rightly view the Lord Jesus and perceive Him to be what He really is and who He is. 'It is I'—as though He would say, What are all your difficulties, mountains and even your sins, to Me? I am above them all. I AM! We read that God appeared to Jacob, 'I am the God of Abraham and the God of Isaac'. Be not afraid. 'I am the Almighty God, walk before Me.' Be not afraid. It is I, the Word made flesh. This view by faith of the Lord Jesus is amazingly confirming to the Lord's people. It is I, the Word made flesh, the eternal Son of God assuming human flesh. There He was; Deity was in Him. Although He was a mere man in the eyes of many, omnipotence was in Him; He was Almighty God in the days of His flesh and had all power in His hand. It is I, your Saviour, your Redeemer, 'And I if I be lifted up from the earth, will draw all men unto Me.' It is I. He Himself is the Centre of all strength, comfort and peace to His people. When the Lord is really with you you have no fear; but when, as was the case here with the disciples, darkness came upon them, the storm rose, the waves beat about them, they were tossed with tempest and the winds were contrary, then they were filled with fear, for the Lord was not there. But then this was to test their faith and confidence in Himself. When we look away from Him we soon sink in our feelings; yet how prone we are to do this! Sometimes we suffer for it too. O how often it is that fears run high and faith runs low. It was so with the disciples. In Matthew we read how Peter ventured to walk on the water, to go to Jesus; while he kept a stedfast eye fixed on the Lord Jesus he was safe enough, but when he looked round at the waves and billows, he began to sink; and he did sink to a certain extent; he began to go down. That is just how it is with us. When we look away from Jesus we fall a prey to temptation and fear, because we have not a stedfast eye. 'Be not afraid', He said; but when Peter began to sink we read that the Lord put out His hand and caught him and said, 'O thou of little faith, wherefore didst thou doubt?' O this doubting, this doubting! It is a wonderful mercy to be delivered from a false confidence in religion; it is very easy to trust in something in ourselves or in an arm of flesh short of Christ; but a stripping time will come one day when we shall know the difference. We shall find if we are trusting in anything of our own, the bed too short to stretch ourselves upon.

What a mercy it will be to be delivered from a false hiding-place and from every refuge of lies and to be brought to confide in Him alone. 'Be not afraid.' It is wonderfully sweet to be able to put our trust in Him, to come up from the wilderness leaning upon Him, not upon anything of our own, or any creature, but leaning alone upon Him, upon His promise; 'He hath said, I will never leave thee, nor forsake thee'. If you get that in your heart you can go through the storm with it, you can go through the darkness with it, you can battle against the contrary wind with it. He is all-sufficient; 'be not afraid'. Look unto Me, that is in heart. 'Look unto Me, and be ye saved, all the ends of the earth: for I AM God, and there is none else.' 'It is I; be not afraid.' Has there ever been an occasion when the Lord has spoken after this manner, when perhaps you have been tossed with tempest and not comforted, when no one could comfort and no one could save but Himself? Then you have heard His voice in your heart saying, 'It is I, be not afraid'. When you can see Him above everything else, then you have no fear. Fears arise from unbelief in the heart and distrust of the Lord's word and providence.

I know it is better to be fearful and trembling than to live in a false confidence about our state; but it is a wonderful mercy when faith is brought into exercise, so that you can really prove that 'In quietness and in confidence is your strength'. It is I; as though He would say, I am above every mountain, above all your fears; lean upon Me, I will bear you through. Be not afraid. Be not afraid of the darkness, the storm, the wind, be not afraid.

Faith never presumes. Nature can at times be exceedingly presumptuous but there is no presumption in faith. There is a wonderful difference between the quiet confidence of faith and the hurried presumption of unbelief. 'In quietness and in confidence shall be your strength', that is your daily strength; the strength of the promise is felt for the day and then you can leave the rest. If you could rise in the morning with this in your heart, 'It is I, be not afraid', it would not matter what you might have before you that day; but if you rise dark in your feelings, troubled in your circumstances, alone, confused, dark, weary, assailed with unbelief, you can be torn this way and that way by the suggestions of the enemy, and have no comfort, no rest. Nothing will take the place of the Lord's coming. When He comes He can still the storm. The waves are in His hand; the waves are under His control. 'He commandeth and raiseth the stormy wind', and yet it is the same hand that makes the storm a calm, 'so that the waves thereof are still'. 'It is I.' O this is a wonderful stillness; it removes your fears and apprehensions; all the darkness and tempest tossing you may have felt subsides under the Lord's presence. 'Be not afraid.' Be not afraid of the future. Why not be afraid of the future? Is there not reason to be greatly apprehensive? There is! The future is dark and gloomy; but if the Lord is our God we can go into the future and live day by day under the comfort and assurance of His sufficiency. Nothing else can produce it but the quieting effect of His Word in us. 'It is I, be not afraid.'

With respect to our young people, who can tell what they may live to see come upon this earth, what troubles, what afflictions? But if the Lord is pleased to bless them with His holy fear and enable them to look to Him and put their trust in Him, they can go on in a gracious confidence that all will be well with them. 'It is I, be not afraid.' Trouble there may be, wars there may be; but

'I am the Lord thy God; I will go before thee; I will not fail thee nor forsake thee'. If ever that has come into your heart, then it has enabled you to cast the future upon Him and live by the day in this sense, 'Give us this day our daily bread'. Be not afraid.

Be not afraid of men. Some of us have been and humanly speaking, have had reason to be so too; but in the prophecy the Lord says, 'Fear ye not the reproach of men, neither be ye afraid of their revilings'. Fear not this. He does not say, There will never be any reproach for My sake. 'Who art thou, that thou shouldest be afraid of a man that shall die . . . And forgettest the Lord thy Maker?' It is when we are afraid of dying mortal men that we forget the Lord our Maker. Forget! 'Who art thou, that thou shouldest be afraid of a man that shall die?' Be not afraid. This does not intend a careless, indifferent way of life but a gracious reliance upon divine sufficiency, whatever may come against us; and things will come. Perhaps you have something before you that may try you greatly and which you know not how to negotiate; this is the word to enable you to walk in it and through it too. 'It is I, be not afraid.' Look not so much to the difficulty but look unto Me. The quietness and confidence that can be felt is wonderful and is always humbling in its operations in your heart, always so; it produces no self-confidence. 'Lord help me', said the woman. 'I will help thee', saith the Lord. Fear not I will help thee, be not afraid. Be not afraid of enemies. David was not afraid when he said, 'When . . . mine enemies . . . came upon me to eat up my flesh, they stumbled and fell'. 'The Lord is my light and my salvation; whom shall I fear? the Lord is the strength of my life; of whom shall I be afraid?'

Be not afraid of death; it will come in the Lord's time and in itself there is every reason to dread it as a gloomy thing; but it is not gloomy to faith because the sting is taken away. 'Though I walk through the valley of the shadow of death, I will fear no evil: for Thou art with me.' Be not afraid. What a mercy it is then when we can hold fast in the confidence of faith when everything else appears to give way. 'The mountains shall depart, and the hills be removed; but My kindness shall not depart from thee, neither shall the covenant of My peace be removed, saith the Lord that hath mercy on thee.'

Well I did not actually anticipate speaking in this way, neither do I know why I have done so, but I hope it may be a word seasonable to some, and that we may feel strengthened in the Lord and have grace to put our trust alone in Him.

Amen.

GOD'S UNSPEAKABLE GIFT

25 December 1952

'Thanks be unto God for His unspeakable Gift.' (2 Corinthians 9: 15)

THE great work of redemption by the Lord Jesus was marked by some remarkable days. It was a wonderful day when He was born at Bethlehem when the promise concerning Him (that had lived ever since man fell in the Garden of Eden) was fulfilled. 'When the fulness of the time' came, the great Redeemer of guilty, ruined man, appeared upon earth born of a virgin at Bethlehem. It was a great day, too, when He offered Himself a supreme Sacrifice by giving Himself for our sins and dying on Calvary's tree. It was a great day, too, when He rose triumphant from the grave, when He burst the bands of death and emerged from the silent tomb, a mighty Conqueror over death and hell. It was a great day when He ascended up into heaven, led captivity captive, and took His seat at the right hand of God, where now He is ever living—living 'after the power of an endless life', 'able also to save them to the uttermost that come unto God by Him'.

There will be another great day, which will be a wonderful day to His people but a day of awful terror to the wicked—that day when (as it is so clearly and definitely recorded) He will come again with great power, majesty and glory, with His angels, to receive all His dear, redeemed people into those eternal heavenly habitations. I have noticed particularly how frequently the Scriptures affirm that all this is for His people. Sometimes it is said, as we have read (Luke 2: 1–20), 'all people' which is your mercy and mine. You will remember I have sometimes said, 'No one can be more thankful for that word "Whosoever" than I am'. But 'all people' must be specified, as all 'the elect of God' gathered from all quarters, of every nation, kindred and tongue. These shall be brought, as we read in Luke chapter 1, to a 'knowledge of salvation . . . by the remission of their sins'. So Zacharias prophesied under the anointing of the blessed Spirit, saying, 'Blessed be the Lord God of Israel; for He hath visited and redeemed His people'. As I recently hinted at a Prayer Meeting, what a wonderful day this would be, what a season to be remembered, if we could feel to say under the blessing of the truth, 'Blessed be the Lord God of Israel, for He hath visited and redeemed *me*'. O, some, I believe, have long earnestly prayed for this testimony in their consciences and I am glad they cannot rest without it. If such were so favoured this day, what a day it would be!

Everything that we receive from God in His mercy is received as a gift, and as a free gift, which is a very mortifying consideration to man's proud nature but is a mercy felt in the soul of a sensible sinner, who, being brought to feel that he has nothing to pay with, has to fall flat, as it were, before the cross and just confess that he has nothing in his hand to bring. To such characters as these the gospel is profoundly sweet and I feel persuaded that it has so been to some of us. In fact, the freeness of the gift has sometimes been the sweetest part of it because it has brought us to this point feelingly 'Where there is neither Greek nor Jew, circumcision nor uncircumcision, Barbarian, Scythian, bond nor free; but Christ is all and in all'. You will never enter into the truth of that graciously unless brought to feel the *freeness* of the blessed gospel.

Here then is a gift. It is pleasant to receive a gift from a friend when that gift is given in affection and love. Often such gifts have touched a tender chord in our hearts, have they not? But all earthly gifts, acceptable as they are (and especially when you can feel that they are a token of affection) sweet as they may be to receive, all—all fall beneath this gift. There was never such a gift as the gift of the Saviour. Referring to this the apostle says, 'who gave Himself for our sins'. There is no doubt, although the apostle had referred in this chapter to the effects of charity and exhorted them to liberality in helping and assisting one another in their affliction and in their need, he evidently winds it up by referring to the greatest of all gifts, even that unspeakable gift; because we must realize, I believe, that there is only one *unspeakable* gift. Indeed, there may be some very valuable gifts of a material nature. One might give all that was in his power to give, for the help and benefit of another, but that would be a gift which could be expressed or comprehended: this gift is a gift that is *ineffable*! It is an unspeakable Gift! No thought can convey what is involved in it; no word can express, no tongue can describe, no 'pen of a ready writer' explain fully, what is involved in this gift. We can, I believe, feel that the gift is like His love; it 'passeth knowledge'. Though it is an unspeakable gift and like to His love that passeth all knowledge yet there is that in it, when it is received, that can be felt. Though it is an unspeakable gift it is not an *unfeeling* gift; it is a gift which, when it is received, will *fill your soul* as nothing else can. Some of you can believe me and can follow me when I say that even in the receiving of the gift, that is when the dear Redeemer was manifested and received in your soul, you could not fully describe it; it was an unspeakable gift even in the receiving of it, but O the sweetness, the peace, the joy, the happiness, the liberty that is felt when the gift is received. It is an unspeakable gift; and seeing that all other spiritual gifts that accompany salvation are, as it were, incorporated in it, it must be said that all spiritual gifts that a sinner receives from the Lord are beyond his powers to express or explain; yet though that is so, if the Lord should condescend to come and bless your soul and you should try to speak to another of that blessing in your soul, that friend would understand what you mean although in itself the gift is unspeakable.

'Thanks be unto God.' Have you ever felt like that? Have you had a moment?—(perhaps that is rather a favourite phrase of mine but still never mind)—have you had a moment when you felt as though your heart would burst and all you could say was 'Thanks be unto God'? Bless His holy Name for manifesting such mercy to a wretch like me? So sweetly did Zacharias prophesy relative to John the Baptist 'Through the tender mercy of our God; whereby the Dayspring from on high hath visited us'. 'Thanks be unto God.' Here then is ground for real praise and thanksgiving from the heart. We may sing the hymns and sometimes it is very sweet to sing His praises when in a little measure by His grace we can sing with the heart and with the understanding—it is very, very sweet. The heart rises, as it were, at such a time in faith and love, ascribing all to Him absolutely—unto Him every time. All is 'to the praise of the glory of His grace, wherein He hath made us accepted in the Beloved'. 'Thanks be unto God.' O, if some of us could say 'Thanks be unto God for this day!' By this I do not mean 25 December or what is usually termed Christmas Day, but if we could say 'Thanks be unto God for a day when the Saviour was born at Bethlehem' and especially if we could say 'He was born to redeem *me* from all iniquity'!

'Thanks be unto God for His unspeakable gift.' Here are one or two points. First of all, considering this briefly, is the Giver of the Gift, whom we believe to be 'God, even the Father of our Lord Jesus Christ', 'the eternal God', the Father in the Trinity of Persons in the Godhead. Let us ever be particular about this, because it has been affirmed quite properly, that salvation is built upon a distinction of Persons in the Godhead. 'For there are three that bear record in heaven, the Father, the Word, and the Holy Ghost: and these three are One.' Here, then is the Father, so frequently spoken of in Scripture in that relationship and especially in the 17th of John in the Redeemer's intercessory prayer. 'The God and Father of our Lord Jesus Christ' gave His only begotten Son. You cannot understand that—I cannot—here is a mystery; here is the great mystery of godliness but it is true, and faith can sometimes receive the sacred truth, 'He gave Him'. And, moreover, He gave Him in the warmth of divine love. O so much is in this. It is not like one saying, O I suppose I had better give so-and-so something, otherwise he will think I am unmindful. No, He gave Him in the warmth of His love. I feel sure of that because it is so clearly affirmed to be so. It is said, 'He so loved the world' that is His people in the world, Gentiles and Jews, 'He so loved the world, that He gave,'—He *gave*—'His only begotten Son'. Possibly that is one of the most familiar Scriptures that we have, but O the beauty of it, the blessedness of it, the mercy of it, He *gave*; nothing else would accomplish the purpose designed; nothing less would fulfil the conditions of the covenant of His grace. He *gave*.

He gave Him in His eternal decrees before the world was, and this is expressed in different ways. Have you thought about this?

It is expressed like this, He did not spare Him. 'He that spared not His own Son but delivered Him up for us all.' He did not spare Him, His own Son; that seems to come very closely home, doesn't it? It was His *own* Son that He did not spare. It was a sharp trial of faith to Abraham to offer Isaac when God said to him, 'Take now thy son, thine only son Isaac, *whom thou lovest'*— (what a way of expressing it!)—'and offer him there for a burnt offering upon one of the mountains which I will tell thee of'. But O, that sacrifice of Isaac is but a shadow compared to this. He did not spare His own Son.

Then it is expressed as 'delivering Him up'. 'He delivered Him up for us all.' And why did He deliver Him up? Was it not for our offences? 'He was delivered for our offences, and was raised again for our justification.' O what an amazing contemplation! It is expressed by sending Him. In this the love of God is manifested that He *sent* His Son into the world as a propitiation for our sins; *sent* Him. Hence we read in Isaiah, 'Behold My Servant, whom I uphold; Mine Elect, in Whom My soul delighteth'.

Let us not overlook the giver of the gift. You never receive a gift, do you, without thinking of the giver? No, it is the giver as much as the gift. Then not only is the giver to be considered but the gift. O what a gift! The gift was Himself. 'When the fulness of the time was come, God sent forth His Son, made of a woman, made under the law.' To contemplate this great gift we may go to Bethlehem for a few moments and consider this amazing grace, this inexpressible gift.

Consider the conditions under which He was born, the place where He was laid; not in a palace, in a grand room with beautiful furniture and everything that the heart could wish; no, He was laid in a manger. All this was to give expression to His amazing humility. 'Though He was rich, yet for your sakes He *became* poor', although at the same time He was the eternal Son of God; but the Word was here made flesh to dwell among us. He is Emmanuel—God with us, the complex Person of our adorable Redeemer, a Babe born at Bethlehem. Think of the place where He was laid.

Think again, too, of the people to whom the news was announced; it was not to the royal family, or an assembly of dukes and nobles, but to the humble shepherds keeping watch over their flocks by night. Is there not an amazing depth of truth underlying all this? They were *the first* to whom the news was broken by the angels from heaven, this host of angels giving glory to God, saying, 'Fear not; . . . for unto you is born this day in the city of David a Saviour, which is Christ the Lord'. O what an assembly, angels from heaven appearing to the meanest, humblest subjects on earth! What a linking together of honour and humility appears at that moment when the shepherds heard the angelic hosts.

Think of the Name that was given to Him. Why did they give Him such a Name as Jesus? Because He came 'to save His people from their sins'. O if what is involved in that Name were brought into our hearts today! A Name so familiar I agree, in the Christian world, so termed, but a Name that is inexpressibly sweet when the dear Redeemer is applied to the heart in a gracious manifestation. Then you can say,

'How sweet the Name of Jesus sounds.'

Here then to consider this unspeakable gift we go in faith to Bethlehem and here we see Deity manifested, Deity revealed. God was manifest in the flesh. Never was such a birth as that, you know; His birth was *unique*. Never has there been subsequently a birth under such extraordinary, inconceivable conditions. The Holy Ghost overshadowed the virgin and said unto her, 'That holy thing which shall be born of thee shall be called the Son of God'.

'No nearer we venture than this
To gaze on a deep so profound.'

Here is Deity revealed, here is man redeemed, guilty, ruined, fallen man, rebels, wretches, steeped in sin, born in sin; here they are redeemed; here we see Satan's power destroyed over those for whom Jesus came.

Just this for a moment and then I must close. The last point is the receiving of the gift. Have you ever received Him? Because the gift will not avail you anything unless you *receive* it. Have you received Him? Perhaps you say that sounds like free will. No, not at all. Have you received Him? We read about this, the apostle Paul speaks of it, 'As ye have received Christ Jesus the Lord, so walk ye in Him'. And John, 'As many as received Him, to them gave He power to become the sons of God'. And when the Lord returned from the country of the Gadarenes 'the people gladly received Him for they were all waiting for Him'. They were in just the right place to receive Him. Have you received Him? Say you, What does that mean? I cannot explain it, but I can tell you this, when the Holy Ghost begins the work in your heart, the first thing He will do is to plough up, 'break up your fallow ground', by a conviction of your guilty sins, and by emptying from vessel to vessel, until in His own time He brings the Redeemer in the power of faith into your heart and you receive Him. O this receiving of Him! It is a choice moment when you can feel He is your Saviour, because to receive Him is to receive eternal life; He brings it with Him, if I can put it in that way; He brings it with Him when he comes. 'I give unto My sheep eternal life.' And if He comes and blesses your soul, what does He bless you with? He blesses you with eternal life! It is a receiving of His love, for the Holy Ghost sheds it abroad in the heart. All other gifts are involved in receiving Him.

But I must leave it. May the Lord grant us some little experience of this and then we shall be able to say

'Thanks be unto God for His unspeakable gift.'

GOD WORKING IN HIS PEOPLE

16 May 1954

> 'Wherefore, my beloved, as ye have always obeyed, not as in my presence only, but now much more in my absence, work out your own salvation with fear and trembling. For it is God which worketh in you both to will and to do of His good pleasure.' (Phil. 2: 12, 13)

In these two verses the apostle describes very principally what real, experimental religion is—that it consists in God working in His people according to His own sovereign will and pleasure, and in their working out their salvation with fear and trembling—that is, as we may believe it, in view of the importance and solemnity of this engagement; with fear, lest we should be deceived in our conclusions, or lest, after all, 'a promise being left us' we should come short of it; or with fear lest after all, our spot should not be the spot of the Lord's people; and with trembling, as being before God in all these things, having a humbling, sober sense of the majesty of God and of our own comparative nothingness.

It would appear then, that true godliness consists principally in three things—in what God has done *for* us; the foundation is there. This being of the first importance, everything else follows upon it. His work is a perfect work, perfect in every feature of that work; it is perfect in creation and providence, and it is perfect in grace! But not only does true godliness consist in what God has done for us, but it also consists in what He is doing *in* us. There is a very, very close connection between the work of Christ on Calvary's cross where the work of redemption was completed, and the work of God in us, which is essentially a saving, gracious knowledge of, and interest in, all that the great Redeemer accomplished on Calvary. Then there is another point in true godliness and that consists in what is brought forth *by* us—the fruits of His grace in our life, walk and conversation. These three points go very closely together, in fact, they are bound together in the salvation of a believer, although all the merit of that salvation is in Christ. *All* the merit is there! but a great many things flow out of it, that come right into the heart and soul of the Lord's dear people, who are the subjects of that salvation.

There is then, involved in the salvation of the Lord's dear people, the glorious, eternal Trinity—the Father in His work in the covenant of grace, His work in the choice of His people, the election of them according to His divine foreknowledge, and also in adopting them as His own children, whereby they are brought into a most blessed relationship, 'heirs of God and joint-heirs with Christ', are 'No more strangers and foreigners, but fellow-citizens with the saints, and of the household of God'. They are then, we must conclude, a very favoured and privileged people, to have an interest in this! The work of the Father also consists in sending forth His beloved Son, the gift of Him, in not sparing Him, but delivering Him up for us all, in causing Him thus to be made sin in bruising Him, in placing the chastisement of our peace upon Him and also in the gift of the Holy Spirit, by whose gracious, effectual teaching His people are brought to a knowledge of these things. Here, then, is the Trinity! We shall never be saved without the Trinity, although we may often feel to be in much confusion in relation to these great things, for many of the Lord's people feel their simplicity—and that is not the worst thing, if it is a means of humbling us before the Lord and working in us that prayer, 'Open Thou mine eyes, that I may behold wondrous things out of Thy law'.

Now the point I want to impress upon you is the fact that, if all these things were done *for* us, in the councils of God, if the Lord Jesus Christ did die for us, if He removed the curse for us, if He paid the mighty debt for you and for me, if He went, as it were, through hell, to deliver us from it—if all this has been done *for* us, then there will surely be, in the Lord's time, something done *in* us. It will be sure to follow, just as surely as these things have been accomplished on our behalf, because we read of the Lord Jesus Christ, that 'He shall see His seed, He shall prolong His days, and the pleasure of the LORD shall prosper in His hand'.

If, indeed, these things have been wrought in us, then there will be—there are *sure* to be—some things brought forth by us, because 'faith without works is dead'. There will be the fruits of that grace in some measure, although you and I, it may be, have to mourn and confess our barrenness—but still there will be the fruits. The point I wanted to impress is the linking of these three things together, so that the fruits brought forth by us are an evidence of the Lord having done something in us, and if the Lord has done anything in us, then that is a proof or witness that God has done all those things *for* us.

So it flows forth in this way and the Lord's children are concerned about themselves, as some of you are, as to whether your name will ever be found 'beneath your Lord the Lamb', as to whether you have any interest in God's eternal decrees, whether His pleasure was toward you from all eternity. Look inside and examine yourself, whether there has been any change wrought in you, and in some hope that there has been a change wrought in you, whether any fruits have been brought forth by you, by His grace. So we read in chapter 1, of the apostle's confidence in these Philippians in this; he was 'Confident of this very thing, that He which hath begun a good work in you will perform it until the day of Jesus Christ'.

I attempted to speak a little this morning about this working of things out, because if there is a real work of grace in our souls, it will have to be worked out, and much of the Lord's people's experience consists in this—in working it out, examining it, waiting upon God to have the matter settled in their own consciences, whether it be real or not. Much consists then in this working it out—that is, in seeking to know whether the salvation accomplished by the Son of God on Calvary was for us, whether that is our own salvation: in that desire to be brought rightly to that confidence and assurance that the Psalmist felt when he was able to say, 'The LORD is my light and my salvation; whom shall I fear? the LORD is the strength of my life; of whom shall I be afraid?' How much of this working out of things has there been with us? Do you know anything of this working out of your own salvation? earnest entreaties, cries, waiting upon the Lord to have the matter made clear and plain in your own conscience? Because if the life of God is there in our hearts, there will be a working out of things. You will look at this point, and that point, and another point, and say, Do I know anything of this? have I ever felt that? have I any real experience of this? You will look at those precious doctrines of divine grace and question whether there has ever been any application of them to your own heart, whether His blessed gospel has come to you 'in power and in the Holy Ghost'; and there will be a fear in this, because of those of whom we read that 'it comes to them in word only', and of the parable of the sower and the seed by the wayside, and stony ground, and so on. There will be a working of things out in your own case in fear and trembling. But after all, this working of things out is by means of God working in us; this is the apostle's answer to the question, 'For it is God which worketh in you both to will and to do of His good pleasure'. This seems to be to show us the truth of what we have been singing (202) that salvation is all of His grace from first to last, because nothing will ever be worked out, but what God has first worked in; and this can be, in one sense, very confirming.

If you find yourself engaged, concerned, anxious, lively before the Lord, in relation to your own case, find yourself having to work things out, examining things, proving things, waiting upon the Lord in things, that means that God has not only done something *for* you, but has done something *in* you. O, how we need to be brought to a point in this! 'It is God which worketh in you to will and to do of His good pleasure.' There is, then, such a thing in religion as having God working in us; in fact, no religion has any divine reality in it, unless God is in it, in His saving, divine teaching. That is what makes it real, and gives it such lasting issues. O, can you look within your heart and feel there a hope that God has worked something in you of His good pleasure?

But what are these things—to come to points? Points, in a sense, without being too cut-and-dried, are helpful, because points rightly used, serve somewhat better to the retaining of things in our memories. There is a working of God in us in several different particulars; in the first place it is God Who works in us a spirit of conviction and a sense of our own ruin and guilty condition before Him. In a sense we all know what sin is in its outward aspect, but very few know what sin is in its inward aspect, as before a heart-searching God. Many have broken the laws of the land and know that they sinned in doing it, who have never had God coming to them, searching them as with candles and opening and discovering to them the innermost recesses of their heart. But this is God's work and there is no real conviction of sin unless it is by God working it in us. Man, by nature is ruined, lost, 'dead in trespasses and sins', but he never really knows that, to feel it and to mourn over it, till God works conviction in him and discovers to him his lost and ruined condition, reveals to him His holy law and, by His Spirit, charges that law home upon the conscience to its own condemnation, bringing there 'the sentence of death'. This is a wonderful work. This brings one to say and feel as the Psalmist, when he confessed before the Lord, 'Against Thee, Thee only, have I sinned, and done this evil in Thy sight: that Thou mightest be justified when Thou speakest, and be clear when Thou judgest'. It is a mercy to be brought there and it is only God brings us there. We can be full of religion of a kind, without ever being brought there; but if we are brought there, by God working this conviction in us, then we shall be 'emptied from vessel to vessel'; we shall lose and have to part with everything that we have, as the apostle Paul did, when he said, 'What things were gain to me, those I counted loss for Christ'. God brings His dear people to a very solemn sense of their own poverty; He shows them that they have nothing to be proud of in themselves, but much to be deeply ashamed of before Him. He works it in us—and He will work it in you. If you are going to heaven, one thing God will work in you is the fact that you deserve hell, and He will bring you to such a place as to acknowledge His justice in it too; He will work this conviction in you, and it is a mercy where that is so, because where this emptying-out business is bringing down, stripping, wounding, killing, there will be a humble, sober sense of the solemnity of eternal things, the value of an immortal soul, and the unspeakable blessedness of being prepared for eternity. Has the Lord ever worked that in you? Has there ever been a time when you have had to fall before Him with nothing but filthy rags, full of shame and confusion of face, like 'Joshua the high Priest standing before the angel of the Lord, . . . clothed with filthy garments'.

Another thing the Lord works in His people is repentance and godly sorrow for sin. Legal repentance is in the power of nature. A person may have very deep remorse for some sin he has committed; a prisoner in the court of justice may have very painful regrets for the things which he is charged with, and brought under the law for. All that kind of repentance can be in the power of nature; but gospel repentance has to be worked in us by the Lord Himself, because it is His own gift, the Lord Jesus Christ being exalted at His Father's right hand to give it. 'Him hath God exalted with His right hand to be a Prince and a Saviour, for to give repentance to Israel, and forgiveness of sins.' Has the Lord ever wrought that in you? Can you look into your own heart and trace it, at any time, in your life? a little real grief and godly sorrow for sin? Perhaps you have to say, as all the Lord's people have to say, I wish I could feel more repentance and have more godly sorrow for my sin, but I am so hard, cold, and indifferent, I cannot seem to bring forth anything good; all I can do is to bring forth sin. Well, that shows how you depend upon God to work it in you, and mercifully He does; and when He does work it in you of His good pleasure, then it will be a sweet repentance. O, it is a sweet repentance then, a repentance joined to joy in your heart, that His free, holy mercy should ever have flowed into the heart of a wretch like you, or like me! Repentance is very sacred where it is real and produced by godly sorrow and a sight and sense of a suffering Saviour; it is very, very sweet.

'A sinner may repent and sing,
Rejoice and be ashamed.'

Well, has God ever worked in you this repentance? It is very peculiar—there is a brokenness of spirit with it. It is not a hard kind of feeling, as though you would say, Well, I must try and work up something good in me, if I can. No, this repentance—well—it just flows out. Sometimes you may get just a little touch of it when you are praying, or you may have just a spot of it when you are going to business, or may get just a little softening of it in the silent watches of the night; but in each instance it has to be worked in. Those rightly instructed will not say, I will exercise a little repentance; no, they have to prove that it is God who worketh it in them; and when He works it in, there is such a sweet communion and love flowing one to the other, 'It is God that worketh in us to will and to do of His good pleasure'.

Another thing that God works in us, is a spirit of prayer and importunity. I say, a *spirit* of prayer because it is what you feel in your heart; you cannot give yourself a spirit of prayer, although you may say many a prayer; but this access that the Lord's people feel, has to be worked in them. Those occasions when you are favoured to get near to God in prayer, when you can take to Him your difficulties, the load that presses upon you, the burden of tomorrow, the concerns of your daily life, your prospects, your fears, the mountains that rise before you, and all these things; when you are helped to take them before the Lord in prayer and have access to Him, unload your heart, cast your care upon Him; all this is done by God working in us a spirit of prayer. In Romans 8, this is proved by what the apostle says of the Holy Spirit. 'Likewise the Spirit also helpeth our infirmities: for we know not what we should pray for as we ought: but the Spirit itself maketh intercession for us with groanings which cannot be uttered.' God must work in us that spirit, to pray for that which is according to His will to bestow upon us. Do you ever find anything of this working in you? the Lord working this in you, thus to wait upon Him, cast your care upon Him, commit your way to Him, and put your trust in Him? It is God which worketh in you.

Another thing God works in His people is a spirit of faith, this also being His precious gift. In John 6 the Lord said to His disciples 'This is the work of God, that ye believe on Him Whom He hath sent'. Many people think they can believe of their own will. It is true they may assent to things and say they believe this or that, but real believing goes much deeper than all this; it is a manifestation of the truth in your soul by the Spirit of God. He will have to work faith in you, because the Lord Jesus Christ is the Author and Finisher of it and it is very, very sweet when a little of this faith is worked in us by the Lord. He can work in you faith to bring you through, to help you over the mountain, conquer your enemies and bring you forth from them all. He can work faith in you to believe that He will bring you through, above all that you ask or think. As I have often said, it is very sweet to believe; it brings such a rest. The walls of Jericho can fall flat when you believe; when God works this faith in you, nothing is impossible! You can take up the challenge then which the Lord gave to Abraham, when He said to him, 'Is any thing too hard for the LORD?' Faith is a wonderful grace! One moment you may look ahead and say, however can I face this or that, how can I come through this or that trial? Then when faith is brought into exercise, when the Lord works faith in you, you can say, He will bring me through, He is sufficient, He is the Almighty God, He will not fail or forsake me. But He must work this faith in us; it makes such a difference when the Lord works faith in us. It is altogether different from one saying, I will make up my mind to believe, I will put my trust in Him. An effort of something in ourselves may often tumble to pieces, because it is, more or less, a resolve of nature in us; but when God works faith there is a getting hold of Him, and when you get hold of Him, you can let go of everything else. As soon as you see God above the ladder, you see everything else at the foot. It is a mercy to have faith to lay hold of God and plead His own promise.

Another thing God works in His people is a spirit of love. Has He ever worked that in you? Has there ever been a moment in your life when you have felt you loved Him? when it has just come like that? when, perhaps, after a long time of bondage, trouble, and confusion, there has been a sweet flowing of His mercy into your soul? Then there is such a reviving, such a turning out of the unclean birds and a taking possession of you by Himself, when the Holy Ghost has shed His love abroad in your heart? O, it is sweet to love Him! The religion of Jesus Christ is a religion of love! I believe that, because love moved Him to do all that He did for His dear people. They are rebels, so faint, and so poor; yet still it remains true that 'we love Him because He first loved us'. 'It is God which worketh in you both to will and to do of His good pleasure.'

Then there are other things. For instance, He works submission. You may be in affliction, under a heavy cross, walking in a heavy trial, and you say, I will make the best of this because all my worry about this and that will not help matters; I will try to leave it all. You may try; but unless God works this holy submission in your heart, it will be a poor leaving, and in all probability you will find it crop up with more force than ever; but when He works submission in you, you can 'lie passive in His hands and know no will but His'. This is altogether different, is it not? because He works it in you. Then just for a few moments you can be torn between tempestuous motion and a very sweet submission. A Father's hand puts submission into your cup, and you can drink it when He works this submission in you, and believe all things will work well for you in His purposes. Has He ever worked that in you? As to this submission, it is felt sometimes just for a few minutes, and when you can feel it just for a few minutes, everything else seems to fall into its proper place, you can say, 'He hath done all things well'. He works it in you; *He* must work it in you.

Not only does He work submission, but He works patience, because He is the God of patience. You may say, I am going to be patient in this, and not let my old nature get the upper hand; and perhaps you have hardly said it, before your old nature gets a bigger victory than ever before; but when God works it in you, you would not move a straw. Then you say, I must walk in this as He helps me by His grace. It is a given patience. The apostle said to the Hebrews, 'Ye have need of patience, that, after ye have done the will of God, ye might receive the promise'. Other things, as endurance, He works in His people, by giving them to prove His sufficiency in their time of need, and helping them through what may appear to be insurmountable difficulties. Has God ever worked anything in you?

Then it says He works in us to will and to do of His good pleasure. He works in us to will, that is to say, He works that will in us. In the Revelation we have it, 'And the Spirit and the bride say, Come. And let him that heareth say, Come. And let him that is athirst come. And whosoever will, let him take the water of life freely.' And you will take it too. Some of you have taken it. There is such a thing as taking the water of life freely, receiving the blessed gospel in your heart; when God works the will you are willing. Not only does He work *to will*, but also *to do*. The works of faith He works in us. James says, 'Faith without works is dead'. The will in this way He works in faith not meritoriously, but in effect—in the fruits which are borne, corresponding fruits. He works a willing mind to do this and to do that. He works a willingness in the heart to do that which will be for His own honour and glory and for the good of His people. He works that work of faith in them, of which Paul speaks in writing to the Thessalonians, 'Remembering without ceasing your work of faith, and labour of love, and patience of hope'. The Lord works this labour of love, you see, whether it may be to any who are sick, or to His cause, or whatever it may be, or however humble; He works a willing mind to do it. He gives both. 'It is God which worketh in you both to will and to do of His good pleasure.' Everything works out according to the pleasure of His own will. Thus it was His pleasure to afflict and bruise His own beloved Son, and so it is His pleasure thus to work these things in His dear people. Everything that is worked in you, is worked in you then by His good pleasure, that is, as He shall dispose, some in one way, some in another, more particularly, or more deeply. Some may be called in one thing more clearly and deeply and some in another; although it is His good pleasure that 'all shall be taught of God'. It is God that worketh in you, so the working out of our own salvation follows this up and shows and reveals the fact that God has been working in us. May the Lord grant us some little experience of these things.

THE WORK OF FAITH AND LABOUR OF LOVE

11 September 1955

> 'Remembering without ceasing your work of faith, and labour of love, and patience of hope in our Lord Jesus Christ, in the sight of God and our Father: Knowing, brethren beloved, your election of God.' (1 Thessalonians 1: 3, 4)

WE made some observations this morning in relation to the apostle's particular feeling of confidence with regard to these Thessalonian believers; that they were the children of God, and were eternally chosen—elect according to His divine foreknowledge—in the covenant of grace. What a wonderful mercy it is to feel that of anyone, and to feel it of ourselves! to feel a right and well-grounded hope, at least, that God had purposes of mercy from all eternity toward us, though we are not deserving of the least of His mercy.

It ought to be noted that the apostle observes three particular ways in which the gospel came to these Thessalonians—he speaks of it as coming to them, or as of their receiving it, 'in power, and in the Holy Ghost'. O what a mercy it is to feel something of the authority and power of the gospel in our hearts! There is something saving in this; it is altogether different from a mere form of godliness, or from just having a formal profession of religion. When the gospel comes into your heart with power, you will feel it, and will be able to say, as we were singing this morning:

> 'The gospel bears my spirit up;
> A faithful and unchanging God
> Lays the foundation of my hope
> In oaths, and promises, and blood.'

Not only did they receive it in its gracious power and efficacy but they received it not as the word of men but as the word of God. The apostle speaks of it 'effectually working in them that believe'. So he states that when they received the word of God which they heard preached by the apostle and Timotheus, they 'received it, not as the word of men, but as it is in truth, the word of God, which effectually worketh also in you that believe'. O what a mercy it is to feel a little, at least, of the effectual working of the truth in our souls! In such a case it is not received as man's word, as though one were preaching something of his own, but as the word of God.

Has there ever been a time with you when you have felt to receive the truth in, and by, the ministry, not as the word of men, not as merely something the poor minister may be trying to say, but as feeling an authority in it, receiving it as the word of God, and feeling it effectually working in your heart?

Thirdly, they received it not only as the word of God, but also in much affliction. 'Ye became followers of us, and of the Lord, having received the word in much affliction, with joy of the Holy Ghost.' So, then, they had some joy in their affliction. The gospel brought a joy to them. They were in much affliction, probably under much persecution for the gospel's sake, but still they counted it all joy when they fell into those divers temptations. So I believe it often is with the Lord's people—the gospel is received in much affliction. Sin is an affliction; and when sin is felt, mourned over, and grieved over in the heart, when one's state as a sinner brings godly sorrow and repentance, there the gospel, as applied to the heart, brings a sweet healing, a joy, comfort, strength and peace.

Here the apostle refers to their 'work of faith'. 'Remembering without ceasing your work of faith.' The work of faith and the trial of faith are very closely linked together; faith will have its work and faith will have its trial. The work of faith may consist principally in receiving what the Lord is pleased to apply to us. The work of faith is in receiving the promises, but not only in receiving the promises—it also consists in receiving reproof, divine chastening, admonitions, and sometimes timely exhortations. When the Lord's chastening hand is upon us, it is the work of faith 'to hear the rod and who hath appointed it'. Unbelief, pride and hardness that is in us all, more or less, will rise up against it, but it is the work of faith to receive the correction; it is the work of faith to render praise for it; it is the work of faith to believe that it is appointed in love, and it is the work of faith to believe that

> 'The lash is steeped He on thee lays
> And softened in His blood.'

It is the work of faith to submit to the will of God in His disposing of matters that may concern us, to be still, and know that He is God, to prove that 'in quietness and in confidence shall be your strength'. And while we are here in this wilderness there will always be 'the work of faith'. Sometimes this work of faith consists in battling with the uprisings of unbelief in your heart. Faith will rise up, and pride and resentment will rise up; in fact, sometimes they seem to prevail and the spirit sinks; but it is the work of faith in the deep waters to lay hold on and cleave to the Rock, and trust alone in an unchanging and all-sufficient God. Sometimes it is the work of faith to go forth in things, in difficulties, in matters that may come in your daily life, in certain hard and, it may be, heavy things that you may have before you in a day. Perhaps you may arise in the morning and have matters of a burdensome and difficult nature that you may feel altogether unfit to cope with. What then? Well, it is the work of faith to take those matters to the Lord, to seek strength to wait upon Him, and ask Him to level a mountain for you or raise a valley for you, if it be according to His divine will.

I must reaffirm what I said this morning, that this work of faith is by His good Spirit; it is not something to play with, or do what we will or wish with; but you may sometimes distinctly feel the work and victory of faith, in being helped to overcome some difficulties or to walk in some peculiarly trying path, to bear some particularly heavy cross, or to be sustained in and under some affliction.

It is the work of faith to receive divine teaching; it is the work of faith to receive the Lord Jesus; it is the work of faith to renounce all for His sake, as the apostle did when he 'counted all things but dung', that he might win Christ, and be found in Him. 'Remembering without ceasing your work of faith.' Although, if I had grace I might dilate a long time more upon this, I would seek this evening to consider the second point.

'Remembering without ceasing your work of faith and labour

of love'. These are, as I hinted this morning, very closely connected. Work and labour imply, of course, the same thing, although perhaps the term labour may indicate some greater difficulty. Some kinds of work may be comparatively easy, but to labour for this or that matter, or in this or that thing, suggests some difficulty and the need of grace and perseverance. So the apostle speaks here of a labour of love. This can be considered in the first place in relation to love to God. It is said in the Scripture that 'we love Him because He first loved us'. That is a very blessed truth—the former is a proof of the latter. You will never love the Lord unless it be that He first loved you. Moreover, that love that you feel toward Him, is a proof of His eternal love toward you. But, O my friends, sometimes, at least, there may be a great labour in this love. Good John Newton said in one hymn,

> ''Tis a point I long to know,
> Oft it causes anxious thought;
> Do I love the Lord, or no?
> Am I His, or am I not?'

This may be a great point then, and here a labour may come in as to whether you do truly love the Lord or not, because sometimes, you see, the old enemy will say, what you thought was a little love to the Lord was just a spasm of natural emotion; you thought you had a little softness, but there was not anything in it after all. People of the world can shed a tear as well as you. All kinds of things he can tell you and then you will find yourself in a dilemma and conflict—Was that which I felt love to the Lord or not? Then there will be a labour. What kind of labour? Well, in waiting upon the Lord for a testimony that it was real. And sometimes the Lord is pleased to give a testimony of this reality by a fresh touch. When you get a fresh touch you can say, This is what I felt before, bless His holy Name; I do not want anything different. You see, we shall never rise altogether above this inward conflict.

I remember in my very early days, going one day to Hanover Chapel. Mr Newton was preaching, and they had that hymn

> ''Tis a point I long to know,
> Oft it causes anxious thought;
> Do I love the Lord, or no?
> Am I His, or am I not?'

and when dear Mr Newton began to preach he spoke like this: You could not have had a hymn more suitable to my feelings than that, for it is exactly how I feel. What?, I said, what? do you mean to say that *you*, a minister and a pastor all these years, have not got any higher than that? Do you mean to say it is a point *you* long to know, after all this, whether you love the Lord or not? Yes, he said, it *is*, and he said there was never a time when that language was more suitable to his own feelings than it was that evening. Well, you see, that left rather a sweet memory, especially since I have been in the ministry myself, because the Lord's servants get into very low water sometimes, even if they do not say much about it; they get into very low water, so that they can preach about it; and in fact, they have to get into low water, and feel as opposite as they could feel to those good things they preach about. But whatever ministers' feelings may be, here is the blessed truth.

This labour consists in a seeking unto God to have love shed abroad in the heart. 'O, when wilt Thou come unto Me?' Lord, do make that love manifest in my poor heart. Can it be possible I am one of Thy children? Make it known to me. Soften this hard, stony, rocky, flinty heart of mine. Lord, I cannot soften it. Grant me a touch of Thy mercy. What is all this? I believe it is a labour of love. But why all this labour of love? Is it not because you do love Him? Because if you did not love Him, although perhaps you do not feel it to your satisfaction, but if you did not love Him, there would be no waiting upon Him to have that love shed abroad; there would be no desire for it. Do you feel something like the Church in the Canticles, where she says, 'Tell me, O Thou Whom my soul loveth, where Thou feedest, where Thou makest Thy flock to rest at noon, for why should I be as one that turneth aside by the flocks of Thy companions?' It seems there was a labour of love there. There was a labour of love in her desire to be brought to places of feeding, to be with the flock and to partake of the same food, enjoy the same company, to mingle with those to whom she felt a union of heart, and, most of all, to be where the Shepherd was, where the Lord comes and feeds His flock. O, this labour of love! Sometimes this labour of love, which is a love to the Lord, is under a dark and heavy cloud with regard to one's state of soul, and in much darkness at times too, and on some occasions in, and under, things of a very weakening and distracting nature. O, in your heart you say, Nothing is so sweet as this love. O that I could but love Him; and sometimes when you are thus cogitating, you may feel it flow in, you get it; the touch comes, the Lord makes Himself precious, and then the labour is well rewarded; not because you merited it, but because of the Lord's great compassion. When that is the case you have to say,

> 'Compared with Christ, in all beside,
> No comeliness I see;
> The one thing needful, dearest Lord,
> Is to be one with Thee.'

Well, do you have any labour of love as toward the Lord Himself?

Love has a labour in another direction from this, although flowing out of it, and that is as the apostle mentions in this epistle, love to one another, love to the brethren in the gospel, which is to be distinguished from natural affection, although there may be both, of course; but the love here is of a spiritual nature, and it is very sweet to feel it; it is an evidence of divine life in the soul, if rightly understood. I know some people have almost based their standing for eternity upon feeling a little love to the Lord's people, because the apostle said, 'We know that we have passed from death unto life, because we love the brethren'. But we need to remember that the love the apostle refers to there is the love that flows out of love to the Lord Jesus Christ. You love the brethren because they love Him, because they love the same Jesus that you love, and that knits your heart to them; it is a gospel love; it is as foreign to natural sentiment as the North and South Poles. It is a spiritual bond that joins and unites the Lord's dear people together, and though, naturally speaking, they may have very much to try them, and to try one another too, in their natural mentality and disposition, still, here it is, and it is very sweet to feel that love in the gospel to the Lord's people. 'Let brotherly love continue.' How blessed it is when this love in the gospel is a means of rightly removing unfriendly feelings or jealousies or differences. This is where the labour of love comes in and it is a very blessed thing when it prevails to the sinking down of other things, which in themselves may be a barrier or a stumblingstone. Even naturally speaking, there is nothing to compare with love. It is said to be the best rag of poor, fallen human nature, and so it is, for after all, apart from anything else, this world would be an arid waste if there were no natural ties and bands of affection, uniting one and another together in that which the Lord has designed. O, it is very sweet to feel a little love in your heart to the Lord Jesus. I remember years ago, working in my shop in Brighton when I felt such a love to the Lord Jesus in my heart that I looked out of the window and said, If I saw a tramp going down the street, if he was one of the Lord's children I could love him, whoever he was. Perhaps you may get a moment like this.

This labour of love may often consist in battling against, and seeking to overcome things of an earthly nature which tend to divide the Lord's people. There can be a flowing together to the goodness of the Lord even when things are somewhat trying and difficult. Should there not be? After all, if we are the Lord's people, as we hope we are, some of us, when we come to think of what He has done for us in delivering our poor souls from eternal death; when we think of His love to us, what He has gone through, suffered and endured; when we think of the love that many waters could not quench and many flames could not burn; when we think of the love from which nothing can separate; then should it not be in the hearts of the Lord's people to labour in this love? that is, should there not be a labour of love one toward another in the gospel, as having professed the Lord's Name? O, so many things are not right, so many things are wrong in me; and we shall never find perfection in the flesh.

Then again, this labour of love in a gospel sense, may sometimes consist in forgiving injuries, and that is a labour of love because, you see, if one should smite you on one cheek, it is not in poor, fallen human nature to invite him to smite you on the other cheek too—and yet that is what the Lord said in His Sermon on the Mount. There can be a very great and profitable labour of love, even in this. After all, you know, if the Lord's love touches your heart, if it does, when it does, if one should injure us when that love is felt, all the harm we can do him is to try and pray for him and that is like 'turning the other cheek also', for that is the best way, and often the surest way, of gaining the victory. 'If thine enemy hunger, feed him; if he thirst, give him drink; for in so doing thou shalt heap coals of fire on his head.' O this labour of love when it prevails in heaping coals of fire on the head of an enemy, indeed it has gained its point and it will make him feel ashamed of his treatment of you and acknowledge it too.

This work of faith and labour of love consists in another point, and that is in endeavouring to 'keep the unity of the Spirit in the bond of peace'. This is a labour of love because the old enemy will always be trying to sow the seeds of discord, if he can, among the Lord's people; he is very busy at that kind of business. Moreover, if he can divide in any way, if he can wedge in with his cloven hoof, he will, and divide the Lord's people; he will divide the church if he can. O what unhappy things have taken place in many churches. This labour of love will consist in endeavouring to keep the unity of the Spirit in the bond of peace. Not peace at any price, just going with the stream, countenancing all things or glossing everything over, as though it does not matter—we will love one another and that is all there is about it, and passing by what is really wrong and displeasing in the Lord's sight—that is not a labour of love in the right sort of way at all, because it can bring the Lord's displeasure upon us. But this labour of love is in endeavouring to keep the unity of the Spirit in the bond of peace, with an eye to the Lord's honour and glory in the church. Many have had to suffer for their faithfulness, many have had to suffer for giving what may be a timely reproof, although perhaps in the tenderest word possible and in a spirit of love, which was a labour of love rightly considered; but there must be faithfulness with it, and a right 'contending for the faith once delivered unto the saints'. 'Remembering without ceasing your labour of love.'

This labour of love consists also in ministering to the needs and necessities of the Lord's people in their afflictions. The apostle James defines real religion in its effects and proofs, as made manifest in this sense; he says, 'Pure religion and undefiled before God and the Father is this, To visit the fatherless and widows in their affliction, and to keep himself unspotted from the world'. I am the last one to say much about this, because of my own shortcomings, but here is the point and, moreover,

James says, 'Is any sick among you? let him call for the elders of the church; and let them pray over him'. The 'elders' may be deacons or ministers or even a private member—'let them pray over him, anointing him with oil in the Name of the Lord'. Here is a labour of love. Now and again, I believe I have felt it sweet to try to pray with the Lord's people in their afflictions; here and there it has been a choice spot, with a little sweet softening of heart in waiting upon the Lord sometimes by the bedside of an afflicted saint. There have, at times, been some very choice moments. This is a labour of love.

Of course, in those days particularly, in which the apostle wrote, and up to more recent times, there is a labour of love in ministering to the necessities of those who may be deprived of the needful things of this life. From the very first the apostles practised and gave direction for the poor to be considered, and to be helped and relieved in their necessities. In writing to the Philippians the apostle makes particular reference to their practical consideration of him, in what they did for him, assuring them that his God would supply all their need.

This labour of love comes in many ways, even in relation to public duties, it is a labour of love, a sacrifice made for the Lord's sick, or in attempting anything for the spiritual welfare or well-being of others, as in instructing children in the truth, or in ministering the gospel for the Lord's sake, in holding any position in the church of God that involves responsibility and anxieties, in taking up the cross for His Name's sake. The labour of love comes in all these things, and of this the apostle felt confident concerning these Thessalonians. 'Remembering without ceasing your work of faith, and labour of love and patience of hope.'

'Patience of hope.' Hope is a grace that relates principally to the future and fundamentally to that which 'the Lord has promised to those who love Him', to the entering into that inheritance which He has laid up for His dear people. Now we will say you feel a hope of heaven in your heart. Well then, what need is there of any patience? You will need patience in this vale of tears, in this path of tribulation, in holding on in hope, until that hope is fulfilled. The patience of hope will consist in this, because many things may come to try it. It may be a hope that seems sometimes almost to be lost sight of. The apostle speaking to the Romans said, 'Hope that is seen is not hope: for what a man seeth, why doth he yet hope for?' But if the hope of eternal life is in you, patience will be needed, patience of hope, because of all the difficulties that may attend your pilgrimage, until that day when it shall be 'Absent from the body—present with the Lord'.

Sometimes the patience of hope is exercised by deferred answers to prayers, in our matters, or in our souls, under or in the fulfilling of some particular promise that we may hope and believe the Lord has given us. If you have a promise given you you may have to go through a great deal before the promise is fulfilled, and this is where the patience of hope comes in. James says, 'Let patience have her perfect work, that ye may be perfect and entire, wanting nothing'.

I shall have to leave it now; but in this verse the apostle says all this is 'in the sight of God and our Father'. All is in His sight, and, moreover, all this labour of love and patience of hope centre in our Lord Jesus Christ. It is a hope that is built upon His love and righteousness, it is a hope that is fixed upon Him. All these three things are 'in the sight of God and our Father', and in the exercise of them and the preparation of handling them, and the manifestation of them, the apostle saw the proof of their election. 'Knowing, brethren beloved, your election of God.' We are not able to prove our election of God by searching the divine registers, by looking into the Lamb's Book of Life of which we read, to see if our name is there, to convince ourselves, but rather in the fruits that attend this divine choice, in the work of faith, and labour of love and patience of hope, and in the power of the gospel in our souls. It is as though the apostle would say, Now, beloved brethren, I see your election of God in this work of faith, I see your election of God in this labour of love, I see your election in this patience of hope; he felt assured of it.

May the Lord grant it to us and may He give us grace to receive what I have spoken, in a spirit of love, and may we have grace to follow Him, and one day, by His great mercy, be with Him where sin no more defiles.

THE PIERCED SAVIOUR

17 November 1957

'For these things were done, that the Scripture should be fulfilled, A bone of Him shall not be broken. And again another Scripture saith, They shall look on Him Whom they pierced.' (John 19: 36, 37)

In comparatively few verses here, we have recorded a matter that will fill heaven! If you and I have an interest in it, it will fill our heaven, and ultimately bring us there, to praise and bless the holy Lamb of God for ever and ever. As our eyes are opened, in any measure, to the solemnities of eternity, we shall realize that the highest honour that God can confer upon a sinful man, is to give him a part and interest in the gospel, in the love of God and in the atoning sacrifice and precious blood of the dear Redeemer, and eventually, upon that ground, open to him the gates of heaven and grant to him an abundant entrance there. On the other hand, the most awful calamity that can befall sinful man, is to live and die ignorant, hard, careless, indifferent, unconcerned about these tremendous issues, die in his sins, and sink to the bottomless pit. O, how can we bless God enough for the gospel? Favoured souls are they, who can feel to have some standing for eternity! Indeed blessed are they, who long to feel the cleansing flood and more so, they who hope they have had a taste of pardoning love, through the precious blood of Christ applied to their consciences. O happy indeed are they who feel a hope of heaven and an interest in these blessed realities!

This chapter records some particulars of the Saviour's crucifixion at Calvary. Though there are heights and depths that must ever confound us, yet here we are assured, without any question, that He did indeed, literally, die a physical death; moreover, that His holy side was pierced and that blood and water issued therefrom. This is referred to in the Revelation; 'Behold, He cometh with clouds; and every eye shall see Him, and they also which pierced Him: and all kindreds of the earth shall wail because of Him. Even so, Amen.' So such a word embraces everyone in this congregation; some will wail because of Him and others will be filled with holy peace and joy. It would seem according to that word, that *all* shall see Him, *every* eye shall see Him, and they also which pierced Him, some to their eternal condemnation, some to their eternal justification. Moreover, is it not also predicted by Zechariah in his prophecy, 'I will pour upon the house of David, and the inhabitants of Jerusalem, the spirit of grace and of supplications: and they shall look upon Me Whom they have pierced, and they shall mourn for Him, as one mourneth for his only son.' There will then be those who will have godly sorrow, contrition—yet mingled with a sacred sense of pardoning mercy and love, as faith views that wounded side, and others who shall call upon the rocks and mountains to hide them from His wrath.

These words are very speaking, are they not? 'One of the soldiers with a spear pierced His side, and forthwith came there out blood and water.' May it not be a noticeable point to observe here, that the piercing of the Redeemer's holy side was not the cause of His death? For we read before this, that Jesus said, after He had received the vinegar, 'It is finished', bowed His head, and gave up the ghost. Are not these some of the most profound, solemn, sacred, and far-reaching words in Holy Scripture? He said, in the midst of that inconceivable agony, 'It is finished'; then 'He bowed His head, and gave up the ghost'. This indicated submission to the will of His Father, that the cup was passing from Him, the bitter ingredients had been taken, and the cup of divine wrath exhausted. Justice had drawn its sword and smitten the innocent Surety, had sought satisfaction and found it, and had no need to go any further. Justice was satisfied there. He said, 'It is finished!' That is to say, when the Redeemer died the work of redemption and substitution was complete. He bowed His head! Ordinarily the head would fall from physical exhaustion, but the Saviour bowed His head in token of submission to His Father's will, indicating thereby that the work was accomplished. O, have we ever heard such a voice, indicating that it was for us? 'It is finished; and He bowed His head, and gave up the ghost.'

'Then the Jews, because it was the preparation day, desired

that the bodies should not remain on the cross on the Sabbath day, and besought Pilate that their legs might be broken and that they might be taken away. Then came the soldiers, and brake the legs of the first, and of the other which was crucified with Him.' They apparently did not go first to Jesus. Are there not things beyond our understanding in this? They went to the two thieves (one a vessel of mercy, and the other a vessel of wrath) and brake their legs to dispatch them. O, sad to think of indeed! a suffering, a lingering death, for still life lingered; so they brake their legs. A solemn thought this! Wonderful indeed that one should have proved to be a vessel of mercy and before he died, prayed, 'Lord, remember me, when Thou comest into Thy kingdom'. 'But when they came to Jesus, and saw that He was dead already, they brake not His legs.' But why all this? 'That the Scripture should be fulfilled, A bone of Him shall not be broken.' They brake not His legs. O, is it not striking to observe, that even those Roman soldiers were directed to fulfil Scripture, though as far as we can tell they may have known nothing about it? That the Scripture should be fulfilled, they brake not *His* legs. 'A bone of Him shall not be broken.'

This was the case with the type—when the children of Israel came forth from Egypt on their deliverance, the paschal lamb was slain and eaten, according to the divine directions, but they were not to break a bone thereof. 'Neither shall ye break a bone thereof', a type of the dear Redeemer in this sense, and, moreover, that the Scripture should so be fulfilled, 'A bone of Him shall not be broken'. A bone may indicate strength in the body, and so may indicate the strength of the dear Redeemer to fulfil all that was committed to Him, and laid upon Him—the bone being a solid part of the body. Yet it may also be observed that inasmuch as the church is His body, mystically viewed, not one member shall be broken, lost, for whom He laid down His life.

'Again another Scripture saith, They shall look on Him Whom they pierced.' There was, then, a literal piercing of the side of Emmanuel after His decease. Seeing that He was dead already, that the Scripture might be fulfilled, they brake not His legs, but a soldier pierced His side, which would have caused instant death otherwise, and this too that the Scripture should be fulfilled. Wonderful thought this! But let us remember that the dear Redeemer had already paid the price, laid down His life. His human soul had entered heaven which we can believe according to the dear Saviour's word to the dying thief, 'Today shalt thou be with Me in paradise'. So the piercing of His side was not the cause of His death, but that the Scripture should be fulfilled. The piercing of the Redeemer's side was also an indication of those two wonderful blessings that should flow from His death in the sanctification and justification of all His dear people. This was the 'fountain opened for sin and for uncleanness', predicted in Zechariah 13: 1. It was necessary then for His side thus to be pierced, that Zechariah's prophecy should be fulfilled and, moreover, that there should thus be a fountain opened for sin and for uncleanness; so His holy side was pierced, and there came out the water to cleanse, the blood to atone, to wash away the filth and the guilt of sin that must otherwise have been our everlasting ruin. O, it is wonderful to get a glimpse, by faith, of this and to feel a hope, in some measure, that His side was pierced for us, and that the precious blood that flowed from His wounded side, was to atone for our guilty, black, vile sins. Well might one say,

> 'Let us our loved Redeemer meet
> Weep o'er His pierced hands and feet
> And view His wounded side.'

O, has it ever been so with you? Have *you* known that never-to-be-forgotten moment, when *you* looked upon Him Whom *you* pierced? Hart says,

> 'They nailed Him to the accursed tree;
> (They did, my brethren; so did we); *So did we*!
> The soldier pierced His side, 'tis true,
> But we have pierced Him thro' and thro'.'

Just a moment's further consideration upon this point. It may be observed by the Scripture, that not only was the dear Saviour *literally* pierced by the spear of the soldier, but there was a deeper piercing by the hand of justice. Justice drew its sword and smote the innocent Surety. In Isaiah 53 it is so declared 'Yet it pleased the Lord to bruise Him'. A profound Scripture this—'It pleased the LORD to bruise Him.' When the dear Saviour was on the Mount of Transfiguration, and when He was baptized in Jordan, the Father's voice was heard, saying, 'This is My beloved Son, in Whom I am well pleased', and yet it pleased the LORD to bruise Him! 'He was wounded' we read (striking words indeed). 'He was wounded for *our* transgressions, He was bruised for our iniquities: the chastisement of our peace was upon Him; and with His stripes we are healed.' O, does that mean you? Does that mean me? Can it be that such poor, worthless worms as we are wrapped up in such a statement? Was He delivered for *our* offences, and raised again for *our* justification? The hand of justice wounded Him—which was a terrible wound; indeed, it must have been a terrible wound!

> 'Many hands were raised to wound Him,
> None would interpose to save,
> But the awful stroke that found Him,
> Was the stroke that justice gave.'

But not only was the Redeemer thus pierced by the hand of justice, but He was pierced also by His people. He was pierced in His heart by His dear people, whose sins were thus laid upon Him, which were a load, a burden, overwhelming, that sunk His soul 'in deep mire', as we read, 'where there is no standing', and into deep waters, where the floods did overflow Him. O, when we think of this, what an awful thing is sin! What a price was called for—to atone for sin and to ransom us from eternal death! 'They shall look on Him whom they pierced.'

'These things were done, that the Scripture should be fulfilled.' So we may conclude by this, that literally speaking, the Saviour was pierced by the sword of the Roman soldier, He was pierced by the hand of justice, and He was pierced by the sins of His people. But it is said here, 'They shall look on Him whom they pierced'. There were some standing by who were eyewitnesses of this, and of the sufferings of Christ, as the Apostle Peter speaks: 'We have not followed cunningly devised fables' in this, it was a literal fact; but the view of faith is deeper—to gaze upon those wounds by faith, is deeper, and can, indeed, be more real where that revelation is given. Some, it may be, saw the piercing of the Redeemer, who had no part or lot in the matter, but some of them had. We read, 'Every eye shall see Him, and they also which pierced Him'.

This flowing forth, then, of the blood and water, sets forth the all-sufficient efficacy of His precious death; it ensures your heaven and mine, if we have a part in it. Is it not an amazing consideration that He should go to such depths as these? suffer such inward pangs of soul, and pains of body, for a wretch like me—or like you? If it were to enter into our hearts, it would make us feel to be wretches that we should be the cause of such inconceivable suffering—and yet, how it would make us love Him, admire Him, esteem Him, account Him All-in-All, Alpha and Omega! It would make Him everything to us if we did but get a glimpse of Him.

'They shall look on Him.' In this the Scripture must be fulfilled! O, if the Lord were pleased to give us some opening up of this, some view by precious faith, by divinely-given faith, which the Holy Ghost is pleased to work in a believing heart, what should we see in the wounded side of our glorious Redeemer? We should see the everlasting love of God! Where can divine love shine brighter than at Calvary? 'In this was manifested the love of God toward us . . . Herein is love, not that we loved God, but that He loved us, and sent His Son to be the propitiation for our sins.' O wonderful love is this! Wonderful love shines forth at Calvary, before the eye of faith, to a sensible sinner who is brought to weep before His cross, to feel a hope that the hell he deserves is put away, and that one day he will see in the realms of bliss, that glorious, exalted Lamb that has been slain. 'They shall look on Him Whom they pierced.'

Another point seen by faith is that by the piercing of His side that fountain is opened 'to the house of David and to the inhabitants of Jerusalem for sin and for uncleanness'. This pure water must wash the filth away; this precious blood must make the atonement. Here, then, is the fountain opened for sin and for sinners too, the precious fountain that Cowper speaks of.

> 'There is a fountain filled with blood,
> Drawn from Immanuel's veins,
> And sinners plunged beneath that flood,
> Lose all their guilty stains.'

Lose them. Lose them! O, have you known anything of that? They lose them! Another writer says of the atonement:

'It rises high, and drowns the hills;
Has neither shore nor bound;
Now if we search to find our sins,
Our sins can ne'er be found.'

O, what amazing grace, mercy, love, compassion and pity flow from His wounded side! Moreover, faith sees in the wounded side of Jesus an open way to heaven, a 'new and living Way' through the rent veil of His flesh. 'A new and living Way!' This is the gospel way as distinct from legal traditions and obligations, that were a shadow of good things to come. This is the good thing that has come; here is a new and living way opened for a sinner, for you, for me; it is a way open, it has not to be opened, it is already open. Jesus Christ declares Himself to be 'The Way, the Truth, and the Life'. Here too a poor sinner has a ground upon which to stand and 'come boldly to the throne of grace'. The precious blood of Christ is his argument, his plea, that upon which he may, by faith, boldly venture and take no denial.

'I can no denial take,
When I plead for Jesus' sake.'

'They shall look on Him.' Here, without pretending to visionary things (although I do not want to discredit what visions some of the Lord's people may have seen) I remember when this was so real in the view of faith to me, that I felt just then it could not have been more real if I had actually been at the foot of the cross when He was crucified. 'They shall look on Him.' Have you known a day or a night when to look on Him has melted your heart, moved your affections, brought forth worship? when you have put your crown on His head and crowned Him Lord of all? 'They shall look on Him whom they pierced.' The wounded side of Jesus brings reconciliation, nearness, removes differences, takes away barriers. 'Ye who sometimes were far off are made nigh by the blood of Christ.' Can you follow the apostle in that?

'The blood of Christ, a precious blood!
Cleanses from all sin, doubt it not,
And reconciles the soul to God,
From every folly, every fault.'

Do you wish for another advocate, another gospel, something more up-to-date, as people say, more modern, more pleasing? O, if the grace of God is in your heart, and your soul is lively, you will say, O, that I could live closer to Him, be more often weeping at His cross, feel in my heart a sweet contrition, hear the echo of that wonderful voice, saying, 'It is finished!' and feel that this mighty work was accomplished for me! What else do we need? We do not need a lot of religious enthusiasm, but we need a bleeding Jesus; nothing more can we wish for, nothing less can we do with. O, that precious blood—invaluable blood! 'They shall look on Him whom they pierced.' Here then, is a welcome to a sinner who may be feeling ready to perish; there is a welcome here. O, but, some of you say, I feel to be too bad, too vile, too black, too sinful, too great a sinner. Who said so? What kind of a woman was she who was first at the sepulchre and who could not leave it, but waited there and was the first to see the risen Saviour? Was it not Mary Magdalene? May not this show the wonderful, sovereign condescension and love of the Redeemer, to appear first to such a character as she had been? O, but, say you, she was given repentance and was forgiven! She leaves me far behind. What do you need in your soul? What do you need, poor thing? O, say you, I need that same blood, 'That same Jesus', that same sacrifice. O, what will satisfy you? O, say you, I know what will satisfy me. If I could but 'look on Him'. But I am dark, confused, ignorant, vile, out-of-the-way. Yes, but what is all this to Him? What does He say? Come unto Me, with all this, with your vileness, wretchedness, ruin, sin, guilt, misery. Come to the cross with it all. Take it there and plead the blood that does for sin atone.

'They shall look on Him.' O, have you had just that sacred glimpse of Him, by precious faith? Then you will get to heaven. Heaven is to be seen through His wounded side, for a poor perishing sinner, who is brought to that place to have to say, 'Give me Christ, or else I die'. What do you think of Him? What is your feeling of this sacrifice? What is your view of this precious blood? How are you moved by His death? O, say you, it is all profoundly blessed, wonderfully real; but I do not know, I seem to be out of the secret, I do not know. Do you want to know? Do you ever pray for the Lord to make it clear in your soul? Do you seek sometimes for that precious blood to be sprinkled on your conscience, so that you can say, I am clean, just God, I am clean? O, say you, that would satisfy me, give me peace, bring me joy, assure me that it will be well with me one day. O, may the Lord grant it then, and may He favour every waiting soul who longs for His appearing, with that sweet manifestation of His dying love. This will be more to you than anything else; it will break you to pieces. It will break your heart—and it will bind it up too. For this precious blood heals the broken-hearted.

> 'Jesus heals the broken-hearted;
> O, how sweet that sound to me!
> Once beneath my sin He smarted, (Did He?)
> Groaned, and bled to set me free.'

O, that personal pronoun there! May the Lord bring it in! We mourn that the Lord seems distant from us in this, but O, may He hear the cry of the poor and needy, and bring a healing, not a slight, partial healing, but a full forgiveness. May He say to some, as He did to the woman who was a sinner, like you, like me, 'Thy sins are forgiven thee'. Here is our foundation, our hope, our trust, our confidence, our peace, our heaven.

But there are our providences, difficulties, burdens, trials, heavy things, disappointments, set-backs, all kinds of things; what about all these? If the Lord is pleased to come and bless your soul, it will help you through a trial better than anything else; it will bring you quietness, confidence, strength. O, say you, if I could believe He had pardoned my dreadful sins, it would bring me through all my difficulties. Has He not done so for some of you? Has He not said, 'I will never leave thee, nor forsake thee'?

May the Lord help us, give us a gracious experience of that which will give us a standing for eternity, bear us through the flood of Jordan, and grant us an abundant entrance into His everlasting kingdom!

SORROW AND JOY

28 June 1964

> 'And ye now therefore have sorrow: but I will see you again, and your heart shall rejoice, and your joy no man taketh from you.' (John 16: 22)

THERE are two things of which it may be said they are a deep concern to us all, however much we may or may not feel it. The first relates to this mortal life here below. We must begin with this which concerns us in many different ways in our daily life and circumstances, our relationships in life and its changing conditions; those times of joy, times of sorrow, times of distress and grief, times of relief with things more according to our natural minds and wishes; and it would be sad to have a temperament that was unmoved by the things through which we pass in this life. They are a concern to us, they have been to everyone of us, and especially to younger friends in the earlier stages of life, our future, our success in life and our relationships and many things which concern us now; but the greater concern by far should be in connection with the life to come, the hereafter compared with which this present life is but as a passing moment. It is a great mercy if we really have a concern about our never-dying souls, about eternity and where we shall spend it, and how we shall spend it, and what it will eventually mean to us. Are we concerned about this? Are you concerned about it? Am I? Does it lie upon our heart, do we inwardly perceive the tremendous issues, does the case of our soul weigh with us as to what the Lord's purpose will be? What a mercy if, even if when young, we are brought to seek God, to wait on Him and to pray that we may be found eventually among His redeemed children.

These chapters, dear friends, relate to both conditions. They were spoken to those troubled disciples under distressing circumstances when the Lord, whom they loved and whose company they had enjoyed, was about to leave them. This was a great perplexity to them. Their minds seem to have been confused about the meaning of the Lord's coming to this earth and assuming human flesh, although the Lord had many times told them. Here He speaks kind, gracious, tender, feeling words of comfort to them in view of the approaching events and the fact that He would for a time have to leave them. He speaks so tenderly to them saying, 'Let not your heart be troubled; ye believe in God, believe also in Me'. He would quiet and console their minds, although He was Himself in trouble enough, fully realizing what lay immediately before Him. I would like to think of this on the part of the dear Redeemer, although untold trouble and distress and pain and suffering immediately awaited Him, so that soon after He said, 'Now is my soul troubled', yet to these poor disciples He said, 'Let not your heart be troubled; ye believe in God, believe also in Me'. He comforted them by the promise made several times to them of the Holy Ghost that should come in due time and with which they would be very graciously endued and filled to qualify them for the work before them.

He refers to their present condition of sorrow and to a future condition of joy, 'And ye now therefore have sorrow'. It is quite easy to see why they were in sorrow; but He says, 'I will see you again, and your heart shall rejoice and your joy no man taketh from you'. I would like as helped to bring forth these three points as they concern us each more or less. This present sorrow, and indication of future joy 'your heart shall rejoice', and thirdly the nature of that joy, 'Your joy no man taketh from you'. The nature of this joy is a point to notice because it cannot be said of any earthly joy, sweet as that may be at the time, that no man can take it from us, because the time soon comes when that particular joy is taken from us, or things come to rob us of that enjoyment.

First of all then there is present sorrow, 'And ye now therefore have sorrow'. As this was true with these disciples then, so on different occasions and at different times is it likewise true more or less with all the Lord's people. Mercifully it is not a life of uninterrupted sorrow, rather it is mingled with times of joy; yet what child of God is there, who has been some years in the pilgrimage to the heavenly city, who has not experienced certain seasons of sorrow? It is true more or less with every one of us. What is it that occasions sorrow? What is sorrow? It is a state of mind occasioned by certain prevailing conditions, or something we are brought into and we may have to pass through; it is grief of mind; and here it is to be noticed how tenderly the Scriptures speak to those in grief. In the Lamentations it is said, 'Though He cause grief, yet will He have compassion according to the multitude of His mercies'. You see when things come upon us over which we have no control whatever, and naturally speaking would have prevented, when in the providence of God they are brought upon us they occasion grief of mind.

There is a natural mind; if we possess the faculties of nature we cannot be other than grieved by many things in these days in which we are living; the state of the nation, the prevailing wickedness, the Sabbath breaking, the contempt of God's Holy Word, and other such things occasion sorrow to a child of God; but there is a different kind of sorrow from this, there is a spiritual sorrow that is peculiar to a living vessel of mercy. Natural sorrow is with all folk at times, but with this difference and it is a very distinguished difference too, when natural sorrows come to the Lord's people those sorrows are tempered more or less with the Lord's consolations. So it is said, 'For our light affliction, which is but for a moment, worketh for us a far more exceeding and eternal weight of glory'. Also the prophet prayed in the Psalms, 'Make us glad according to the days wherein thou hast afflicted us, and the years wherein we have seen evil'. Things are balanced. No child of God is forbidden to sorrow under loss or bereavement, or other distressing circumstances. How can it be otherwise? How can affectionate parents be other than sorrowful under the loss of a child, as has recently been in the sudden loss, of which we have heard, of a dear child of about two years, or if a husband should lose his wife or a wife her husband, or the children their parents, or the loss of a dear friend. These things cause sorrow but not despair. We are not forbidden to sorrow, but that sorrow is to be regulated. It would not be right for a person professing grace to be overcome with sorrow because it would evidence the lack of consolation in the case. The sorrow should be regulated as I believe it is; we may grieve but not rebel. This is the difference. There can be grief in the heart of a child of God without rebellion, without resentment against the will of God concerning the dispensation. There can be a right giving up, a subjection to the Lord's purpose under things very painful to flesh and blood and to our natural affections. It is a mercy to feel something of this.

There is then sorrow under losses, afflictions, bereavements, changes and almost innumerable things; but still there is a sorrow peculiar to a child of God. What is that? It is a sorrow occasioned by sin. Not sin generally speaking, but by a sense of sin that is felt in his own heart by divine teaching, as being guilty in the sight of a holy God. That religion is a poor religion, and that profession a poor profession, where there is an absence of sorrow and grief for sin. Why so? Not so much because of the possible consequences of sin, but because sin was the cause of such grief to the Lord Jesus Christ Himself. Our sins were the occasion of greater grief to Him than ever they can be to us, if we can believe that. In the prophecy we read of Him, 'Behold, and see if there be any sorrow like unto my sorrow'. What was the sorrow of the precious Redeemer? The burden of the sin of His dear people for whom He stood substitute. This occasioned Him grief and sorrow so that He was a Man of sorrows and acquainted with grief, and it is a mercy to have a religion with this ingredient in it.

Have we got this? Do we really grieve on account of sin because this grief is of a godly sort. This is not a natural sorrow arising from loss of some kind but it is godly sorrow arising from grace, from the Holy Spirit's divine awakening, from His gracious teaching when we are shown what guilty, wretched sinners we are in the sight of a just and holy God. When we are brought down before Him to confess our sins in His sight, to plead for mercy through the Lamb's redeeming precious blood. Do we know anything of this sorrow? I have to say I do not know the affliction of this sorrow that I should do as a minister. It is a very real sorrow, and I have known what it is to be grieved on account of my sins. When was this? More particularly when I saw by faith those sins laid on Him and when I saw that great work of redemption finished for me. Then I was grieved on account of my sins. It is a mercy to have a little godly sorrow; this godly sorrow works repentance; this is an important point to notice. It is this which proves it to be godly sorrow. If it is not godly sorrow in your heart it will never work repentance; but godly sorrow brings the soul into the sacred experience of repentance, that repentance that is sweet to feel though so closely attended with grief and sorrow on account of our sins. As we feel sorrow on account of sin so shall we feel joy on account of forgiveness.

There are many things that cause sorrow. The Lord's absence causes sorrow if we are exercised; darkness and uncertainty about our case, the hiding of His face and other things of this kind cause sorrow to exercised people. Does this cause any sorrow to you? Are you and I exercised rightly with regard to this, and do we know anything of this godly sorrow, this sorrow for sin, this repentance that needeth not to be repented of; that is to say we shall never need to repent of the repentance we have toward God, never. We may sometimes feel sorrow in that we know so little of what this repentance is; here is matter of sorrow.

'Ye now therefore have sorrow.' This sorrow with these disciples was because they could not visualize or foresee the necessity of the Lord's departure from them, or that He would be seen again by them, and what would result and issue from His sufferings and death. It was a sorrow occasioned by a darkness that was upon their minds at that time. Does not this come into personal experience? There may be sorrow now with some of us because we may not be able to foresee or visualize the design, purpose or ultimate issue of certain things that we may now be passing through. 'Ye now therefore have sorrow.' This is the first point and if we have grace in our souls we shall not want to skip over this, or conclude that there is no necessity for this sorrow, because godly sorrow is one of the most wholesome experiences a child of God can have here below. It is so sanctifying in its nature, and humbling in its effects. It brings us down, it brings us into sensible fellowship with a suffering Christ, it gives us to perceive the necessity and ultimate issue of His own sufferings. We shall have sorrow, we shall have it in our lives, we shall have it in the nation, we shall have it in our souls. You may have it in a number of different ways beside these, so that sometimes you may heave many a sigh secretly. 'Ye now therefore have sorrow.'

There is a second point, 'But I will see you again, and your heart shall rejoice'. Here you see the Lord refers to the fact that though for a season He would be taken from them, and would be put to death, yet He would rise again from the dead and they should see Him again after His resurrection from the dead and that would bring them joy, take away the sorrow they felt by reason of His being taken from them for a time. So it came to pass, as we know in the latter part of this Gospel, and the other Gospels, where it is said that the Lord appeared to them, 'Then the same day at evening, being the first day of the week, when the doors were shut where the disciples were assembled for fear of the Jews, came Jesus and stood in the midst, and saith unto them, Peace be unto you. And when he had so said, he shewed unto them His hands and His side. Then were the disciples glad when they saw the Lord.' This was a joy to them, it was the same Jesus that had been taken from them, that was nailed to the cursed tree, that had poured out His soul unto death, and evidenced the height of divine love towards them by His substitution and death. It was the same Jesus that appeared to them there when they were assembled together and demonstrated His identity by showing them His wounds in His sacred body occasioned by nailing Him to the cross, and the wound in His holy side occasioned by the spear of the soldier. 'He shewed unto them His hands and His side. Then were the disciples glad when they saw the Lord.'

'I will see you again, and your heart shall rejoice.' Though we have not been favoured like this, have not that joy in a literal sense which they had to see Him after His resurrection, there is joy, a particular joy that pertains to the Lord's dear people, that arises from the resurrection of the Lord Jesus Christ and His appearing to them as a risen and exalted Saviour in the exercise of their faith. So Peter says, 'Whom having not seen ye love'—that is, these poor scattered converts—'Whom having not seen, ye love; in whom, though now ye see Him not; yet believing, ye rejoice with joy unspeakable and full of glory.' The joy here to a believer is the joy of faith when the Lord appears to him, it is the joy of His presence. He sees us again after a season of darkness and trouble and conflict and fear and absence. He comes again; this 'seeing' means coming to us in a spiritual way.

As His absence causes sorrow so His presence causes joy. This I believe follows with every living child of God; His sweetest joy is the Lord's presence with him in his soul's feelings, even if that be but for a few moments. It is the joy of heaven, it is the sweet joy he feels because he can say, The Lord is my God. Thomas said, 'My Lord and my God', and when he said that he was unquestionably filled with joy. So it is with the Lord's redeemed family. He shows Himself through the lattice, He standeth behind our wall showing Himself through the lattice of His Word, Gospel and ordinances, and His waiting people get a glimpse of Him again, He comes to them, He removes the cloud between and they get a fresh glimpse and it is as sweet as it was before.

'I will see you again.' This can have another point; it may be a time of darkness and absence and bondage now, and the Lord knows whether this is so; His omniscient eye is always upon His people; He sees them under every condition and in every distress. 'I will see you again.' This can be a confirming promise to those who may at this present time be attacked by the enemy. 'I will see you again, and your heart shall rejoice.' Faith may lay hold of this promise under present conditions of sorrow; the promise has a strength in it, it is the strength of an unfailing Jesus, 'I will see you again, and your heart shall rejoice'. What is this joy? As I have hinted it is the joy of His presence. It is the joy of the Gospel that is brought into the heart, it is the joyful sound of the everlasting Gospel that is heard in the heart of a poor sinner who has been mourning over his sins before the Lord. What can bring greater joy into the heart of a poor sin-sick soul who may have feared that hell would be his portion, and had every reason to fear so too as far as his own condition is concerned? But says the Lord 'Your heart shall rejoice'; so it will when He comes again.

This joy incorporates all the precious blessings of the everlasting Gospel, they flow into your heart poor sinner when the Lord comes again. He brings all these good things with Him, like a friend coming to your house with a basket of good things, just those very things you may need, so does the Lord come with His hands full of the blessings of redeeming grace to these poor sorrowing ones. 'Your heart shall rejoice.' He causes the heart to sing for joy when He comes, joy unspeakable; a sweet joy this. It is the joy of liberty, the joy of interest in His love and grace, the joy of pardon in His precious blood, the joy of being justified through His obedience to the law on our behalf. More than all, it is the joy of Himself. He Himself is the joy, He comes into your heart and fills you with Himself, 'I will see you again'. I can almost hear some say, I wish He would come again, and perhaps I can hear some say, I do not feel He has ever come. This same truth applies, 'I will come to you'. In an earlier chapter He says 'I will not leave you comfortless: I will come to you', and if He has come to you and then departed, He says 'I will see you again', and this to be a comfort and support to us in the trial of faith and waiting for His appearing. So 'Your heart shall rejoice'.

Thirdly, 'Your joy no man taketh from you'. Why is it a joy that no man can take from us? Because it is the joy of heaven, for it *is* a heavenly joy. That is the reason why. It is the joy of the Gospel. In the first chapter in the Epistle to Peter, Peter says, 'Wherein ye greatly rejoice, though now for a season, if need be, ye are in heaviness through manifold temptations'. Yet still they were rejoicing greatly, not on account of these temptations, but on account of what the Apostle had referred to, that there was an inheritance laid up for them in heaven through faith unto salvation. No man can rob us or destroy this joy. This is the joy of hope sometimes felt in the heart in sweet anticipation, it is the joy of love, of prospect, and no man can take that away however much they may persecute and oppose and indeed may be a cause of much natural trouble and distress; they cannot take away that which the Lord has put into your heart, it is a spiritual, heavenly joy, a joy to be known in its fullness one day when we have finished with earth and everything here below. With a child of God that will be to enter into that joy and no man will take that away from him then; no man can take it away now. They cannot take the consolation away.

It is true that we do not always feel this joy; many things come to interrupt it. We may have to say we have known very little of it; but no man can take it away because it is the Lord's gift, it is a heavenly gift, it is the joy of one day being with Him, 'In my Father's house are many mansions: if it were not so, I would have told you. I go to prepare a place for you. And if I go and prepare a place for you, I will come again, and receive you unto myself; that where I am, there ye may be also.' No man can take that away. To take that away they would have to take your heaven away and no man can take your heaven away if the Lord has opened one for you. Here is a sweet word of consolation to the Lord's poor people in this valley of tears and losses and sorrows. 'Ye now therefore have sorrow: but I will see you again, and your heart shall rejoice, and your joy no man taketh from you.'

Amen.

REASONING TOGETHER

14 December 1966

> 'Come now, and let us reason together, saith the Lord: though your sins be as scarlet, they shall be as white as snow; though they be red like crimson, they shall be as wool.' (Isa. 1: 18)

THIS remarkable prophecy has a great many references to the Messiah, the Lord Jesus Christ, and His ultimate appearance in human flesh; to His coming in the fullness of time to fulfil the will of His Father to send Him and to redeem His Church and deliver her from the bondage of the law and the terrible curse under which she lay because of her guilty condition; to provide a righteousness so that she shall be presented without spot; and all to redound to the glory of God in a manifestation of His infinite wisdom, mercy and grace in the recovery of poor, lost, ruined sinners from the Adam fall and to make their standing in Christ far more secure than was their standing in Adam. As we look through this blessed prophecy we can observe the Lord's appointments in all these particulars that were then yet to be fulfilled. If we have faith to view this and to look back upon the fulfilment of all that is here indicated we may have great cause to bless God for His mercy and for His Gospel and so to be satisfied with that provision of salvation, to want nothing else beside it for our poor, perishing souls, and if we have felt that, to wait too for a sweet renewing of it in our own hearts.

The verse I have read has been upon my mind today; as you can see it has both an invitation and a promise. The invitation is to come and reason together. This is what the Lord says, 'Come now, and let us reason together'. What amazing condescension is this on the part of the Majesty of heaven to invite poor, guilty people to come and reason with Him. There is something more than an invitation, there is one of many very blessed promises of the result of this and what the Lord Himself would say to these poor reasoning people. He says, 'Though your sins be as scarlet, they shall be as white as snow; though they be red like crimson, they shall be as wool.' I have been thinking today that the two great things that concern us are SIN and SALVATION—to know our sins forgiven; to feel that these scarlet-dyed sins, these double-stained sins are washed away so that not a stain remains, not a speck; 'they shall be as white as snow'. What is remarkable about this verse is that it seems to stand by itself, to be distinct, not necessarily connected with what goes before or what follows. It stands forth like a shining light in the midst of the dark background here recorded, of the conduct of the people, of their forgetfulness of God and in consideration of their not showing the gratitude of a beast who does respond to his master's voice. 'But Israel doth not know, my people doth not consider.' Then there is their completely corrupted condition 'From the sole of the foot even unto the head there is no soundness in it; but wounds, and bruises, and putrefying sores: they have not been closed, neither bound up, neither mollified with ointment'. Well, might we not conclude that a people in such a condition might be justly banished and punished for their sins without any promise of mercy. There seems also to be such sacrilege; their services appear to have been hypocritical; although they went through some performance yet their heart was not in it. 'Bring no more vain oblations; incense is an abomination unto me; the new moons and sabbaths, the calling of assemblies, I cannot away with; it is iniquity, even the solemn meeting. Your new moons and your appointed feasts my soul hateth; they are a trouble unto me; I am weary to bear them.'

How profoundly solemn is all this; consider the position of the people, their general conduct. In those days we know there were godly people, there were many who feared God and desired to serve Him; but here is the sacrilege of the feasts, the base conduct of the people generally speaking. It seems to describe our present condition with all the vanity and worldliness and forgetfulness of God and His Word and His ways, sacrilege and mockery under the cloak of religion; all the ritual and things that must be dishonouring in the sight of a Holy God. Yet a word like this seems to shine forth and burst through the black cloud like a voice from heaven. It seems a remarkable statement to make and is in a way in parenthesis. We could read the verse before and that which follows and they would be quite well connected. The Lord warned them of the consequences of their sins and exhorted them to sanctify themselves and humble themselves before Him as a people; but even so this amazing promise bursts forth in the midst of all this, in the forgiveness of sins. This appears to be a striking feature in the prophecy of Isaiah. In the chapter we have read the Lord solemnly reproves them for their guilty condition and yet momentarily breaks forth like this, 'Come now, and let us reason together, saith the Lord: though your sins be as scarlet, they shall be as white as snow; though they be red like crimson, they shall be as wool'. Here is the freeness of God's grace and mercy, and the superabounding of His grace over the abounding of sin. He hates sin, but here is the invitation, 'Come now, and let us reason together'.

I have been looking at these two words, 'Come now'. It does not say, 'Come ye', or 'Come thou', or 'Come sometime', but 'COME NOW'. This appears to be a matter that should have no delay; now is the day of salvation; 'COME NOW'. This is the Lord's invitation and we have this in a number of places, as you know. The Lord Himself said in the days of His flesh, 'Come unto Me, all ye that labour and are heavy laden, and I will give you rest'. There are a number of invitations to poor, needy, sensible sinners who venture before the mercy seat to 'Come now'. Why come now? Because of the urgency of the matter, because of the greatness and importance of it and because of the consequences and ultimate result of living and dying unforgiven, COME NOW; lose no time; no matter is as important as the salvation of a sinner's soul. 'Come now and let us reason together.' This coming is the venturing of faith as it was in the case of the Syrophenician woman who came to the Lord Jesus to plead with Him. The Apostle says, 'Let us therefore come boldly unto the throne of grace, that we may obtain mercy and find grace to help in time of need.' 'Come now.' This is a point to notice, the throne of grace is open, and open night and day to those who knock by the way, 'Come now'. This is drawing nigh as it is said in Psalm 73, 'It is good for me to draw near to God'; it is good for me, he found it to be so.

'Come now' then, come now, repenting sinner; come, approach this throne of grace; come with all your sin and guilt and ruin and misery and death, come now and let us reason together. And what can be said about this reasoning? How can a guilty sinner reason with a holy God, one who is separate from Him on account of sin? In view of the merciful invitation we are warranted to venture near, to come to the throne of grace; but what can we plead, how can we enter into this debate? The Lord says, 'plead together' as though He would say, You say what you have to say and then I will say what I have to say. Let us plead together; it is an invitation. Here is an opening of the mouth for the dumb. But what can we plead with the Lord, what can we reason with Him? It is perfectly true that on our part we cannot plead anything good of ourselves; we cannot take something which we may think to merit the favour of God, as, to use an illustration, Naaman did when he went to Elisha to be cured of his leprosy. He took with him a substantial present and hoped that he might obtain favour with the prophet with all that he had brought to load him with; but that was to no purpose whatever. 'Go and wash in Jordan seven times, and thy flesh shall come again to thee and thou shalt be clean', cleansed of thy leprosy. Not, O what wonderful presents! I can do no other than pronounce you clean. Yet there is that in a poor sinner to want to take something that he may think will please the Lord, something that may seem to have some merit in it. We cannot plead acceptably upon that ground; we have no good works to plead to merit the favour of God. Good as good works are as the fruit of His grace, and love to Him, we have to come to this mercy seat and plead our own unworthiness, our guilty condition, that we have nothing but sin, that our best is stained, and dyed with sin, that our all is nothing worth. So we have no argument from that point of view. We find Job saying, 'O that I knew where I might find Him! that I might come even to His seat! I would order my cause before Him, and fill my mouth with arguments.' O, they could not be arguments of his own goodness, for he had to come down to this, to repent in dust and ashes and to say, 'Behold I am vile'. No, we cannot plead our own goodness, or strength, or merit or anything of that kind. All we can plead is our guilt and sin and need. Let us plead together.

From another point of view there *is* something that a poor, guilty, helpless, wretch can plead. What can he plead? He can plead the blood of Christ as a healing balm for the wounds of his sin. He can plead in this debate what the Lord has promised, and that the Lord Himself has said, 'Put Me in remembrance: let us plead together: declare thou, that thou mayest be justified'. The Lord Himself can say to such an one in pleading with Him or debating with Him, with all this guilt and sin, that there is no reason why he should keep away from Him, but all the more reason why such an one should venture in humble confession and plead for mercy. There is something to plead; not anything in ourselves to merit the Saviour's esteem, but there is a blessed Gospel to plead, there is a divine promise to plead, there is the Lord's own Word to plead. There is that to plead which faith may hold Him to, and He Himself has said, 'Put Me in remembrance', say all you have to say. 'Let us plead together.' There is also the power and wisdom and grace of Christ to plead. He has said that none shall be turned away who venture in faith. This coming to the Lord is really believing in Him. 'He that cometh to Me shall never hunger and he that believeth on Me shall never thirst . . . him that cometh to Me I will in no wise cast out.' Never will the Lord turn one away. There is no Scripture to confirm that He will, for He has said 'All that the Father giveth Me shall come to Me; and him that cometh to Me I will in no wise cast out'. Here is something to plead. What a wonderful mercy it is! With all our guilt and vileness we have something to plead, and we have the atonement to plead, we have His own Word that He will not cast us away, we have His own invitation to plead. 'Let us plead together', as though the Lord would say you can be quite free to make all the confessions that you feel necessary or to remind me of whatever you feel desirable, 'Let us plead together'.

'Let us reason together.' The reasoning here appears to be based upon the matter of forgiveness. Now what does the Lord have to say about this? Is it not remarkable what the Lord says in response to the reasoning of a poor sinner who ventures to that Throne of Grace to reason with the Lord? I take this to be the reasoning of faith, the argument of faith; this is not carnal reasoning but it is the exercise of faith upon Christ, it is a bold venture, taking no denial. As one says:

> 'I can no denial take
> When I plead for Jesus sake.'

The reasoning is centring in the blessed mediation of the Lord Jesus Christ; for His Name's sake, that is it, that is the point that we come to with all our reasoning, for His Name's sake; and no other ground but this. What does the Lord say in response to all this? He says, 'Though your sins be as scarlet, they shall be as white as snow'. He goes straight to the point; no going round about it, 'Though your sins be as scarlet, they shall be as white as snow; though they be red like crimson, they shall be as wool'. This is the Lord's reasoning. O, what condescending grace is this! This is not upon the grounds of the law or upon the grounds of abstract justice, for if the Lord only reasoned upon that ground He could do no other than banish us for ever from His presence. If I may put it like this, it is not to the throne of justice that a poor, venturing sinner goes to reason with the Lord; it is not before the throne of His justice, for no mercy can be shown there under the law; the terms of that are 'Do and live, sin and die', that is the law. The throne that a poor, guilty wretch ventures to is the Throne of Grace, the Mercy Seat that was sprinkled with the blood when the high priest went in once every year. The bloodstained Mercy Seat is the place of meeting. It is the place of meeting where the Lord comes and has contact with a sinner, the Mercy Seat. This is where the two parties plead together. Here it was that the Lord said, 'There will I commune with thee'. There will I meet with thee. Have mercy upon me for Christ's sake, for Christ's sake; that is the argument you venture to use, which the Lord will never turn away. He will never turn away one who comes seeking mercy for Jesus' sake. He does not belittle sin, 'though your sins be as scarlet'. That is of the deepest dye. Though they be as scarlet and red like crimson—it does not say just a faint mark, but as scarlet, they are deep, double-dyed sins; this indicates the heinousness of them, they are deep-dyed sins. Yet, even so, although this is true, and it is enough to close the mouth apart from the precious blood of Christ, here is the promise, 'They shall be as white as snow' and 'They shall be as wool'. This indicates the complete removal of every stain, every mark, every spot. They shall be as white as snow; this appears to indicate the complete removal of guilt, so that this guilty person stands before God pardoned and cleansed and justified with nothing between. If the Lord brings an experience of pardon into your heart this will be one of the effects; there will be nothing between you and your God. It will fill you with peace. You will know something about what dear Watts says where he writes of the blessed atonement of Jesus Christ and its sufficiency.

> 'It rises high, and drowns the hills;
> Has neither shore nor bound;
> Now if we search to find our sins,
> Our sins can ne'er be found.'

White as snow, WHITE AS SNOW, not a sin to be found, not a blot, not a stain! This takes us to Psalm 51 and the prayer of the Psalmist 'Purge me with hyssop, and I shall be clean: wash me, and I shall be whiter than snow'. Not, I shall still have a few stains left, but 'I shall be whiter than snow'. 'Though your sins be as scarlet, they shall be as white as snow.' This does not mean that our poor flesh is made perfect in ourselves, but we are perfect in Christ, perfect in Christ. But notice at what a tremendous cost is this wonderful cleansing. Our sins are as scarlet, red like crimson, but nothing less than that red flowing blood from the Redeemer's sacred side can cleanse these crimson sins. Blood must flow, that red, rich stream of blood must flow to wash this load of guilt away and wash away the stain. One says of the stream,

> 'What stream is that which sweeps away
> My sins just like a flood,
> Nor lets one guilty blemish stay?
> 'Tis Jesus' precious blood.'

Nothing else can. This means not only or simply that we are forgiven, but justified, 'That thou mightest be justified'. The perfection of His obedience, the obedience of Christ, is the argument of faith for this robe of righteousness to be put upon us to cover us so that there is not a sin that can be seen; all is hidden from the eye of justice. It is a great word in itself; it is a blessed word; it is a word that may bring hope into the heart of a despairing one who has nothing of his own to plead. One who is made sensible of his guilt and sin may venture to the Throne of Mercy like this,

> 'Just as I am without one plea
> But that Thy blood was shed for me.'

Amen.

A SYMPATHISING HIGH PRIEST

6 December 1970

> 'Seeing then that we have a great high priest, that is passed into the heavens, Jesus the Son of God, let us hold fast our profession. For we have not an high priest which cannot be touched with the feeling of our infirmities; but was in all points tempted like as we are, yet without sin. Let us therefore come boldly unto the throne of grace, that we may obtain mercy, and find grace to help in time of need.' (Heb. 4: 14–16)

IT would be a wonderful evening if we should be favoured to feel the witness in our hearts so that we could say of the sufferings of a dear Redeemer, 'this we know, that it was all for us'. There may be some for whom it *is* who do not feel they could lay claim to such an assurance, but who may have to say, O that I could feel it *was* all for me! Where this is the case may the Lord be pleased to grant it, so that you can walk up and down these verses and feel an experimental interest in the sacred, blessed truth that is here concerning the Lord Jesus Christ in His office as a great high Priest. Words must be poor when we attempt to speak upon such a subject as this, but after all the life blood of the Gospel centres in the Priesthood of the Lord Jesus. There has never been a priest like Him and there never will be. We may read about the high priests and the priests in the Old Testament but none can compare with Him. He has no comparison; the main point here consists in the fact that He is able to save to the uttermost poor lost people, not through what somebody else has done for Him, but what He Himself has accomplished.

In this office are three things that might be mentioned that are necessary and are involved in the Priesthood of Christ. One point consists in taking our nature upon Him, without which He could not be a priest; another, the sacrifice that He offered without which He could not take away sin; and the third the position that He occupies as having passed into the heavens where He exercises that blessed office and disposes the blessings of grace to His poor, needy people upon the earth. There He is, our great High Priest. He is great here particularly in His sympathy, but He is great in a number of different ways, He is great in His love. 'Greater love hath no man than this, that a man lay down His life for His friends'; but our blessed High Priest did, and that for some of you. I hope it may be His blessed will that it proves to be for everyone, even as we have been singing.

He is great in His knowledge, wisdom and understanding; nothing is concealed from His penetrating eye. There is no creature that is not manifest in His sight; all things are naked and opened unto the eyes of Him with whom we have to do. He is our great High Priest. This comes into our lives. Do we feel to need wisdom? Then this great High Priest is made this unto us for He of God is made unto us wisdom. Do you need a righteousness? It must come from this Priest. Do you need strength? It must come from Him as a priest for ever after the order of Melchisedec.

'Every grace and every favour
Comes to us through Jesus' blood'

'Seeing then that we have a great High Priest that is passed into the heavens.' This is a blessed proof of His divine personality, as was His resurrection from the dead. When the work of redemption was completed He ascended up from this earth to heaven. We read that His disciples saw Him go up until He vanished out of their sight; He ascended up and passed into the heavens. I do not know how you may feel about this, but I know it has been a consoling thought in my heart many and many a time that we have a Priest in heaven, a living Jesus, made a priest mediatorially after the order of Melchisedec, and His life now as a Priest is an evidence and demonstration of the satisfaction and acceptance of His sacrifice, and all His dear people stand perfect in Him. All their sins are washed away for ever and they are justified by His obedience unto death. O what a glorious Person He is. I am sure I may repeat what I said this morning; as you may be helped keep your eye fixed on Him when you pray; also, when you read keep that eye fixed on Him for that is where your blessing must come from.

He is a great High Priest passed into the heavens, Jesus the Son of God, therefore, 'let us hold fast our profession'. This will present many difficulties because of the opposition that necessarily attends this holding fast our profession. There is the power of unbelief within us, temptations without, cross providences, hard things, afflictions, losses, a path of tribulation, darkness, fears, apprehensions; many, many things will make it a difficult matter; but, as I believe I mentioned this morning, it is a profession of faith in Christ, for that is where the soul anchors, it is a profession of faith and confidence in His precious blood to purge our load of guilt away. It is a profession of the perfection of His righteousness to present us without spot before God one day.

The secret of this holding fast is union with Him; 'I in them'. The vine and the branches indicate this; when the branches are in union with the vine then it lives and is fruitful. So does a living soul that is in union with Christ. There is no continuing without this, no holding fast in a gracious saving way if there is no union. This holding fast is looking to Him, trusting in Him, casting our care upon Him, committing our way to Him, leaning upon Him, holding fast with a 'Lord help me'. 'Hold up my goings in thy paths, that my footsteps slip not.' O what a wonder it will be to come through, to be brought through, to overcome at last, to be victorious. We need grace to keep our eyes fixed on Him in spite of all opposition. 'Let not all this terrify, pursue the narrow path.' Press on, 'forgetting those things which are behind, and reaching forth unto those things which are before'. Press toward the mark.

The point I would like to speak on for a little while is just this matter of the priesthood of Christ in His compassion and sympathy. It is said by the Apostle here that 'He is touched with the feeling of our infirmities'. By infirmities you know we may understand some kind of weakness or disability or affliction. Indeed, it may apply to any trial that we may have to walk in, in which we may feel we have not strength of ourselves to do so. He is touched with our infirmities, the feeling of our infirmities. They can be infirmities of the body, in some particular limb, or an infirmity in relation to the hearing or the sight, as we read of one who had an infirmity for so many years who was waiting at the pool. We read of what the Lord said to the ministers of John, 'Go your way, and tell John what things ye have seen and heard; how that the blind see, the lame walk, the lepers are cleansed, the deaf hear, the dead are raised'. All these are infirmities. We may term them afflictions, I know, but they are infirmities in the sense that they indicate some particular weakness. As a deaf person is not able to hear because of that infirmity, so a dumb person is not able to speak because of this infirmity. There are many infirmities, and sometimes these can be for the time being through taking a mistaken view of things. This was the case with Asaph; he came to mistaken, premature conclusions. This can be an infirmity. Good Asaph said, 'Has God forgotten to be gracious? . . . Will He be favourable no more?' This was an infirmity, a mistaken conclusion, he said so. He said 'This is my infirmity: but I will remember the years of the right hand of the most High'.

Now, dear friends, we are all subject to these infirmities. Do you not feel it? Sometimes this can refer to the matter of prayer. We have an infirmity in this matter. What is this? The Apostle refers to it in the Romans, 'The Spirit also helpeth our infirmities: for we know not what we should pray for as we ought'. Here is an infirmity. This may seem difficult to understand; but we may not always know what is best for us or what the will of the Lord is concerning us. We can be very much in the dark, and may pray for things that nature desires, without real subjection to the Lord's will. Here is an infirmity; but 'The Spirit helpeth our infirmities: for we know not what we should pray for as we ought: but the Spirit itself maketh intercession for us with groanings which cannot be uttered'. How does the Spirit help these infirmities? By strengthening us, holding up our hands in prayer and imparting that importunity so that we feel able to come boldly unto the Throne of Grace in the boldness of a living faith. This is how the Spirit helps our infirmities. He may also do this by presenting Christ before our view as all-sufficient to supply every need, and thereby urge us to earnest pleading by the Spirit of grace and of supplication.

Here are these infirmities, then. Now the Lord Jesus Christ Himself has no infirmities that are consequent upon inherent weakness and sin. We know all afflictions and death itself result from sin, from the fall of man. The dear Redeemer has no infirmities inherent in Himself, but He understands the infirmities of His poor dear people because of what He has passed through Himself. Whatever infirmity you may labour under He can understand it sympathetically. Are you suffering pain? He can understand that pain because He suffered such pain, as He did when He suffered that cruel death. Are you insulted, persecuted, opposed? So was He. He was insulted, persecuted, opposed and hated. He can understand your trials and afflictions in this way. Oh, say you, but I am tempted by the devil—so was He. As you know, He was tempted in the wilderness. Say you, I am tempted to unbelief and distrust of God; so was He by Satan, tempted to a distrust of God's providence; for when He was hungry He was tempted to turn stones to bread. That was a temptation from Satan. When you feel to be assailed by Satan you may remember that so was your Saviour assailed by Satan. Oh, say you, I am tempted to pride and presumption—so was He. Are you tempted to idolatry?—so was He.

The point then is that, whatever your temptations are, this great High Priest can understand them. But there is something more than this, more than understanding them. This is that He is touched by them. He is touched by the feeling of your infirmities. This can be very, very sweet. This being touched with the feeling of our infirmities appears to be first that He walks with us in them. As it is in the prophecy by Isaiah, 'When thou passest through the waters, I will be with thee; and through the rivers, they shall not overflow thee'. You are afflicted by these infirmities, but He walks with you in them, He is touched by the feeling of your infirmities, and not only so but He supports you under them, He does not leave you to shift for yourself; He supports you in them. He bears you through them. He supports you with His staff and rod; He does not leave you to fight your battles alone; He is the captain of your salvation made perfect through sufferings. Some of you may understand me; you may have felt a particular sense of the Lord's presence with you in a furnace of trial, supporting you with a promise, holding you up, walking with you in the trial, carrying the burden for you, bearing you through it. So it has been a sanctified trial, because the Lord was with you in it, and blessed His word to you when you were passing through the waters.

He is touched with the feeling of our infirmities. He may touch your heart with His love, melt you in repentance and contrition for sin, bring you near to Himself, carry you as a lamb in His bosom through the rough and rugged track that you may have to travel along in this path of tribulation. He is touched with the feeling of our infirmities, and was in all points tempted like as we are yet without sin. We are poor sinful mortals. We are liable to fall a prey to temptation. He was tempted in all points, yet He was perfectly holy. Although He was tempted He was never tainted, although He suffered being tempted, He never fell by any temptation. Oh no, He knows just how to take you up in His arms and carry you through, as though He would whisper in your heart, I have suffered all for you. He will take you up in His arms, so to speak, and carry you through a furnace or bear you through a river, help you, bring you through and give you to feel a sweet peace and quietness in it. This is being touched with the feeling of your infirmities.

> 'Touched with a sympathy within,
> He knows our feeble frame;
> He knows what sore temptations mean,
> For He has felt the same.'

This is an incentive in the mind of the Apostle to come boldly unto the Throne of grace, as though he would say, You have these infirmities. How can you carry them, how can you walk in them, how can you endure them? Here is a direction, 'Come boldly unto the throne of grace' with your infirmities, your weakness, your temptation, your sins, your fears, your failings. This boldness is the boldness of faith. Faith is what I may term a confidence, not a presumptuous boldness. It is described in one of the Psalms, 'I am the Lord thy God, which brought thee out of the land of Egypt: open thy mouth wide, and I will fill it'. Ask for great things, 'large petitions with thee bring'. 'Open thy mouth wide.' This is a confidence then. Why go to this throne of grace? Because we have nowhere else to go. It is the only avenue of soul relief, of deliverance. Let us come boldly. You may say, My case is too bad. Who said that? The Lord never said so. We need to be careful about listening to what the devil says. The Apostle James says, 'Resist the devil and he will flee from you'. How can we poor things resist the devil? I would say the best way is to come boldly to the throne of grace, for that is what the devil cannot abide. The weakest saint upon his knees can gain the victory.

> 'Satan trembles when he sees
> The weakest saint upon his knees'

This is the best way of resisting him.

What various matters there are, your soul, your body, your providences, your circumstances and many things. This is an open door. 'Let us come boldly to the throne of grace, that we may obtain mercy, and find grace to help in time of need.' That is the reason why we are exhorted to venture with this boldness. First of all that we may obtain mercy. What is it that we need mercy for? Mercy in forgiveness, grace to strengthen. When it comes to the matter of mercy this is a great thing, for this forgiveness is an act of mercy; this can take us to Psalm 51 where the Psalmist says, 'Have mercy upon me, O God, according to thy lovingkindness: according unto the multitude of thy tender mercies blot out my transgressions', and so on down through the Psalm. If the Lord should be pleased to bring that forgiveness into your heart and give you to feel it, He will only do it as an act of mercy toward you or me or anyone else, not because we have any claim upon Him. It must be an act of mercy; in fact it is mercy all the way. 'Have mercy upon me, O God.' This is what the Lord Jesus is exalted to give. He is 'a Prince and a Saviour to give repentance to Israel and remission of sins'. Oh what blessed peace He gives, what joy, what life, what liberty, what assurance! All is an act of mercy. In this blessed word we have those promises that He will do this, 'If we confess our sins, he is faithful and just to forgive us our sins, and to cleanse us from all unrighteousness'. He is faithful because He has promised, and just because He has given satisfaction, so that the pardon of sin does not clash with the holy character of God.

It is an amazing wonder that we may obtain mercy and grace to help in time of need. It is always a time of need; but there are particular times of need, when that need is so particularly felt that you come to the place of one of whom we read that she said,

'Lord help me'. 'Grace to help in time of need.' This can be when we are under some infirmity, pressing hard upon us, some particular affliction, some trial, some hard thing that you may have to walk in that is like water wearing the stones. These things bring us down so that we feel to have no strength left except it be to pray, 'Lord help me'. Then this grace is given, 'grace to help in time of need'. Venture boldly to the throne of grace that you may find grace, obtain it, feel it, experience it. It is a confirming word. It is what so many of the Lord's people have felt in a time of trouble, sorrow, affliction, when life has been in jeopardy, heavy outward trials that have been very hard to bear, but not too hard for the Lord to give strength to hold you up and bring you through.

The Lord said to the Apostle, 'My grace is sufficient for thee, for my strength is made perfect in weakness'. In this way you may find and feel your shoes to be as iron and brass; you can walk in them and they will be sure to fit. You have to bring these infirmities to a mercy seat that you may find grace to help in time of need. They are sure to come, they have come, they do come; and what a mercy it is when a waiting soul finds the Lord in a time of need, and feels that inward support, that divine sympathy; this is when this great High Priest is touched with the feeling of our infirmities. I hope I have been helped to say a few things that are according to the Gospel and according to the experience of the Lord's people. May we be favoured to prove that we have such an High Priest who is touched with the feeling of our infirmities and that a throne of grace is open for us to venture to, that we may obtain mercy and find grace to help in time of need.

Amen.

STILLNESS IN TROUBLE

6 October 1971

'Be still and know that I am God.' (Ps. 46: 10)

WE have read a little in Job of the words of Elihu, that God is just in all His ways, although from a natural point of view it did not appear to be so, because Job was one who feared God, a perfect and upright man and one who eschewed evil, and yet all those desolating calamities came upon him which were enough to crush the strongest spirit. Naturally speaking one might say, 'Why?' to many things, to some things in our own lives. We may say why should this be, or why should that be, of things which may be mysterious to us, and may perhaps occasion much inward conflict, as some things do. Even so, we find that God has a purpose in all He does or permits, as far as that expression can be considered consistent. Elihu said in the light of all this, 'God is great and we know Him not'. Even in the reading of Holy Scripture in some circumstances, in the lives of godly men, we may be somewhat confounded by the trials they had to pass through; yet in each case the Lord brought them through, blessed them and made their latter end better than their beginning. It is a mercy when faith holds fast in the face of everything that seems confounding to reason. They are two opposites and can never really flow together. Here we walk by faith not by sight, and sometimes it has been a walking by faith in very dark paths, deep trials, much tribulation, much affliction; yet even so God, we believe, has a wise and tender purpose toward His people in all the disposings of His providence. It is a great thing when rightly we can 'be still and know that He is God'. This Psalm is very confirming, comforting, strengthening, and consoling. 'God is our refuge and strength, a very present help in trouble.' It does not say we shall have no trouble, for we shall, and the Lord's people have some troubles the world have not. There can be similar circumstances, but the Lord's people have exercises in and under them that are peculiar to a living soul.

'God is our refuge and strength'—this seems to be the language of the church more than a particular person—'Therefore will not we fear, though the earth be removed, and though the mountains be carried into the midst of the sea; though the waters thereof roar and be troubled, though the mountains shake with the swelling thereof.' Not, God is our refuge and strength, therefore it will always be calm, quiet and peaceful, and there will be no roaring waters, swelling mountains, or the earth being moved and carried into the midst of the sea. Notwithstanding all this, 'There is a river, the streams whereof shall make glad the city of God, the holy place of the tabernacles of the most High'. This seems to bring us into a new condition of feeling; the quietness of a river with its streams quietly gliding along, notwithstanding all the commotions of the earth. There are living communications of divine love and mercy to poor sinners who put their trust in Him. So the author could say, 'The Lord of Hosts is with us; the God of Jacob is our refuge'. It is a mercy when we can feel this, it will bring a confidence, a rest to the mind and spirit.

The Psalm is a beautiful one. It begins and ends with the same language, 'God is', 'the God of Jacob is'. 'God is'—it is a mercy when we can feel that 'God is', not simply that there is some supreme Being but that God is the God of His people, the God of Jacob is our refuge, therefore, all our matters, our life and everything connected with it, are in His hand; 'all my times are in Thy hand'. It is a mercy when we can feel something of this and 'be still and know that I am God'. I would like to speak of this in three or four particular aspects.

First of all as a warning; for we may look upon it as being a divine warning that seems to come in after what has been recorded in the Psalm of the power of God in making desolations in the earth and making wars to cease unto the end of the earth. The Lord has indeed made desolations in the earth; He has done this all through the ages of time. He has made desolations in the way of solemn judgements that have fallen upon the ungodly, and there have been desolating wars. All through the Old Testament we can see that the Lord has made desolations in the earth, in the terrible flood, in the burning of Sodom, and in the wars that have cost such dreadful loss of human life; and as far as the children of Israel are concerned, in their captivity, and ultimate dispersion, so that for generations the land was a wilderness and the temple just a mass of ruins. He made desolations; He makes desolations still in the exercise of His divine sovereignty in some ways that may confound us and this is like a warning voice to 'be still' to warn us against revolting under the Lord's ways and dealings in things that may come upon the earth, or our nation, or the church, or individual persons. It is true they cause much distress and grief, as the things that have just this week taken place in the death of these four poor children.* It is extremely sad; but the warning to us is against revolting under the ways of God, however mysterious they may be. This appears to be the case with Elihu in his address to Job. His great point appears to be to acknowledge the justice of God in those things that Job had to pass through. This may seem at times very, very difficult, but this word, 'be still' is as though the Lord would warn us against the spirit of rebellion, resentment, and fretfulness in view of the Lord's ways and disposings of His providence. Sometimes these involve very heavy things, they stagger us, they wound us, they grieve us; but grief is different from rebellion. One can feel grief under distressing circumstances and yet not be rebellious, revolting, and resentful in our spirit against the ways of the Lord. This is a warning; yet how often there has been this murmuring spirit, characteristic of the children of Israel; although the Lord had done great things for them, yet how soon they rebelled against God and Moses. They continually murmured; this is very solemn, because they suffered much chastening on this account, desolating things sometimes under solemn judgements, though the Lord did not forsake His people. We can be grieved without being bitter, rebellious, and resentful. There is a point in this; I believe in the trials of the Lord's people there can be grief without bitterness. It is rather a sweet spot in a way, and there is a stillness in it; although it may be hard to bear with some things, as it is now with us, yet even so they are all in the Lord's hands. It is true that we *are* grieved, yet grief is not sinful in itself; but

* The reference is to the tragic death in a fire of four Sunday School children.

rebellion, pride, bitterness, resentment, is the uprising of our poor old fallen nature. Yet we feel it sometimes, do we not? This is then a warning against revolting.

How sad are some things with us now; we all feel sad and grieved; but even so with the Lord's dear people there is a spot into which they can be brought and can feel as we have been singing,

> 'My Father's hand prepares the cup,
> And what He wills is best.'

To come there is very sweet; then we can feel a little stillness. It is one thing to *read* comforting words; we can easily read comforting, quieting words in the Scripture; but what we are not able to do is to bring them into our hearts, so that we can feel the consolation of them in a gracious and spiritual way. When we do, we can feel a little stillness. How does the Lord do this, then? Why, sometimes the Spirit of the Lord may bring a fitting word with some power into the heart that brings a quietness with it. 'When He giveth quietness who then can make trouble?' Sometimes it can be without any word at all. It can be a sacred influence that you feel upon your spirit, although it may be more than you can seem to understand. The Spirit of the Lord can bring a quieting influence into the heart when one is perturbed and distressed, and then there is a little stillness. If we could command of ourselves what is in this Psalm, we need not be perturbed about anything really; neither need we when we can feel in our hearts this gracious stillness. It is not a fatalistic attitude; it is a gracious stillness; but here is the warning, 'Be still', as though it were a word of warning to a rebellious, fretful one, 'Be still'. It is nature that rises up, but it is grace that falls under. Nature will never fall under the disposings of God's ways in an acceptable manner. It is grace alone operating in the heart that can bring a stillness, to the comfort and peace of mind of a troubled one. Here is the warning then and this is the first point—a warning against the possible consequences of fighting against God, of revolting, rebelling, resenting the ways of the Lord with us.

A second point consists in what is involved in this stillness. It is experimental, it is the Lord speaking here, 'Be still and know that *I* am God'. It is the Lord speaking, and the Speaker must give the blessing; it is beyond our command, naturally speaking; but there is something very sweet in it. One of the ingredients in this stillness is faith. Does not this link up with what I referred to on the past Sabbath Day when the Lord said, 'Let not your heart be troubled, ye believe in God, believe also in Me'? It is faith in exercise that can see a Father's hand toward us in His dispensations, painful as they may be, that can bring a stillness. It is confidence in God, a sacred confidence, which seems to rise above all the frettings of our poor nature; this brings a little stillness. Faith is a wonderful grace, especially when we are enabled to feel it brought into exercise upon the Person and work of the Lord Jesus Christ as we view it in the Gospel in what the Lord suffered for us, especially when we contemplate Gethsemane. This can make our own sufferings appear comparatively light, as light afflictions which are but for a moment; this can bring a little stillness. I believe this fellowship with the Lord Jesus Christ in His sufferings can be very sacred; it can bring a spirit of confidence, faith can view what He suffered for us, the curse that He was made for us, and feel some hope that we are thereby delivered from it. This can bring a little stillness, and some consolation in the path of tribulation here. It is when we realize that He has conquered sin, death, and hell for us at a higher cost than we can conceive; it is that view of a suffering and now exalted Redeemer by precious faith, that sight of Him, that lifts us above the things that drag us down and confuse us, grieve and stumble us, that brings a little solemn stillness.

Perhaps you have felt something of this just now and again even in the night seasons when the Lord has visited you and given you to feel the comfort of a word or promise, possibly when you have been enveloped in trouble. This brings a stillness, and you can believe that all is ordered well, and that as we read, 'all things work together for good to them that love God, to them who are the called according to His purpose'. Then there is a little stillness when we are taken away from self and the reasonings of our poor depraved nature, and faith becomes as an anchor in the soul that holds us to Christ. It is when you get just a little communion with your best Friend that you can feel a little stillness.

This stillness consists in a submission to His divine will. A submission to it does not mean being callous about it. This submission is a particular experience, when just at that time you can be passive in His hands and know no will but His. That is very sweet, but nature cannot produce it; the Lord only can bring that stillness into your heart, and then you would not have anything altered just at that moment. Your will is swallowed up in His, as you will remember when the dear Saviour was there in the garden He said, 'Not My will but Thine be done'. When the Lord is pleased to bless you in your soul, and favours you to feel a union with Christ and some fellowship with Him, in some small measure, in His own agonies, then you can say the same: 'Not my will but Thine be done.' This is very different to saying I must put up with it; I must try and be brave; I will stand up to it as well as I can, others have—No!—this is when the Lord is with you, when you get some glimpse of His amazing compassion, and that He was made sin for you, when you can feel that your soul and body belongs to Him and that one day you will be with Him for ever, and will leave all your troubles behind for ever. Then you can be still. This is a very sweet spot; I know we cannot produce it but here it is, 'Be still and know that I am God'.

This stillness has in it a patience. Some people are naturally impatient, but now and again the Lord comes over our natural resentment and imparts a gracious patience; not a natural but a gracious patience. Then you can submit yourself to His divine will and accept the bitter ingredients in the cup, feeling that it is as we have been singing what the Father has prepared. This is an injunction then, 'Be still and know that I am God'.

Now there is a third point—there is also the consolation. Wherein does the consolation consist? It is in the text, 'Be still and know that I am God'. The consolation, comfort and strength of the stillness consists in a knowledge of God. The Lord says so. 'Be still and know that I am God.' He does not just say that there is a God or some kind of supreme being; for that may not bring you any sweet consolation. What brings a stillness is the knowledge of God as our covenant God, as the God of Abraham, Isaac and Jacob, your covenant performing God. When you feel that sacred relationship to Him then you can at times feel a little stillness. He was the God of our fathers though they had their trials, some sad and heavy things, as did dear old Jacob; so that he said they would bring down his grey hairs with sorrow to the grave. Job must have felt a little stillness after he was stripped of practically everything, of all his possessions, and even his sons. He must have felt a little stillness when he said, 'The Lord gave and the Lord hath taken away, blessed be the name of the Lord'. What an amazing thing to say. Here were these three friends sitting there seven days and seven nights in absolute silence, but Job must have felt a little stillness, to say the Lord has only taken away what He gave, and He has as much right to it and more than I have. There must have been a little stillness there. This was just the opposite of what Satan predicted; Satan said, 'If you touch his property he will curse you to your face'. What a liar he has been in the experience of the Lord's people! Here is a stillness then that consists in the knowledge of God as a covenant God. When you can feel that that covenant made with Christ incorporates you, that all those covenant blessings are yours (although your house be not so with God), it can bring a little stillness; then you can feel that He is your God and Father in Christ, not an abstract God, but your heavenly Father. If that is true you are blessed with all spiritual blessings in Christ; and to have some feeling of this brings a little stillness. How much sweeter is this than the murmuring and revolting spirit which will often rise up. We find one saying,

'My God, my Father, blissful name!
O may I call Thee mine?
May I with sweet assurance claim
A portion so divine?'

When you can feel that spirit of adoption in your heart, that He is your Father, it will bring a little stillness, and a very sweet stillness too. Your Heavenly Father is over all your providences. 'Your heavenly Father knoweth that ye have need of all these things.' Not only so, but it is when you can feel that this God is your Saviour and Redeemer in Christ. 'Thus saith the Lord that created thee, O Jacob and He that formed thee, O Israel, Fear not: for I have redeemed thee, I have called thee by thy name; thou art Mine.' We can read it, but if it comes into your heart you will feel a little stillness. In fact, you will feel broken down in spirit before Him, amazed that He should show such mercy and compassion to such a poor wretched sinner. This brings a little stillness; then you can feel that God is your refuge. 'God is our refuge and strength.' When you really feel the consolation of this, when you feel you have His divine protection, being sheltered under the Rock of Ages; especially when you feel a taste of His pardoning love in your heart; then you can feel a little of this sweet stillness. Why, say you, why should I murmur or repine? He has pardoned my awful, guilty load of sin; He has given me an interest in His amazing love, has prepared a heaven for me. As you realize this you will feel a little stillness.

Well, I have said a few things, but there is a sweet spot here, and although some things are making us feel very sad just now I hope we may come into this a little, and feel a touch of the Father's love in our hearts to us, in a sense of what He has done for us, in the prospect that is before us, and the hope that we have of eternal life, and feelingly sometimes in the prospect of heaven. This will greatly help us to 'Be still and know that I am God'.

Amen.

EPILOGUE

The Funeral Addresses

The address by Mr J. C. Neville at 'Ebenezer' Chapel, Clapham at the funeral on 24.1.80

Reading: John 14

DEAR FRIENDS, memories crowd upon us on an occasion like this. One would seek grace to be kept from sentiment and emotion but you will understand I feel that it is no easy thing to officiate at this solemn, though blessedly sacred service. We cannot know, and love in the truth, a man for forty-five years without feeling the sorrow and loss; and that I know applies to many of you friends, the church here, the friends that have come from causes where the Lord's late dear servant laboured in so many different churches, acceptably and fruitfully through grace. He had received his ministry from the Lord and that which by the Holy Ghost he was favoured in his own soul to taste, handle, and feel, and this by the same blessed Spirit he was enabled to declare in love. The ending of this ministry is a loss, and we might just say that Mr Frank Gosden also, since our dear pastor died, has himself been taken.

Dear Mr Delves had a good religion, a religion of the Holy Ghost. It was begun by concern in his soul when he was 17 in a heavy temptation from which he was delivered, but through which he was brought to feel solemn condemnation in his own conscience and came, as he has related, to that place we *must* be brought to, to have the sentence of death in his conscience. Under those exercises for a period he was brought very low. In one serious illness with no comfortable prospect then of eternity, he came near death but was in a solemn condition of felt hopelessness. When he was recovered and the first time he could go to the Lord's house (he was then beginning to attend Galeed), he went with this language in his heart, only one thing, 'God be merciful to me a sinner'. Mr Popham was led in the course of his discourse to say, 'There may be someone here who can only pray the publican's prayer', and our dear friend has related how he was almost ready to get up and say 'I am the man'. Mr Popham said, 'If that is the case, go on in that way, it is the right way'.

I come to the time when he was graciously delivered in his soul. He had many helps under the preaching of Mr Popham and also under godly Mr Dickens of Rotherfield, and there came that time when the Lord so blessed his soul. First he ventured to write to Mr Popham a little of what he had been brought to feel and know, and after that was much exercised lest he ought not to have written. Some of you, with myself, will understand that. That evening as he was working at his bench came that memorable time (some of us have heard him speak of it), when the Lord shone with a sacred light into his soul and he was favoured with a view of the Lord Jesus Christ suffering for his sins on the cross and that word was received in his heart, 'Yea, I have loved thee with an everlasting love, therefore with lovingkindness have I drawn thee'. It seemed to come to him to ask, 'What of the Father?' and this word came, we have just read together, one which ever remained as having a particular sweetness to our late friend, 'He that hath seen *Me* hath seen the Father'. By reason of that he was enabled to go before the church and to give his testimony and was received. Only yesterday afternoon one of the godly members still remaining at Brighton from those days, Miss Lewis, said to me she had never forgotten the savour of that church meeting. Feeling the exercise of the ministry from that time, in due course he was sent forth by the church at Brighton, and for nearly 50 years enabled to preach the Gospel he had received and loved and commended. Many of us who were favoured with that ministry for a period of years have great cause to feel thankful, though ashamed; thankful if by the Lord's great mercy there has been some inward teaching received through it, all of grace; ashamed that we have profited so little and been so poor in the following on in those things. Nevertheless we can thankfully say that dear Mr Delves's ministry, in one's own case from the beginning of his pastorate here until we were removed in providence, was made a ministry of teaching, not only of comfort; I have gone away from this chapel with a reproof in my heart; not that he ever spoke unkindly, I do not mean that, but in his speaking the truth and the Spirit conveying reproof into one's heart. There have also been some sweet confirming seasons as we have sat and listened to the preaching.

The time came when the Lord said 'I will come again, and receive you unto myself'. How blessedly the comfort and substance of the Gospel was manifested in his declining days, as well as in those days when he laboured so abundantly. In his weakness, he was yet favoured to feel the sacredness of those things which he had received and the Lord confirmed them in his heart.

I have a paper handed to me concerning some of the things which he said in the last two years, and I think it would be right to read some of them to you. He said this, 'Yes, I shall soon be landed, I have seen Him by faith and He was the chiefest among ten thousand and the altogether lovely; but soon I shall see Him *face to face*'. 'I feel as though I might go at any time but all is settled and my soul approves it well', remembering that particular blessing he had in an affliction later in his life when it was sweetly whispered in his heart, 'ALL IS SETTLED: ALL IS SETTLED: ALL IS SETTLED'. Some of you have heard him speak of those words. Our concern should be (I hope this might be brought into any heart, if there should be any, without concern), as to whether it was settled for *us* in the eternal covenant of redemption and grace, and what Holy Ghost teaching we have in our hearts as the evidence of that, and what there is of spiritual light and knowledge of the Gospel felt from time to time. That religion he had was a good one, he did not take it up, God gave it to him, and as God gave it to him He maintained it in the power of His grace in his heart, and so he could speak in those later days. To a minister that visited him Mr Delves said, 'I am drawing near the end' and the minister said, 'Now is the time you want something real and solid'. He replied, 'I have got it, He has given me a yea. Yea, I have loved thee with an everlasting love, therefore with lovingkindness have I drawn thee', so that word remained, not only as in the truth of it, but in the substance of the truth received and enjoyed in his soul—what sacred things friends. We can, amidst our own sorrow, feel so deeply thankful for that abundant grace manifested and testified. His life was a testimony, and his last months of weakness and death were a testimony. The Lord tenderly brought him down. He was favoured in his soul, not without conflicts. We who knew him knew sometimes a little of the conflicts preceding a sermon, and yet in all these things he was divinely supported and the Word of God's grace remained in the strength and power of the Spirit in his heart. 'This poor old body is coming to its end, but the prospect is wonderful, wonderful, and loudest of the crowd I'll sing with shouts of sovereign grace', repeating 'Loudest of the crowd'. 'You won't have me much longer but I have a good hope that it is well and desire to fall into the Lord's hands.'

In the chapter we read, the Lord Jesus speaking words of comfort to his then sorrowing disciples, spoke of Himself as the Way, the Truth, and the Life, spoke of the promise of the Comforter, the blessed Spirit's teaching which is so vital to us, and spoke of the inheritance, 'In my Father's house are many mansions; if it were not so, I would have told you'. He suffered those inconceivable sufferings and having overcome sin and death and hell He rose again to be exalted at the Father's right hand. He said, 'I go to prepare a place for you'; He is their forerunner, their representative. As the priest of old had the names of the tribes on his breast, so our Great High Priest has entered into heaven with the names of all His poor redeemed people, poor, guilty sinners, brought to know and mourn over their sinnership and all that belongs to us by nature; but He has entered the prepared place and He has promised to come again and receive them unto Himself. May the Lord help us to look upon this event as the fulfilment of Christ's promise, so it is, 'If I go and prepare a place for you, I will come again, and receive you unto myself'. The moment a saint dies the redeemed spirit is before the throne and enjoys what in a little measure is tasted by the Lord's people here, but he enjoys it then in the fullness and uninterruptedness of it, without a veil between.

Now my friends, the Lord help us to consider, 'How stands the case my soul with thee?'

> 'Poor soul, what is thy hope?
> On what dost thou depend?'

What is there in your heart, in mine, that can really bring that comfortable hope in the prospect of what is before us, to all of us in due time? We can feel sometimes, can we not, that we are at this point, 'If ever my poor soul be saved, 'tis Christ must be the way'. A good line of teaching, but O that we may have confirmed our interest in, and union to, the Lord Jesus Christ. May there be many blessed with the fruits of grace. Many of us feel a sadness and an ashamedness for our lack, but where the grace of God is there shall the fruits be made known. It is a mercy if we have a right concern, but not rest in concern. In fact if it is a *real* and right concern you *cannot* rest there. Some of us can hope the Lord has given us, not in the measure that our beloved friend was favoured to have, but that upon which we can say our hopes depend. Mr Delves's hope was not based upon his works, though the fruits of grace were manifested, springing from the possession of that root. His hopes did not rest upon his many labours, though they were so manifold; nor upon his preaching, though it was so solid and savoury; no, his hopes depended, as expressed in the lines of the tablet at the side of this pulpit:

'Fearless he entered Jordan's flood
At peace with heaven he closed his eyes;
His only trust was Jesus's blood
In sure and certain hope to rise.'

That is our comfort for him, but may the Lord grant us to seek to be followers of them who through faith and patience now inherit the promise.

I have so many memories it would not be prudent, nor would time permit, to mention all; nor would it be God glorifying in a certain sense because we can get the flesh mixed up with things which brings a death upon them, but there are those times when as the Lord favours with some reflection I can say from my heart it has been a sacred privilege to sit under his ministry for many years, and I would have been glad to have done so still. When the time came for the exercise I had long had about the ministry to be brought forward he was a good counsellor and a kind friend. He never pushed it, but when that time came (I think it was the Lord's day before the church meeting) in the afternoon he was preaching elsewhere and I had, and took, the opportunity to go as a hearer and I remember as he preached that afternoon my heart began to say, 'This is what I have got to leave', and I believe it came, 'No, let me rather freely yield, what most I prize to Thee', and just then next to the comfort of a hope in God's mercy the ministry here was the thing I most prized, the house of God. I have been a poor sort of hearer but I believe that it was to me many, many times a place of sacred feeding.

The world, when it ever thinks of death, and our unbelieving heart to some extent is the same, would tend to turn the thoughts away; and at funerals they must have flowers and organs and things like that to make it seem more cheerful. There is no need for that at the death of the saint. It is a sad thing, but as the Lord is pleased to shine through the gloom of the hour and article of death and give a sacred view of that to which death ushers the saint of God, then there is a sweetness indeed. We hope, as I believe our late dear friend would have desired to be said, that what we have said concerning him is what he was by the grace of God. The crown is on the head of Christ and will be placed there; sometimes here in faith and desire, then in the full blessedness of it. May this be our hope.

I would just mention again how we do feel thankful that our dear friend was enabled to attend so lovingly to him, with others that helped as well; and she has been sustained in it and we do hope that the Lord's mercy may be continued in her soul and guide her in all that concerns her still. We feel for the dear young pastor here and do pray that, as he has been sent forth from this church, but more important, anointed by the Holy Spirit, he may be favoured with that light and life in his ministry, with power, that there may be still the accomplishing of the purposes of grace as there has been over the many years, forty-two years, our departed friend laboured in the pastorate here.

I should mention the manner in which he was enabled to give counsel and guidance in the affairs of the denomination; in the Committee and Bethesda Homes, for which he was ever ready to give his time and his attention and kindly help. The second time I saw Mr Delves (not the first) was when there was that meeting in 1934, the 'God honouring movement', when the re-affirmation of our separate position was made; he was one of the tellers—I feel there is a voice in that, may the Lord help us to maintain in a gracious way that separating line and enable us to hold fast that in a day of some degree of drift, we may be mercifully helped, with all the weakness that sometimes some of us may feel, to stand fast in these ways.

I will leave these remarks and I hope you will in love bear

with the felt inadequacies of them. When the Lord Jesus was about to leave the disciples He gave the promise of the Holy Ghost—the Holy Spirit remains, dear sorrowing friends. You have not the ministry of your former pastor, but you have the ministry, and above and beyond that, and where the grace and exercise of these things are in the heart, you have the Spirit of God to teach you—to teach us, and be with us. May He pardon us and help us for His name's sake. Amen.

(The Service in the Chapel was concluded with Hymn 1156—one which was particular to Mr Delves)

The address by Mr P. H. Brunker at the internment at the 'Dicker' Chapel Graveyard.

THE article of death is a solemnity in the case of both believers and unbelievers. It is a solemnity in all cases because of sin. The Scripture declares 'As in Adam all die' and it is true of us each who are yet in the land of the living that we are in Adam; we are under the sentence of death by reason of sin. The world do not regard this solemn scene as a solemnity, they either dishonour the Almighty with unwarranted and rebellious grief or they dishonour Him with a casual hardness. The dead professor dishonours the Almighty by a false joy and instead of realising the solemnity profanes the solemn ordinance. But with a child of God, as it is this day, the grave is made a solemnity by something far greater and far more solemn than sin and its consequences. It is made sacred and savoury by the precious blood of Christ; and we have now laid to rest all that is mortal, the precious dust, of him who lived to exalt the precious atonement. We trust that many of us have gathered to acknowledge that it is that aspect of his ministry that has been life and power to our souls, which makes his memory dear to us. It is the savour of the name of Christ who is now exalted 'Far above all principality, and power, and might, and dominion, and every name that is named' that takes the sting away from this solemn occasion. If we are favoured with a glimpse of the sweetness of redemption that our late dear pastor really felt and experienced and knew and rested upon, both in joy and sorrow, then we have reason to rejoice with joy and with trembling.

I would just make brief reference to our condition as mourners: I would refer to the church of God, that part of it among which our late dear pastor moved. We have read separating words, 'Blessed are the dead which die in the Lord'. Though the majority here are gathered, I believe, out of respect and love to him who has departed, the question to ask ourselves is whether any vital savour has abode in our spirits of the testimony of our late dear friend, for all that is of the flesh will pass away. It may sustain the sentiment and notion but it will not do when you and I come to be laid in the grave. If we have a testimony that Christ is precious it shall be well.

We have reason to mourn as a denomination; may the Lord give us grace to enter into the desolation which is felt in Zion. The church at Clapham particularly feel their loss, the removal of a dear and loving pastor, but in this loss for us as a church we need grace to examine ourselves, to mourn over our poverty and to desire that the unction, the savour and the power of the Gospel ministry, which was long echoed in our midst, might abide with us. My desire is, 'Lord take not Thy Holy Spirt from us'. May He sanctify the loss. And finally I would refer to those in relative bonds. I do not leave them till last out of lack of respect, but I would faithfully say this, that the ties of nature are not to be compared with those of the Spirit, and blessed are we if we can feel a spiritual union with him who being dead yet speaketh.

I would leave these remarks—may I just refer to one point about the life and death of dear Mr Delves? As some of us heard at the chapel he was favoured with a special and sweet revelation of his Redeemer. Not long before he died, when feeling a slight cloud upon his spirit, he revived and said to me, 'Our standing is not dependent upon great ecstasies of joy but upon the finished work of Christ'. Lest any should feel that is dry doctrine, on one occasion in response to my reference to that Scripture 'Unto you therefore which believe He is precious', a few days before he died, he lifted himself up in the bed and looked at me and said, 'He has been many, many times'.

May the Lord pardon where we have failed in speaking and anoint it with His unction and grant that His Spirit may rest upon us, that we may see our hope for eternity upon Calvary and hear the language of our dying, victorious Lord, 'IT IS FINISHED'. In Corinthians we read (and O that our mourning, our sorrows, our ambitions, our joys might be subservient to this kingdom of grace), 'Then cometh the end, when he shall have delivered up the kingdom to God, even the Father'. This sacred occasion marks one more step towards the consummation of that kingdom of grace. May the Lord pervade our meeting with a sense of His own words, 'Thy kingdom come. Thy will be done'. Amen.